RED HOT MAMA

Red Hot

MAMA

THE LIFE OF SOPHIE TUCKER

LAUREN REBECCA SKLAROFF

UNIVERSITY OF TEXAS PRESS ❧ AUSTIN

Requests for permission to reproduce material from
this work should be sent to:
Permissions
University of Texas Press
P.O. Box 7819
Austin, TX 78713-7819
utpress.utexas.edu/rp-form

The paper used in this book meets the minimum requirements of
ANSI/NISO Z39.48-1992 (R1997) (Permanence of Paper). ∞

Book design by Lindsay Starr
Typesetting by Integrated Composition Systems

Library of Congress Cataloging-in-Publication Data

Names: Sklaroff, Lauren Rebecca, author.
Title: Red hot mama : the life of Sophie Tucker / Lauren Rebecca Sklaroff.
Description: Austin : University of Texas Press, 2018. | Includes
bibliographical references and index.
Identifiers: LCCN 2017037715
ISBN 978-1-4773-1236-0 (cloth : alk. paper)
ISBN 978-1-4773-1633-7 (library e-book)
ISBN 978-1-4773-1634-4 (nonlibrary e-book)
Subjects: LCSH: Tucker, Sophie, 1884–1966. | Singers—United States—
Biography.
Classification: LCC ML420.T89 S55 2018 | DDC 782.42164092 [B] —dc23
LC record available at https://lccn.loc.gov/2017037715

doi:10.7560/312360

For my mom, Ellen Sklaroff, with love

CONTENTS

RED HOT MAMA

INTRODUCTION

◇————◇————◇

*I*n the first half of the twentieth century, children of immigrants created the world of American entertainment. These newcomers honed their talents and built an industry on the stages of palatial vaudeville theaters, in the noisy offices of Tin Pan Alley songwriters, amid the scurry to promote multiple motion pictures. Although they felt the rush of creativity and camaraderie, life was not easy. Estranged from families who clung to Old World values, always wondering whether they would be welcomed or rejected, these determined men and women navigated the geography of American politics, beliefs, and instincts. They changed their ethnic names, updated their clothes and makeup, and over time became the most influential figures in show business. By the time the United States restricted immigration for a new generation in the 1920s, no one rivaled these former outsiders in catering to the desires of American consumers.

Sophie Tucker was one of these ambitious second-generation immigrants who found their home on the stage. Born to Russian-Jewish parents, Charles and Jennie Kalish, as the family sought refuge in the United States, Tucker came into the world with virtually nothing. Yet over the course of six decades she rose to the top as show business royalty, alleviating audiences' troubles, bringing families together, and exciting people in ways they had never experienced. Tucker succeeded in living outside all of the expectations for her gender while becoming beloved by fans and industry heads alike.

Despite fame in her own day and her subsequent role as a hero to Bette Midler, Tucker is not as well remembered as some of her peers. When she is, it is as an overweight blonde woman, bedazzling in diamonds, sometimes appearing jokingly on the Ed Sullivan show, bawdy and risqué for her time. Historians position her in a long line of Jewish women who have performed outside convention, such as Molly Picon, Fanny Brice, Joan Rivers, and Sarah Silverman. These characterizations are undoubtedly true, yet Tucker was much more complex, and there is infinitely more to know about her life history.

Tucker began her career in 1907 and continued working until her death in 1966, becoming a giant in popular culture. She performed on an almost daily basis for sixty years, with a career spanning and shaping the major technological developments of the modern era—vaudeville, radio, film, and television. Tucker's life reflects a common struggle to belong in a new, changing nation. Yet she was also irreplaceable. More than most of her contemporaries, she understood how to keep her act fresh, how to change branding when audiences grew tired, and, most important, how to connect with her fans, the press, and entertainment moguls. She learned how to entertain with her own signature flair, inimitable by others in the business.

Tucker's career longevity is astounding; there are not many who can claim sixty years in entertainment and the public eye. Her time in the limelight paralleled and intersected with that of many famous actors and entertainers, including Eva Tanguay, Clara Bow, and Shirley Temple. She outlasted all of them. Unlike others who could not move across genres or who fell into one archetype, Tucker was determined to constantly adapt to changing tastes and fads. Whether this meant rebranding herself from "America's Renowned Coon Shouter" to "Last of the Red Hot Mamas," or moving from cabaret work to musicals to film, Tucker was always thinking ahead. Even in her fifties she happily embraced becoming a piece of nostalgia, inviting audiences who had grown up with her to celebrate a relic of their youth. "Aunt Sophie," as fans often called her, was a constant in their lives. She accepted the charge to learn more songs, sing with more gusto, and adore her fans more deeply than anyone in the industry, becoming a force unto herself. Tucker could never stand still, even at the end of her life, when she called *retire* a dirty word.

She pioneered strategies for staying relevant. With the help of her astute agent, William Morris, Tucker learned the value of working internationally. Beginning in the mid-1920s she traveled to Great Britain, where she found a bevy of new fans and established a larger-than-life reputation as an international sensation. Every time she returned to the United States from performing across the Atlantic, she made a major debut with new songs and tales of adventures abroad, including her three command performances for British royalty. She thrived while traveling and opening herself up to new publics; she performed in Australia and South Africa, and she visited Israel three times. Although performers now travel the world as a necessary part of their career, Tucker was blazing new ground for her time.

In addition, she developed a marketing strategy that kept her current, rivaling social media marketing decades before its existence. Tucker compiled the names of every individual who saw her shows and always alerted audiences when return engagements were scheduled. She welcomed interviews and sent thank-you notes to reporters and critics who covered her. It is no wonder that even into her seventies, she never lost the interest of the media in the United States and abroad. Stories of her continuing returns to popular nightclubs such as the Latin Quarter and Copa City amazed the public.

Tucker moved through show business with an authority that few other women commanded. Whether she served as a mentor, as she did for Judy Garland, or a partner, as she did with Eddie Cantor and

George Jessel, she was able to dictate the parameters of her career. She ultimately became an equal to her male peers: she was the first woman honored at the all-male Friars Club and the first female president of the American Federation of Actors, and she received many other honors that had previously been bestowed on men. Combining maternal concern with a sense of humor that was like a man's, Tucker was remembered as everyone's pal, neither sexually threatening nor dangerously ambitious. Her weight and unconventional beauty ironically allowed her to move into spaces that women did not traditionally occupy, and once she was at the top, she would never back down.

Fiercely independent from a young age, Tucker delivered songs about women's empowerment and sexual satisfaction, and she warranted respect that was a product of her own experiences. Much of her repertoire was comedic and lighthearted, but it came from a place of deep conviction that women could succeed outside of marriage and motherhood. Songs such as "I Don't Want to Get Thin," "Life Begins at Forty," and "You Can't Sew a Button on a Heart" spoke to her firm belief in women's self-acceptance no matter their size or age. In an environment of slender, perfectly coiffed celebrities, Tucker stood as an alternative model of womanhood. Her use of double entendre and tales of her own sexual expertise encouraged women to feel less ashamed of their autonomy. She provided reassurance that their own racy thoughts were more common than they imagined. In making her anxieties and delights part of her act, Tucker gave her audience license to examine many of society's norms and turn them on their head.

Tucker helped pioneer many of the elements that have made the female entertainers who followed her so successful. The risks she took during her career relate to all women who move into the spotlight with fierce, unapologetic determination. Comedians such as Rivers and Amy Schumer, who candidly speak out about topics most people keep in their minds, follow the style Tucker developed in the early 1910s. Joking about taboo subjects in a self-effacing way was always part of Tucker's strategy to draw audiences in, and biting performances such as the television show *Girls* and Julia Louis-Dreyfus's foul-mouthed character on *Veep* profit from this form of irreverent humor. The singer's acute sense for rebranding is now mirrored by superstars such Madonna and Beyoncé, whose albums and concerts move from bubble gum pop spectacle to political provocation. Whether or not Miley Cyrus and Taylor Swift have ever heard of the Red Hot Mama, she helped shape the mechanisms that bolster their base of frenzied fans, with letters and postcards replaced by Twitter and Instagram. Decades before the birth of the most famous current entertainers, Tucker affected many of the performance vehicles these stars now readily embrace.

Tucker paid a steep price for her personal freedom. She abandoned her infant son, her only child, when she left her native Hartford for the dream of stardom in New York City. Shunned by the Hartford community and having disappointed her parents, Tucker spent years working to prove that her choice was worth the pain she had inflicted on her family. She was always connected to her siblings but never in the way that she identified with other troupers in show business. Although she always hoped for a fulfilling partnership with a man, her status as a wealthy headliner prevented personal relationships from lasting. Married and divorced three times in an era when divorce was not widely accepted, Tucker sought to create the most satisfying personal life she could. Eventually she would come to accept that her career and her fans supplied her with the love she always hoped for in marriage, and she became content to live her life alone.

Far from perfect, Tucker often had trouble sharing the spotlight. She was critical about areas in which she had less control, and, at least in the beginning of her career, she always put herself before her family. Although she was uniquely generous to fans and charities, like many big stars she could be incredibly self-absorbed. She had a large, compassionate heart, but her attention to the needs of others was never entirely disconnected from self-promotion. Midler captured this essence best in "Those Wonderful Sophie Tucker Jokes" on her 1977 album *Live at Last*, claiming that Tucker would ask people to "Kiss my *tuchus* and plant a tree for Israel at the same time."[1]

Social justice became a defining mission over the course of Tucker's career. From the time she met her closest African-American friend, former entertainer Mollie Elkins, backstage at the Ziegfeld Follies in 1909, she was increasingly aware of racial inequality and dedicated herself to improving conditions for her black counterparts on the stage. A major contributor to the Negro Actors Guild, Tucker counted many black luminaries as her friends, including Bill Robinson, Noble Sissle, Josephine Baker, and Nat King Cole. In the black press she was known for her generosity. Publications such as the *Pittsburgh Courier* and the *Chicago Defender* covered Tucker's engagements regularly, as well as her advocacy for black songwriters and performers. African Americans attested to her strong belief that people of all races and creeds could pursue the kind of dreams she did as a child of immigrants. Although Tucker did not publicly speak on behalf of the NAACP or other civil rights organizations, she was dismayed by segregation and worked to break down racial boundaries on stage and among audiences.

Tucker's commitment to Jews in the United States and all over the world was steadfast, even though she never identified herself primarily as a Jewish performer. Following in the path of her mother, who always helped people in need, she donated to a wide variety of Jewish charities, with contributions reaching into the millions by the 1960s. Whether she was helping Jewish prisoners celebrate the High Holidays or working to develop youth centers in Israel, she seemed to never decline a request for aid, and the larger political community came to regard her as one of the most reliable donors. Tucker's large contributions did not all go to Jewish organizations. By the time of her death in 1966, she had raised approximately $4 million (about 30 million in today's dollars), and beneficiaries included the Catholic and Episcopal actors guilds in addition to Jewish and African-American organizations. To be sure, Tucker's giving focused more on Jews in the period after the Holocaust, particularly with the creation of the state of Israel, but she never stopped giving to people in need, no matter what their faith was.

Her charity work brought her into conversations with figures such as Albert Einstein, Eleanor Roosevelt, and White House administrators. She was always foremost a performer, but her talent as a philanthropist blurred the line between entertainment and politics. Tucker pioneered the kind of broadscale charity that we now see in the Elton John AIDS Foundation and Bono's aid to Africa. At most of the charity events she attended, particularly in her early years, she was the only woman donating. In many ways, she was always publicly perceived as a contemporary of men like Cantor, Jessel, Al Jolson, and the Warner brothers, rather than of the female performers who made headlines at the time.

Tucker lived large. She wrapped herself in furs, enjoyed hobnobbing with the rich and famous, and adored New York, Chicago, and London. Yet Tucker's story is also about the personal nuances that made her so accessible. In an era when women were not considered funny, her comedic timing was spot-on, and she later inspired entertainers such as Carol Channing. Self-effacing, brutally honest, and a good listener, she encouraged people to feel close to her, and she kept hundreds of the fan letters she received.

She also studied her craft with precision, attending the rehearsals of other performers she had admired and inspecting audience reactions in new cities before she went on stage. Later in her life, Tucker was deeply disappointed by degeneration of the entertainment industry, brought on by youngsters who, she believed, wanted quick fame without acquiring the necessary amount of training. She lived in an era when talent was cultivated, honed, and perfected for years before major money came in; there were no shortcuts in her world. She relished live performance not only because she could see the audience responding, but also because, for her, successful performances were the most legitimate marker of stardom.

One of the most unusual roles Tucker played was that of her own personal archivist. In 1907 she began saving press clippings that mentioned her, pasting them into large, bulky scrapbooks. This may have begun as a way for her to show her family what she had accomplished, but over the years it became a more intellectual venture as Tucker witnessed the end of vaudeville and the rise of technology-fueled media. Filled with programs, speeches, birthday cards, sheet music, and other ephemera, Tucker's four hundred personal scrapbooks are one of the greatest archives of show business. The singer hoped that historians would want to learn about the world she helped shape: the vaudeville years when live music, audience participation, and family fare reigned supreme. These scrapbooks, which she donated to the New York Public Library and Brandeis University, were a gift to the public, another way for her to offer a piece of herself candidly and without restriction. It is highly unusual for a performer to personally organize and donate this much material for archival use, but for anyone who knew Tucker, it was not a surprise because she wanted people to understand her story.

Ironically, even though she left us with so much personal history, Tucker has become lost to our cultural memory. Samson Raphaelson, author of *The Jazz Singer* (on which the famed movie is based) declared in 1925, "Jazz is Irving Berlin, Al Jolson, George Gershwin, Sophie Tucker."[2] The men he lists are canonical American entertainment greats, while Tucker remains virtually unknown. Historians have given white women less attention than their male counterparts in the entertainment world, and Tucker's life was not particularly scandalous. Perhaps her fame was eclipsed by that of women who stirred the public through notoriety, such as Marilyn Monroe. Recent attention to African-American history has rightfully introduced Bessie Smith, Billie Holiday, Dorothy Dandridge, and other black female performers to new audiences. This biography encourages writers and historians to do the same for the countless once-famous women who defined the vaudeville era.

Much of Tucker's seeming erasure naturally relates to her aging audiences; as new generations admired new celebrities and rock and roll, disco, and later hip-hop took their place on national playlists, she faded from our collective consciousness. Her work was not sampled or reinvented by later artists. Yet her music is meaningful, whether in the astounding confidence expressed in her campaign anthem, "Sophie Tucker for President," her promotion of wifely independence in "My Husband's in the City," or her tribute to her own mortality in "Some of These Days." Though it has not been preserved in the Great American Songbook along with the music of her colleagues

Irving Berlin and Cole Porter, much of her work should be remembered as wholeheartedly.

Tucker's life represents all that is possible with a mix of talent and fierce determination. Many celebrities possess these traits, but Tucker used untraditional means to achieve the stardom she dreamed of as a young girl. It was not just that people admired her or enjoyed listening to her music; they felt they knew her as an individual. Realizing this, the singer gave fans more and more of herself, through her autobiography, personal anecdotes in her repertoire, and the correspondence she maintained with many all over the world. Reality television and ubiquitous paparazzi may lead us to believe that we know everything about celebrities today, but Tucker was entirely progressive in engaging her fans on the most personal level. Over time details changed in her biographical interviews, and there were aspects of her life that she did not wish to display; however, the guidance she offered—treat people with respect, work harder than ever, and never give up a dream—remained constant and universal.

There are many reasons Tucker is sometimes called outrageous, from her over-the-top costumes and saucy remarks to her effort to become owner of the Boston Braves baseball franchise. More than outrageous, though, Tucker was exceptional. As performer, activist, feminist, and pal, she meant many things to many people. On October 1, 1953, New York's swanky Waldorf Astoria Hotel overflowed with the most illustrious celebrities of the day, all of whom were there to attend a golden jubilee dinner for Tucker. With over a thousand people in attendance, including Jessel, Milton Berle, Tallulah Bankhead, and civil rights leader Ralph Bunche, it was a sensational show business gala. Tucker was resplendent in her gold and diamond gown, and her signature bouffant hairdo had taken on a silvery tone. She savored the testimonies to her accomplishments and received overwhelming acceptance from her family, fans, colleagues, and friends. This was not the end of her career; it was the pinnacle.

The golden jubilee celebration was a far cry from where Tucker began. She was born to a family that would soon enter the United States as outsiders, when becoming American was all they could hope for. Tucker looked beyond the safety of a national identity, clinging instead to the promise of her name in lights, with thousands cheering and watching her next move. How she turned this childhood fantasy into a reality is a story of tremendous motivation, courage, and a longing to delight audiences more than they could ever imagine. She was both a dreamer and a realist, never backing down from her goal of becoming one of the most formidable women in show business.

1

BREAKING WITH
TRADITION

*U*pheaval, dislocation, ostracization, clinging to faith. This is the way many Jewish Americans remember their family history, and Sophie Tucker was no different. Sophie's father, Charles Kalish, was born in the current-day Ukraine in December 1855 and married Sophie's mother, Jennie Yacha, in 1876.[1] Perhaps as much as seven years older than her husband, Jennie was a strong, steady woman who intended to raise a large Jewish family and contribute to village life as most women did.[2] The couple lived in relative peace under the reign of Alexander II, who was far more tolerant toward Jews than former, more fervently anti-Semitic rulers. Under Alexander II, Jews could attend some universities, were permitted to travel more freely throughout Russia and, in general, fared relatively well economically. At no time in Russian history were Jews free of fear and persecution as "enemies of Christ," but in the Kalishes' first years of marriage, they could enjoy life in their homeland.[3]

This state of relative security would come to a halt when terrorists assassinated Alexander II in March 1881 and the much more reactionary Alexander III came to power, setting off violence against Jews across Russia. Over a hundred communities were plundered, and pogroms forced Jews from their homes and businesses. By 1882 the government had instituted a series of laws that prevented Jews from living in thriving urban centers and limited their access to secondary schools and universities. Jews were disproportionately recruited for army service and were prohibited from serving in any high-ranking capacity.

Denied basic citizenship rights and protection under the law, people like Charles Kalish scrambled for alternatives where their families would be safe. Larger structural issues, such as overpopulation and economic insecurity, had already made emigration appealing, and as persecution ran rampant, people fled en masse. With all of these factors weighing heavily on their minds, Charles and Jennie decided to emigrate to the Unites States, where tales of opportunity abounded. Steamship companies offered reduced-price tickets, allowing more people to flee their homelands. It appears that Charles left for the United States around 1885 to establish himself in a more free and promising land and to earn enough money for his family's travels. Although Jennie had trouble bearing children at first, by the time Charles departed, she had given birth to a son, Philip, and was newly pregnant with her second child.[4]

After Charles landed in New York, he moved to Boston, perhaps to reside with family, but more likely because living conditions were more desirable there than among the swelling Jewish population in New York, the port of entry. Between 1881 and 1894 almost 2 million Jews came to the United States, primarily from Eastern Europe, and unlike members of other immigrant groups, who often returned to Europe after some time in the United States, they came to stay. While many Jews feared that they would not be able to uphold religious traditions in a more secular America, the violence and persecution in Eastern Europe had made their homelands unlivable. This wave of immigrants was largely composed of families, with the majority of people ages fourteen to forty-four. Most were skilled workers with experience in the clothing trades, in working with machinery, and with buildings and furnishings. Although settlement was not easy, skilled workers could find jobs in the industrializing United States, where the need for labor in all areas was escalating.[5]

By the mid-nineteenth century, a sizable population of Jews already resided in the United States. The first wave of immigration, from the mid-1820s through the mid-1870s from Central European countries such as Germany and Poland, was spurred by limitations in Europe on Jews' occupations, areas of residence, and even right to marry. By the time that Charles Kalish arrived, approximately 250,000 Jews lived in the United States.[6] Their presence greatly influenced new settlers' ability to acclimate. Although the religious practices of assimilated Jews differed from those of the new immigrants, those who had arrived earlier nonetheless set up relief organizations for the new refugees. In 1881 the Hebrew Immigrant Aid Society was established to coordinate the settlement of incoming people. Upon landing at Ellis Island, immigrants could read Yiddish-language advice manuals prepared by Jewish aid societies. Still, Jewish Americans were not a homogenous group. Differing religious practices, economic opportunities, and countries of origin often prevented Jewish men and women from working together amicably. For some of the most devout Orthodox rabbis, immigration to the United States was viewed as an abandonment of faith because it made it more difficult for Jews to observe the Sabbath and keep kosher.[7]

It is unclear exactly how Charles Kalish earned a living when he was alone in the United States during initial settlement, but he apparently earned enough money to secure his family's passage to America. Jennie had a difficult road ahead of her as she set out in a hostile environment. Travel from her Ukrainian town, through Poland, and most likely to a port in Germany was precarious in the harsh winter, and she spoke only Yiddish and Russian. Traveling while pregnant and caring for a young child made the journey even more harrowing. Tales of of Jennie's determination and her eagerness to meet up with her husband became part of family legend.

Somewhere during this unthinkable expedition, Jennie's second child, her daughter Sonya, was born. The birth date of this child would always be contested, especially as she rose to stardom and faced fears of aging, but it appears that January 1886 is the most likely month of her birth. We will never know whether kind strangers saw Jennie in labor on the side of the road and welcomed her with open arms to give birth in their home. As Sonya, later to be called Sophie, would write in her autobiography, "Mama had guts; *dreistige* as we Jewish people say. She could always do what she had to do, or thought was her duty."[8] Jennie and her children arrived in New York in 1887, eager to meet up with Charles in Boston.[9]

The Kalish family became the Abuzas soon after they arrived in the United States. How a family of Russian-Jewish immigrants took on the Italian surname is another mystery surrounded by specula-tion. While fleeing conscription into the Russian army, Charles Kalish had met a man named Charles Abuza, who became his friend and traveling companion. It seems that Charles Abuza grew seriously ill, and when he died, Charles Kalish took the Italian's papers and entered the country with a new name. Census records indicate that all family members came as Abuza; there is no record of Charles, Jennie, Philip, or Sonya Kalish. Although this story is quite fantastic, it was very common for Jewish immigrants to change their names before or after settling. Al Jolson was born Asa Yoelson, Eddie Cantor was Isidore Iskowitz, and Nora Bayes was Eleanor Goldberg. These partic-ular name changes were in part influenced by the desire for market-able show business monikers; in Sophie's family's case, the change was in response to European and American anti-Semitism.[10]

The period between 1880 and 1920 witnessed tremendous changes in American life for all residents as immigrants arrived from nations around the world. Newcomers from Italy, Hungary, Turkey, Poland, and Slavic areas in Eastern Europe made up more than 80 percent of all immigrants, and they filled the ranks of a new industrial work-force. By 1900, two-thirds of immigrants lived in cities, with the larg-est urban centers, such as Philadelphia, Boston, and New York, facing swelling increases in population. The varying ethnic groups clustered in distinct neighborhoods, developing their own newspapers, mutual aid societies, stores, and fraternal organizations. From 1860 to 1900, the number of industrial wageworkers had tripled, and organized labor was beginning to exert its power through nationwide strikes. In 1886 the American Federation of Labor was created to address the needs of this heterogeneous population of skilled workers.

Cities were undergoing tremendous technological developments when the Abuzas came to America, as electric trolley systems, skyscrapers, and modern infrastructure such as the Brooklyn Bridge were built. Public libraries and parks satisfied municipal goals for uniting the rich and the poor; New York's famed Central Park was developed in 1873. A budding consumer culture encouraged the growth of department stores, such as Macy's and John Wanamaker's, which employed mostly female salesclerks earning respectable salaries. While not all cities industrialized as rapidly as New York, Boston, or Chicago, smaller urban areas aspired to have the same facilities as their larger counterparts. The ranks of a middling class grew as more women and men worked as teachers, secretaries, and office managers, or in other white-collar jobs. With more disposable income and a longer lunch break, they often filled the audiences of vaudeville performances and other productions that Sophie Tucker would later headline.

If immigrants were making a home for themselves along the northeastern corridor of the United States in the late nineteenth century, African-American life was at a low point. Freed from the yoke of slavery, black men and women in the South were forced into a cycle of debt-inducing sharecropping and were physically terrorized by white men and women. As Jewish immigrants of Sophie's generation came of age, African Americans were segregated and stripped of the most basic rights, actions that were cemented in the Supreme Court decisions in *Plessy v. Ferguson* (1896) and *Williams v. Mississippi* (1898). By 1900, the large majority of African Americans who lived in the South were effectively prevented from voting and were legally confined to "for colored" areas. Jews who had fled Eastern European pogroms and were faring better in the United States were often sympathetic to the plight of African Americans. Many African Americans were moving from rural to urban areas in the South and beginning to migrate to northern cities, and they were relegated to the lowest-paying jobs and excluded from many industrial trades. Race riots, lynchings, and the proliferation of demeaning stereotypes were part of the American experience for black men and women.

Although Americans did not exercise the wide-scale oppression of Jews witnessed in Europe, the United States was still a "full-fledged anti-Semitic society." The belief that the United States was a fundamentally Christian nation cut across class lines, and many people perceived Jews to be dishonest, self-motivated, and racially inferior. Jews were excluded from many prestigious educational institutions, and even some Jews who had risen to positions in national politics, such as Oscar Straus and Bernard Baruch, were restricted from elite fraternal societies. Catholics in particular were hostile to new Jewish immigrants, and Catholic leaders of various national origins expressed vitriol in books and widely circulating newspapers. Many elites felt that a large proportion of the 16 million immigrants who came to the United States between 1890 and 1914 were uncivilized and far from a normative Christian ideal. Jews, who made up about 10 percent of this group, were singled out as the least likely to become true Americans. For many political leaders and reformers, the "Jewish Invasion" threatened key tenets of American society. Jews, unlike other immigrants from Europe, could never come to be regarded as truly white.[11]

While life in Boston was shaped by the settlement dynamics that affected Jews in cities across the Northeast corridor—overcrowding, job insecurity, language barriers, and the difficulty of religious observance—Charles Abuza's earnings were sufficient for the family to move to Hartford, perhaps with the aid of the Hebrew Immigrant Aid Society. This organization undertook initiatives to transplant families from cluttered ghettos to cities with smaller Jewish populations. Sophie was eight at this time, and her family had grown since they came to the United States. Her younger siblings, Moses and

Annie, were born in 1889 and 1892, respectively. By 1896, the family had leased a space at 189 Front Street and had established a kosher restaurant downstairs and living quarters on the second floor. Sophie's family home became central to the budding community of newcomers. Unlike New York's crowded, competitive atmosphere for skilled workers, Hartford had a less contentious melting pot environment among the city's Italians, Irish, and Jews, and it offered more opportunity.[12] Hartford also did not exude the rigid anti-Semitism that Boston's elite Brahmin society perpetuated.

By 1880, Hartford had become home to approximately eight hundred Jews, mostly from Germany, and Hartford's Jewish population later increased into the thousands, reaching nearly seven thousand by 1910. Hartford was apparently a relatively welcoming place, with the city's leading newspaper, the *Hartford Courant*, mentioning Jewish issues and religious observances. In 1890 the newspaper notified citizens that Yom Kippur, the Jewish Day of Atonement, would be observed and explained the details of the holiday; in the same year, the paper featured a book review about Jewish history. By 1890 Jewish merchants had been incorporated into the middle class; they were involved in the sale of jewelry and had built reputable department stores.[13] Yet for newer immigrants, life was difficult, and poverty was a reality for most. Sanitation, reliable electricity, and refrigeration were often hard to come by. It was not uncommon for many families to share a home, with a dozen or more children sleeping on the floor. The threat of disease loomed, as well as the day-to-day scramble for work.[14]

Perhaps because the family had already built a life in Boston, the Abuzas fared better than most recent immigrants. Front Street was at the heart of Jewish commerce, and the area bustled with all kinds of economic and social activity. Peddlers and pushcart owners filled Hartford's East Side, along with fish markets, bakeries, and pharmacies owned by Jewish families. The Abuzas lived in less congested quarters than many, and their riverfront restaurant drew people from the nearby docks. Sophie recalled that although her family was poor, her mother always saved food, clothing, and other needed items for those facing harder times. Jennie's generosity was etched into Sophie's mind from a young age, and later, when Sophie became successful, she would do the same for others in need.

The Abuzas' restaurant quickly became a fixture in town, and Sophie and her siblings worked hard in the kitchen, waited tables, and tended to the needs of customers. Jennie's delicious, inexpensive kosher food, including Old World delicacies such as pickled herring and potato kugel, attracted people in the neighborhood as well as those traveling in and out of Hartford.

The restaurant business often fluctuated, however. As Sophie recollected, "It seemed as if our family finances always followed the thermometer," and cold Hartford winters slowed the flow of customers.[15] Charles's predilection for card games also wore on the family's resources, brought all sorts of unsavory men into the Abuza home, and complicated Jennie's fears for her family. Nevertheless, these kinds of struggles were not uncommon, and Sophie knew that she was part of a community that was constantly working, constantly struggling to get by. As an elementary-age child, Sophie washed dishes, ran errands, prepared food, and cared for her younger siblings. Schoolwork and time with friends often took a back seat to the financial needs of the family. This was the case for most working-class families at the turn of the century, and for children in rural areas, school could barely compete with the schedule of the harvest. African-American children rarely had the opportunity to progress beyond a few years of elementary education, if that. Working full-time, with no hope for education by adolescence, was not at all unusual.

In this context, it was quite bold for Sophie to know from a young age that she would not grow up to follow in her mother's footsteps. Sophie had the choice to remain in modest stability in Hartford, without the kind of movement and disruption so many young people had to endure. Although Sophie never complained about the difficulties of her childhood, she recognized a path to a very different kind of life and capitalized on the kinds of opportunities the restaurant could provide her. Her decisions along the route to adulthood would only intensify the sense that she was different from others in her family and community. Over time her empathy would grow for individuals who, by choice or by necessity, were outside of mainstream life.

The Abuzas' family restaurant would become Sophie's first gateway to performing, to the chagrin of her mother and others who viewed the theatrical profession as scandalous. By the 1890s, all kinds of amusements were developing across the country—vaudeville, nickelodeons, amusement parks, and other types of theater. Immigrant talent fueled most of these developments, and the people on stage and in the audiences represented a spectrum of ethnic contributions. Yiddish theater featured prominently in Hartford, and venues such as Germania Hall and Parsons Theater, which held more than a thousand people, attracted Jews living on Hartford's East Side. Yiddish versions of Shakespeare and the works of other playwrights were performed by some of the most prominent artists of the day. The Abuzas' restaurant's prime location and kosher food made it a regular spot for Jewish performers who traveled through Hartford. Sophie reminisced about waiting by the stage doors to take actors to the restaurant for "the best meal in town for the least money."[16]

Yiddish theater actors made an enormous impression on the young girl. Waiting on giants such as Jacob Adler, Boris Thomashefsky, and Bertha Kalich allowed her a glimpse into another world, and Sophie used extra money she earned at the restaurant to soak up shows at Hartford's other venues. As much as she adored the Yiddish players, she recognized that "Jewish plays" didn't have the drawing power of American theater in general. Her father, who often sold tickets for Yiddish shows, was often left with hundreds of vacant seats. Vaudevillians such as the Howard Brothers and the Empire City Quartet, who also frequented Abuza's restaurant, represented larger success in show business, with marquee performances in cities across the United States that Yiddish troupes could never produce. As much as she felt a sense of pathos for entertainers exhibiting Old World language, customs, and humor, Sophie began to understand that real stardom demanded talent that appealed to broader audiences. Entertainment was a priority for most residents of Hartford, and the *Courant* included a section on the plays coming through town on a regular basis. Yiddish-speaking immigrants might have found these attractions less desirable and too expensive, but their Americanized children relished the opportunity to envelope themselves in a national theater.

As she moved through grade school, Sophie began to recognize that she was special. Compliments from her music teacher on her big, sturdy voice gave her the confidence to sing in the restaurant. Entertaining at Abuza's had a similar function to performing in restaurants in other ethnic communities, as Italians, Japanese, Greeks, and other groups frequently employed singers to keep patrons amused. As she revealed her talent to customers, her mind was flooded with a teacher's remark about her fantastic "personality," and although she may not have completely understood the meaning of the word, it encouraged her to continue molding her performance style. More constant shows at Abuza's drew in extra earnings and increased her interactions with customers in the entertainment business. With more and more excursions to the theater, the young girl absorbed all she could to build a repertoire of songs. She would mimic the artists eating in the restaurant, and they gave her the lyrics to their songs. But this wasn't entirely necessary, as Sophie had an amazing ear for music and a memory that would later allow her to recall not only hundreds of songs, but also names of audience members. Day after day, Sophie got her musical training at Abuza's while offering a performance quality that entertainers at other restaurants could not produce. Her repertoire was completely informal and sporadic; there is no indication that she took any music lessons, and her only practice time was while she was working.[17]

With the money she earned from singing, Sophie visited the theater whenever she could, and her knowledge of the ditties written by Harry Von Tilzer, Witmark and Sons, and other offspring of immigrants expanded with more live-performance exposure. She would experiment with various singing styles for customers in the restaurant and listen to their feedback. By the time she was a fixture in the restaurant, Sophie knew all of the popular hits; piano players offered this music at all of the popular leisure sites, and people bought sheet music at a rapid pace. She took in everything that she was told and hungered for more instruction. Sophie's training thus began with observation, and she remained open to suggestion throughout her career, never afraid of criticism.

By the time Sophie was thirteen years old, she felt entirely comfortable performing for larger audiences. Yet she had serious obstacles to face, particularly her weight; at the age of thirteen she weighed 140 pounds.[18] Although fleshy, voluptuous women had been viewed as ideal in the period between the Civil War and 1890, preferences began to shift toward slender, athletic figures for women. Advice columns urged women to build muscle rather than relying on corsets, and smaller standard clothing sizes began to dictate norms for women's figures. The dieting literature that proliferated in the 1890s emphasized that not only was a slender figure an indicator of self-control and middle-class identity, but obesity was often associated with immigrants and women of color. Racial stereotypes abounded concerning overweight Irish and Jewish women; the *American Jewess*, the first English-language magazine published for Jewish women, in 1895 featured dieting advice so readers could avoid being perceived as the "stout Jewess."[19]

In this context, Sophie's weight would be a great struggle as she imagined a career on the stage. She never embodied the physical traits desired by most producers and directors who were casting stars in the newly emerging American entertainment industry. Although Lillian Russell, one of the most famous women on the stage, weighed over two hundred pounds at the height of her career in the early 1900s, the public fixation on slender bodies intensified with time. So too did the stigma against obesity as Sophie moved from adolescence into adulthood. Her performances at amateur concerts at Riverside Park, coupled with years of entertaining in the restaurant, led her to believe she belonged in the theater, but Riverside Park audiences identified her as "the fat girl." Still, her comic timing and amazing voice, even from an early age, alerted audiences to her desirable presence. When Sophie heard roaring audiences, she realized that inviting laughter could perhaps be just as important as showing off physical beauty.[20] She also understood that her relationship to audiences was paramount.

Charles and Jennie were aghast at the prospect of their eldest daughter mingling with the show business crowd, which many people regarded as scandalous and irresponsible. Although serious actors were gaining more respect over time, the newer crop of budding vaudevillians and burlesque performers were not to be trusted, certainly not with a young impressionable girl in their midst. Sophie's parents equated a career in show business to the activities of gypsies in Russia, who allegedly took advantage of others and had no real family ties. Any parents would have expressed these fears with a daughter considering an independent life on the road, but for a Jewish family, Sophie's dreams also went against the fiber of religious and social customs.

Eastern European culture remained deeply engrained in the mind-set of immigrants, and even though material circumstances made it difficult for people to uphold traditional gender roles, expectations continued that families would preserve Old World patterns. Within Judaism, men and women held very different positions, and intellectual life—particularly the reading of religious texts—was at the center of male training. Women were raised to marry and tend to housework. Immigration disrupted much of this arrangement, as skilled labor often replaced rabbinic training for men and some women worked outside the home to provide for their families. However, married Jewish women worked outside the home in much fewer numbers than married women from other immigrant groups. Even if Jewish women were granted some temporary freedom as wageworkers, it was with the assumption that they would marry and maintain Judaism in the home. Education, paramount in Jewish life, was extended to sons much more than to daughters. Families' investment in their sons' education often came at the cost of further schooling for daughters, and some women worked to support their brothers in high school or college.[21]

In the United States the turn of the century was a period of changing gender norms that challenged all of these beliefs. Victorian ideologies emphasizing separate, domestic spheres for women were slowly giving way to a more modern notion of women's roles in politics, education, and the workforce. A heterosocial culture among the working class—men and women of the opposite sex spending time together in the new dance halls, nickelodeons, and other leisure sites—became more predominant as the century progressed. Middle-class reformers often viewed these kinds of friendly interactions between young men and women with skepticism and even condemnation. Among immigrant families, unassimilated parents were often outraged at this kind of behavior among their children. Yet this was the world that Sophie inhabited, and with her peers she embraced new possibilities for girls, along with a rejection of her mother's lifestyle. The streets and parks that Sophie frequented were at the center of a new kind of American socialization, especially in light of the overcrowding so many faced at home.[22]

When Sophie's mother told her that after school her primary task would be to find a good Jewish man and marry him, her daughter cringed at the idea.[23] It wasn't just that the teenager was looking for a life that included more than washing dishes and helping her husband succeed, but also that her romantic interactions with boys had been fairly limited. Sophie felt that young men always viewed her as a friend, but never as attractive. She was angry that boys were only interested in her when she would pay for them to accompany her to the theater, using the wages she earned from singing in the restaurant. This message—that she could only become popular if she had the resources to befriend and support men—would remain with her throughout her adult life. Extroverted, affectionate, and funny, Sophie longed for love and friendship from her family, customers in the restaurant, her peers, and eventually young suitors. Her constant dreams of life on the stage did not prevent her mind from wandering to the kinds of things most adolescent girls contemplated, especially boys. Sophie's need for attention, particularly in a family of four children, led to the feeling she expressed upon graduating from high school: as she recalled, "More than anything in the world, I wanted to be *wanted*."[24] Not only did she relish the opportunity to stand out, she desperately hoped for huge, all-encompassing, unconditional love. For her, this could never be felt within the conventions of Jewish domestic life.

When Louis Tuck, a popular, handsome, charismatic boy from the neighborhood, expressed an interest in taking Sophie to her first dance, she was in disbelief. Louis was one of nine children born to Simon and Frida Tuck, who emigrated from Russia around the same time as Sophie's family. Many of the neighborhood girls were crazy about Louis, and Sophie was taken in by his attention, having doubted that any boy would want to be more than a friend. She felt attractive and desired for the first time. She was not the "fat girl" asked to sing at Riverside Park, but a normal teenager, enthralled by the rush of the dance, especially because so many girls seemed jealous. After that night, the two began to spend time together. Jennie was not entirely pleased that the new couple was going out as much as they did, as she still needed Sophie to work at home. Yet seeing her daughter on the road to courtship must have reassured Jennie that her daughter would become a proper Jewish wife eventually.[25]

Sophie and Louis could not wait to marry, and they did not give real consideration to the gravity of marriage. As the second eldest boy in what must have been a very crowded home, Louis viewed marriage as a way to "have fun," and perhaps to gain independence from his family. Graduation came, and Louis immediately proposed to Sophie and persuaded her that their life together would be carefree. Disregarding all Jewish traditions regarding marriage preparations, a synagogue wedding, and most of all the approval of parents, Sophie and Louis hastily took the train to Holyoke and were married in secret in May 1903. Sophie told her mother she was going to a matinee with a friend, as she usually did on Saturdays. Her written recollections about the actual event are very brief, most likely because her memories about the aftermath were much more significant.[26]

Returning home to tell her family that she was now Mrs. Louis Tuck was not easy. Jennie and Charles Abuza were naturally stunned and immediately concerned for their daughter's reputation. They suggested that the marriage be kept a secret until a formal Orthodox wedding could take place, and the couple accepted, having taken little time to consider the consequences of their nuptials. Sophie had never asked Louis, a beer wagon driver, how much money he earned, and it was unclear whether they could live alone without outside family support. Still, there was no choice but for the Abuza family to give Sophie a wedding with all the trimmings, and the community came out to congratulate Jennie on her daughter's success in finding a husband. Despite the financial hardships the family often faced, it was clear that the marriage of her two daughters had weighed heavily on Jennie's mind. She had saved every penny she could for a reputable reception and linens for the girls' hope chests.

Initially, Louis and Sophie were able to establish themselves in their own apartment, which Sophie viewed as incredibly luxurious. But Louis's earnings could not support the couple living independently, especially after Sophie learned she was expecting their first child. There seemed like nothing else to do but to move in with Sophie's parents, who by this time had moved to a larger space on Morgan Street, where they could take in boarders. Determined to see both her sister and her younger brother receive a good education, Sophie took their shifts in the restaurant.

The couple were no longer paying rent, but it seemed that Louis was never responsible when it came to saving for the future. When their son, Albert, the first Abuza grandchild, was born in February 1905, Sophie begged Louis to move out of her parents' home to get a more lucrative job that would provide for their family. Louis had little interest in furthering his career and was content with Sophie earning money in the restaurant while he continued to work as a truck driver. He furnished his wardrobe with fine clothes and accepted the status quo, immune to the chattering of neighbors who wondered why a married man would allow his in-laws to unnecessarily support him.[27]

For Sophie, one thing became clear. This was not the life she could continue to live, and while helping her mother in the kitchen was her responsibility as a child, it was not going to be her job as a grown woman. As vaudevillians moved through the city and continued to hear Sophie sing at the restaurant from time to time, they encouraged her to enter show business. She didn't need encouragement from others; she had wanted to sing professionally since she was a young girl. Louis's unwillingness to get a better job only intensified the fire in her belly. She told him that if he could not become more financially responsible, they would need to separate. And so they did. Louis moved to live with his sister and left Sophie to tell her parents that the marriage was not going to work.

In turn-of-the-century America, divorce was frowned upon, particularly in religious communities. In the general population very few couples divorced; there were fewer than two divorces for every thousand marriages in 1870. Courts required evidence of adultery, desertion, or a grave action on the part of a spouse, and in general, divorced Americans were labeled as suspicious or morally bankrupt. Some couples separated, but the decision to seek a divorce, particularly at the urging of the wife, was a serious matter. This was even more the case in Jewish society, where arranged marriages were still customary and Orthodox Jewish couples were expected to maintain traditions and to create large families. Sophie had not only married impulsively, but she was now willing to break her marriage vows. This kind of boldness was unimaginable for Jennie and Charles Abuza, who warned their daughter against such an unacceptable, unforgivable action. They had insisted that no one know that Sophie and Louis had eloped, and public knowledge of their separation would be devastating to the family.[28]

Sophie had made up her mind, though. At the time she told her parents she was separating from Louis, they didn't realize that she was also planning to leave her son, to leave Hartford, and to pursue a life on the stage. With the money she had earned from working in the restaurant, she planned her departure, telling them she needed to take two weeks off to potentially reconcile with Louis. Sophie knew she was never coming back, and as she waved to her infant son in her sister's arms, the guilt overwhelmed her. She remembered telling herself, "It's only by getting out, making something of yourself, making real money, that you can do the most for Son and for Mama who has done so much for you."[29] At this time the Abuzas were not struggling financially; the restaurant was stable, and the family home had additional rooms to rent. While the financial needs of family may have provided a more legitimate justification for her decision in Sophie's mind, she was leaving for her own desires. Caring for Sophie's infant son would not make Jennie Abuza's life any easier. Sophie's sixteen-year-old sister, Annie, whom Sophie had urged to pursue a good education, would be left to primarily care for Albert. When the headstrong Sophie walked out the door, she perhaps had not fully considered the ramifications for her family, including the added responsibility and the gossiping neighbors.

Sophie traveled first to New Haven and then to New York, doing the unthinkable for a Jewish woman of that era, especially one from a respectable, hardworking family. As she prioritized her own independence over her responsibilities for her husband and son, she took the first step in building her career. Yet the guilt she felt about leaving her family would never die down, as much as she told herself, and later the public, that her move to the theater was the only way to support Albert. The truth—that she wanted to pursue her passion more than care for her child—was too difficult to admit. After a week in New York City, she finally told her parents that she was gone for good. She remembered declaring, "I have decided I can do big things and have definitely made up my mind that you will never stand behind a stove and cook any more."[30] Sophie discouraged her folks from trying to bring her home and told them to take care of Albert. She was on her own, and no one could stop her from trying to become a star.

2

FINDING A PLACE
IN THE CITY

*S*ophie arrived in New York City when the world of saloons, smaller theaters, and nickelodeons was evolving into a mass entertainment industry. By the early part of the twentieth century, a host of wide-scale cultural institutions was in full swing, managed primarily by second-generation immigrants. From the magic of Harry Houdini to the lyrics of Irving Berlin, the work of hyphenated Americans, many of them Jewish, influenced the arena of cheap amusements. A talented woman with a big voice, Sophie was not the only young person with big dreams of making it on the stage. Legions of young adults flocked to the Big Apple to try their hand at stardom, offering a brand of talent America had never before seen.

Much of the success of these new bastions of entertainment relied on managers' ability to move beyond the Victorian norms of the previous century, when men and women had occupied separate spheres. Fathers and sons were thrown into the rough-and-tumble manly pursuits of sport, saloons, and fraternal organizations. Women, on the other hand, were guardians of hearth and home, permitted to attend appropriate, often chaperoned leisure events such as museum visits, educational lectures, and theatrical performances. The result was that amusements were crafted for polarized audiences, either as rowdy spectacles or delicate, contained performances. American culture was hierarchical and highly dependent on the gender of the audience.

The most successful entrepreneurs in American history were those who would change this structure and democratize audiences. Italian-American Tony Pastor, a former circus performer, singer, and songwriter, was deemed the "father of modern variety." Recognizing the challenge of transforming what began as rough, masculine, working-class theater, he hoped to create something that a rising middle class with a largely female audience could also enjoy. As Pastor recalled, "I had long believed that the variety show should attract the patronage of women and families." So he "took the lease of an opera house at No. 201 Bowery."[1] Here, Pastor began to set the stage for respectable theater. Success at the Bowery venue allowed him to establish theaters at other locations in the city. By 1881, when Pastor moved to Fourteenth Street, in the center of the commercial Union Square theater area, he had proved that theater was a province for all to enjoy.[2]

If Pastor made it possible for Americans to freely enter theaters with their families, B. F. Keith and Edward F. Albee would take the lead in defining the context of performances, capturing a kind of American attention that had never been previously witnessed. These native New Englanders were incredibly savvy businesspeople, and they transformed Pastor's concept of variety into the incredibly lucrative, fanciful notion of vaudeville. Albee, a former tent boy for P. T. Barnum, and Keith, no stranger to the world of traveling circuses, teamed up to create universally amusing, continuous entertainment. Performers ranged from stunt animals to singers to midgets, but the key was that shows never stopped between 10:00 am and 10:00 pm. Keith and Albee knew that tastes ranged across audiences and that it was critical to draw in women and children during daytime hours. As a form of entertainment not defined by strict artistic principles, the genre included all kinds of acts, as long as they qualified as morally unobjectionable.[3]

When they decided to feature a version of Gilbert and Sullivan's opera *The Mikado*—expensive for patrons of high theater but a fraction of the price in vaudeville—crowds came in droves. The combination of both a legitimate opera and shorter, more playful acts fueled the careers of Keith and Albee, who by 1893 owned theaters in Philadelphia, Boston, and New York. Pitching vaudeville as moral, clean entertainment, they encapsulated the diverse flavor of Pastor's earlier downtown ventures and moved the shows to cities across the nation.[4]

Keith and Albee were no different from other Gilded Age entrepreneurs, such as Andrew Carnegie and Nelson Rockefeller. They altered individual stage shows into a vertically integrated monopoly on vaudeville. Newly formed circuits included booking agents, theaters, and all other aspects related to the enterprise, which allowed them to dominate the industry. Others, such as Marcus Loew, F. F. Proctor, and the Shuberts, would compete with the Keith-Albee organization, but the latter had established a model for a modern, standardized form of mass entertainment. As acts toured along well-established routes and agents took control of performers, vaudeville set a precedent for the kind of amusement that could be successfully consumed by a national market. Most cultural developments—film, radio, and later television—would mimic this structure. Sophie entered the industry at a time when it was still in a formative stage, and she had the ability to shape the genre in ways that its creators were open to accepting.

When she arrived in New York with only the money she had earned working at Abuza's, vaudeville greatness was still just a dream for Sophie. Although she had relatives in the city, she decided that family would prove a distraction. Fearing that the judgment she received from her parents would also manifest among her cousins, she decided to live on her own, opting for a dingy hotel on Forty-Second Street that cost a dollar and a half a day. The small amount of money she brought with her would not last for long, yet she stood firm in her conviction that she could dazzle the leaders of Tin Pan Alley and begin working steady gigs. Abuza's Restaurant customers such as the Howard Brothers had told the young entertainer that New York would love her and that songwriting giants like Harry Von Tilzer would relish the opportunity to work with such a unique singer. Dressed in the finest outfit she had brought with her to the city, Sophie spent her first morning in New York set to do Tin Pan Alley using Willie Howard's card to introduce herself. This was it, she believed: the opportunity she had left everything behind for.

When Tucker entered the offices of Tin Pan Alley in 1906, a commercial revolution in music was already underway, transforming the focus from melodies that had little national appeal to songs that were purchased, played, and internalized by most Americans. From 1870 to 1910, the rate of piano production skyrocketed as more people of all classes saw the piano as a standard fixture in the home. Music education was prevalent at the time, and new technologies like the player piano and phonograph would further propel the sale of commercial music.[5]

Creating catchy tunes became very appealing to creative entrepreneurs in the fluid, largely open market. Beginning with Charles Harris's smash hit "After the Ball," performed by idolized conductor John Philip Sousa at the World's Columbian Exposition in 1893 as well as vaudeville stars of the day, hundreds of thousands of Americans purchased sheet music based on a standardized sound. Once "After the Ball" had demonstrated its cache, Harris was able to move his small Milwaukee office to New York and become a songwriting fixture. Other aspiring songwriters began setting up offices on Fourteenth through Forty-Second Streets, surrounding the theater district, including Midwesterners Von Tilzer and Paul Dresser as well as New Yorkers such as the Witmark brothers. These individuals and many others would tap into the pulse of American values: marriage, courtship, family, racial ideas, and politics. One Tin Pan Alley chronicler exclaimed, "Tin Pan Alley lives, not on private emotions, but on tie-ups with current events, passing moods."[6]

Sophie knew that a new kind of music—ragtime—was taking the nation by storm, and she was ready to become part of the craze. Tin Pan Alley began to flourish even more with the introduction of this new genre, a syncopated piano sound that rebuffed the constraints of more traditional Victorian music. Although ragtime was initially suspect due to its association with African-American musicians, by 1910 it was a respectable genre, considered fit for middle-class consumption. Dependent on the piano, ragtime caused a flurry in the sale and distribution of sheet music, with Tin Pan Alley songwriters and publishers as the primary beneficiaries. As "the modern American music industry came to power during the revolution of ragtime," sound was completely transformed. The difficulty of playing ragtime compositions led to the popularity of the mechanical player piano, which allowed technologically reproduced sounds to be heard without actual musicians.[7]

With all of these changes taking place, the music industry was ripe for new talent. By the first decade of the twentieth century, mostly Jewish songwriters and publishers replaced the gentiles before them. They had a background in sales and a long period of assimilation in America, and they had discovered how to work within the American economic system with little public recognition of their Jewish heritage.[8] Adaptation to life in America and rejection of traditional values united these young people in ways that produced a broader youth culture beyond the neighborhood of Tin Pan Alley. Their Judaism was not formalized, but it played an important role in the creation of America's songbook. Often melodic patterns frequently sung in Jewish prayer made their way into popular standards, as did Yiddish phrases, which were sung by both Jewish and gentile performers.[9]

The position of Jewish men in the entertainment industry, first on Tin Pan Alley and later in motion pictures and talent representation, is connected to skills they honed before they entered the business, but also to the precarious position they occupied in the larger industrial structure. Anti-Semitism intensified with the great wave of Eastern European Jews entering the country, and many executive positions, white-collar managerial jobs, elite clubs, and, by the 1920s, many Ivy

League colleges barred Jews from their ranks. Jews were among many marginalized peoples, including other immigrant groups and particularly African Americans, who capitalized on access to a nascent entertainment business. This industry did not have the same rules regarding who belonged and who did not that had long been cemented in other businesses. If racist charges of Jewish dominance over Hollywood and other areas of entertainment were grounded in the large representation of Jewish studio heads and directors, it was because the entertainment industry was a place where they could settle in with the least amount of resistance.

Jewish stereotypes also abounded on stage and elsewhere, evoking protests within the religious community. Jewish groups viewed William Shakespeare's most notorious Jewish character, Shylock in *The Merchant of Venice*, as an embodiment of negative stereotypes, and attempts were made to ban the reading of the play in public schools.[10] In a 1910 sermon Rabbi Joseph Silverman of Temple Emanuel-El in New York City, one of the most prominent voices in the campaign against negative representations, warned of the dangers of Jewish caricatures in the media and urged theater owners to turn away any acts demeaning the Jewish faith. Although New York theater owner Percy Williams agreed that he would not employ anyone who "offensively caricatures the Jew," this policy was not adopted by everyone in the business. For decades the problem was compounded by the widespread use of anti-Semitic humor, often reinforced by Jewish performers themselves.[11] Challenges from both gentiles and Jews claimed that the "Stage Jew"—a minstrel version of a Jewish man or woman—was a product of money-hungry Jewish theater managers and entertainers who did not reflect or promote proper Jewish values.

In the opinion of some German Jews who had been in the United States for fifty years or more, corrupt Eastern European immigrants were a leading cause for American anti-Semitism.[12] When Bertha Rayner Frank, the sister of US Senator Isidor Rayner, was denied access to a luxury hotel in Atlantic City that had a house policy "opposed to Hebrews," it caused a stir on the front page the *New York Times*, drawing public attention to the prevalence of anti-Semitism within the most elite circles. A spokesperson from the Marlborough-Blenheim Hotel responded that although Ms. Frank and other "prominent Hebrews" were perfectly acceptable guests, other, more questionable Jews of a lower class and character were not welcome. This incident and many others mobilized Jewish organizations to act against the infringement of Jews' civil rights, but they never quite dispelled the notion that some Jews were better than others.[13] This context prevented Sophie from publicly expressing her identity as the daughter of Eastern European Jews, and although most of the Tin Pan Alley crowd was Jewish, most did not call attention to their religious heritage.

Sophie had familiarized herself with all of Harry Von Tilzer's greatest hits, and when the time came for her to perform for him, she was met with an answer she was not expecting: "Drop in again someday."[14] She moved along to other Tin Pan Alley music houses but encountered the same tepid response. For days Sophie returned to the neighborhood but made little progress. With money running out and prospects looking dim, she resorted to the tactic that had earned her fame as a child—singing in neighborhood restaurants. She relocated to a cheaper apartment on Second Avenue, and in exchange for meals she performed for customers at Eighth Street's Café Monopol under a new name, Sophie Tucker.

Tucker was beginning to build friendships with people she met in her neighborhood, and while she worried about how she could stretch the little money she had, she begged for information about singing opportunities and learned that off Broadway, on Fortieth Street, the German Village had a reputation for employing singers at cheap rates. As Tucker made her way to secure a gig in that area, she viewed the harsh reality for many women without work: they hustled on the street as a last resort. When she arrived at the first German Village club, things became dicey while she waited to talk to the manager. First she was propositioned as a prostitute by a drunk customer, then she was denied a job because the manager felt she looked too young. Tucker realized that she had to look the part of a professional singer. "I didn't have the word for it, but that night I tumbled to the idea—'New Yorkish.'" Tucker remembered proclaiming,

"Sophie Tucker was going to have to look and act as if she belonged to Broadway."[15]

Body image would always be a huge part of Tucker's career. As she transformed herself from the country girl from Hartford into a New York sophisticate, she gained confidence, even though her finances were dwindling. She bought a fashionable outfit on installment and practiced styling her hair until it looked more glamorous. When she made her way back to the German Village, she landed her first job in the fall of 1906, singing for fifteen dollars a week. The three-story building had different sections dedicated to a varied clientele, with new customers at the top and wealthier patrons on the first floor. The underground rathskeller was set aside for agents, managers, and other established industry personnel looking for new talent. Tucker exercised her marketing savvy from the get-go, discovering audience preferences and memorizing hundreds of songs to deliver on command.

Although she started out performing on the third floor, for less important customers, her fan based grew quickly. Singing every evening required changes of wardrobe, and Tucker used some of her earnings to furnish herself with the latest fashions. She was far from being able to afford the minks and sequins that would become her staple look later on in her career, but she knew that the skirts and "lace peekaboos" would hold her audiences' attention. Understanding that her body type was not like those of other aspiring singers, she worked to flatter her curvier figure. She also enhanced her song catalogue and was finally becoming more familiar with the men of Tin Pan Alley. The "boys" were starting to get to know the young up-and-comer, and they gave her material to try and tips on delivery.

Tucker possessed an unusual kind of business acumen. Every individual she came into contact with—managers, bus boys, song pluggers—were potential customers whom she never forgot. She hoped to move down to the German Village's centrally located rathskeller, not only to gain more attention from patrons, but because she knew that industry leaders such as Florenz Ziegfeld and A. L. Erlanger often came by to survey new acts. Tucker had a knack for being in the right place at the right time, determined to stir conversation and offer a unique sound that would imprint her image in people's minds. Lacking the kind of physical beauty that many slimmer, more delicate starlets relied on, Tucker knew to trust other, more valuable components in her arsenal.

To her delight, Tucker moved downstairs in the German Village when another singer moved on to a larger venue, and her paycheck rose to a hundred dollars a week. It was good work, although the area was under constant police surveillance because crime was frequent, and the neighborhood maintained a seedy character. The singer had befriended many of the women working in the Village and at other sites in the Tenderloin District, some of whom worked as prostitutes to support families or children. Watching these women hand over money to men who acted as if they owned them made Tucker cringe, and although she never passed judgment on the business of hustling, she knew she would not let any man control her. She tried to help other women when she could, hiding a portion of their money in her room so they could hold on to some of their earnings.

Tucker began to worry about the longevity of her job at the German Village because various forms of nightlife were under city investigation. Politicians and reformers were becoming increasingly concerned with the vices of the city, with particular concern for young women. By 1910 women made up 20 percent of the workforce, and young women in particular were moving away from closely monitored, family-centered work into factories, shops, and offices. New amusement resorts, dance halls, and theaters provided mixed-sex company, and female sexuality was expressed much more openly. To the chagrin of parents, teachers, and other authority figures, lines were quickly becoming blurred when it came to the behavior of young women. Working-class daughters threatened the easy classification of women as either completely chaste or sexual deviants.[16] Officials in the legal system felt a pressing need to control female behavior and sexuality, and progressive reformers worked toward instituting a series of changes in juvenile homes, settlement houses, and prisons. Within the courts, there was an effort to steer women away from delinquency and to curb the environmental factors—bad mothers, unregulated workplaces, vulgar amusements—that supposedly stimulated female desire.

In this atmosphere, Tucker was taking a major gamble. When she entered the German Village, she was initially assumed to be a prostitute, and future work in these kinds of places would subject her to police suspicion and public condemnation. Unmarried and moving about the city on her own, the singer shed all expectation of female propriety, particularly for a daughter of middle-class restaurateurs. Unlike the white, middle-class women who filled the ranks of the swelling suffrage movement and organizations like the Woman's Christian Temperance Union, Tucker was not determined to purify either the ballot box or the urban ghettos. She was an entertainer looking for access into show business with no chaperone. Tucker's lack of attention to her special needs as a woman and her boldness in entering the male-dominated terrain made her early experience in New York remarkable.

Tucker seems to have consistently sent money home to Hartford, and she wrote letters to her parents encouraging them to take good care of Albert and to bring him to New York, to buy necessary material items, to make sure her father went to the dentist, and other more mundane requests. She promised she would keep sending a portion of her weekly paycheck. Yet her parents most likely never responded to her letters during her initial experiences as a singer because they were humiliated and angered by their daughter's unforgivable actions. It does not appear that Tucker ever saw Albert during her first year in New York; she was apparently completely isolated from her family and the Hartford community.[17]

While many immigrant families were appalled at the notion of their children entering show business, some became more accepting when financial security materialized. Tucker's relationship with her parents was different from that of many of her contemporaries, in part because they had established a greater degree of financial success than many new immigrants. The Abuzas did not depend on their daughter to help them secure better conditions. Jewish performer

Belle Baker's parents, initially disgusted by the idea of stage perform-ing, were able to recognize its advantages once their daughter had moved the whole family away from their crowded East Side home. The Marx Brothers' mother, Minnie, reveled in the financial oppor-tunities show business provided for immigrants who had nowhere else to go. Having grown up as an orphan on the streets of New York's Lower East Side, Eddie Cantor moved through the rough streets to the rougher Bowery theaters and finally to major stardom in the big-time vaudeville arena. Cantor's rags-to-riches story was one born out of the dire circumstances of his childhood; Tucker's was not. Her parents were entrenched in concerns about both their daughter's welfare on the road and the traditions they wholeheartedly believed in as obligatory for Jewish women. It took years after she first moved to New York for them to accept her career choices.[18]

As a mother of an infant son, Tucker had not just gone against the grain. Abandoning her husband and child was truly bold, and not com-mon even among performers of the vaudeville era, most of whom did not have children as they rose to fame. Many of her contemporaries would go on to marry and divorce with frequency, but leaving Albert in Hartford without any communication for what may have been over a year was unusual by any measure. The singer's descriptions of her relationship with her son during that first year in New York men-tion caring for Albert financially and getting her mother out of the kitchen—something it seems Tucker wanted for her mother more than Jennie Abuza ever expressed herself. Her autobiography is nearly absent of feelings of guilt, missing Albert, or pondering whether she had made the right decision to leave. Although Tucker's autobiograph-ical narrative was constructed for her fans years after she had reached the height of fame, she was unwilling to admit that her reasons for leaving her child had nothing to do with providing for his future. She had never even considered bringing him with her to New York, and in the course of two years, it appears as if she saw Albert only a few times when her parents or sister brought him to New York after her first year in the city.[19]

Although she was content to remain at the German Village to maintain a living in the beginning, she jumped at the chance to move up in the industry when the opportunity struck. Friends she had made on Tin Pan Alley encouraged her to audition during an amateur night audition at the 125th Street Theater, where she lined up with other hopefuls to perform for manager Chris Brown. This was an important opportunity to dazzle the producers and booking agents who supposedly frequented amateur nights. With shaky nerves she appeared in front of Chris Brown, holding a vast repertoire of music. Brown was pleased with Tucker's voice but not her appearance: "This one's so big and ugly the crowd out front will razz her. Better get some cork and black her up. She'll kill 'em," he declared. With that, Tucker was blacked up with burnt cork, a red bandanna, a pair of black cotton gloves, and a "grotesque mouth." Shoved onto the stage for a potentially unwelcoming audience, Tucker delivered six songs with great success, so much so that Joe Woods, an established booking agent, offered her a job on the small-time vaudeville circuit.[20]

In what seemed like an instant Tucker was a "Coon Shouter," and she was not the first woman to hold the title. Many before her, including Anna Held, Nora Bayes, May Irwin, and her contemporary Fanny Brice were adept in this style of performing. Coon songs were a popular staple of minstrel shows and vaudeville acts by the second half of the nineteenth century, originating when white male minstrels impersonated African-American women in the 1870s. When women began to enter vaudeville in the 1890s, they were performing the works of Tin Pan Alley lyricists, who often expressed racist sentiments as part of their own Americanization process. Racial stereotypes abounded as they, longing for the old world of plantations, made African Americans the butt of every joke. Coon songs imagined America before the chaos of industrialization. Offering a great deal of cultural capital to writers, performers, and audiences, they allowed immigrants to imagine themselves as truly white against the degrading image of African Americans.[21]

Abhorrent to us now, blackface performance was a mainstay when Tucker was establishing herself. Brice, Al Jolson, Mae West, Eddie Cantor, and many others perfected the art of blacking up to complete the performance of debasing, racially oriented music. Blackface could disguise what Chris Brown considered to be Tucker's unacceptable appearance, but it also provided many performers with the ability to take on new identities. Second-generation Jewish immigrants were determined to shed their ethnic traits, and by putting on burnt cork they could assume a racial stereotype that native-born Americans had donned for decades. Once they became black, they could become less Jewish, less different. In the most famous case of blackface expediting the assimilation process—the first talkie film, *The Jazz Singer*—Jolson, as the son of a cantor, becomes a show business star by putting on a racial disguise. On the stage and screen, and even on radio's *Amos 'n' Andy* show, blackface dominated American culture and propelled the popularity and success of some of the most noted white entertainers of the twentieth century.[22]

Tucker was one of several women who capitalized on their heaviness as the butt of a joke. As expectations for women to be svelte and dainty became stronger, those who aspired to be on stage but did not fall into these categories faced real obstacles. Famous female performers of the 1890s, such as Irwin, Fay Templeton, and Marie Dressler, who were overweight and lacked conventional beauty, used racial disguise to further their comedic talents. With the ability to move into artistic territories usually reserved for men, these pioneering women used coon songs to introduce their own brazen personalities. Audiences often saw Tucker's initial performances in blackface as refined; this gave her a status on stage that immediately distinguished her from others.[23]

Tucker's elevated status as a "World Renowned Coon Shouter" was far from how she imagined the road to stardom. When the singer was performing from 1907 to 1909, she felt that blackface obscured the skill she had accrued in the German Village. The confidence she had felt disappeared, and the words of Chris Brown—"so big and ugly"— haunted her. Although she was proud to be part of a real vaudeville troupe, paid fifteen to twenty dollars a week and traveling up and down the east coast, she abhorred the racial disguise. Although she had earned more in the German Village, the dangerous nature of that neighborhood, the steadiness of her new employment, and the opportunity to move up to a major vaudeville house made the change worthwhile. Still, the very act of blacking up was demeaning; burnt cork proved messy and difficult to remove, and it stained her white satin costume. She made the most of the opportunity but would not share this news with her family. At one of the first performances near her hometown, in Meriden, Connecticut, Tucker cringed at the idea that someone from her hometown might come and recognize her. "I couldn't bear to have them know I went on in blackface," she recalled.[24]

Life on the road was lonely, and Tucker had trouble connecting with the other performers. Moving through New England and smaller towns in Pennsylvania, New Jersey, New York, and Ohio, she longed for companionship but remained focused on perfecting her act. She attended to every nuance of performance, rather than the attractions and nightlife that others in the company were drawn to. The theaters she performed in were often small and far from sanitary; still, Tucker found ways to keep her growing collection of costumes and makeup tidy and organized. She recalled with pride that her dressing room was "always clean and neat."[25] She capitalized on the opportunity she was given, and over the course of a year, she had moved to the top of the program.

The singer's routine got stronger as she learned how to improve her makeup from blackface comedian George LeMaire, as well as how to satisfy the desires of audiences with particular songs. Calls for encores became more frequent, and Tucker began to feel more of the acceptance she had longed for. She internalized the important rule of ingratiating herself with the crew and orchestra while familiarizing herself with the publicity men who came to watch. With these individuals imprinted in her mind, Tucker knew that industry leaders, along with the hundreds of people who watched her perform, could not be forgotten. Their names were etched in an address book that would become larger after every show. When she came back into town, she made sure to let both her friends in show business and the men and women she had met during performances know she had returned. Her voluminous collection of business cards included hundreds of names of music publishers, agents, and entertainers, as well as others in random trades whom she met along her way. While her early work in blackface was still on a small-time vaudeville circuit, Tucker felt she was headed somewhere great. She wistfully remembered, "I suppose the determination to get ahead, to have my name up in electric lights over the theater someday, made up for some of the discomforts and inconveniences."[26]

Critics were amazed by Tucker's act, declaring that she offered something completely new and exclaiming that a "remarkable versatility is just being heralded."[27] The singer took her art to a new level, and the personal touch she provided made her "equaled by none in her line," as one reporter claimed. Although newspapers sometimes got her name wrong in the beginning, calling her Ethel Tucker or Sadie Woods, it was clear she had made an impression.[28] For many, Tucker's singing was particularly pleasing to the ear, unlike the performances of others who placed more emphasis on shouting or unruly forms of behavior. As one reporter exclaimed, "Her personality is so likable, her humor so fetching, her manner so breezy and confidential that you are just glad to sit back and let her have her own way."[29] Audiences found the fact that Tucker was a white woman quite remarkable. "So completely does she deceive her audiences that not until the end when she removes her black gloves and fluffy wig do they realize that she is not a negress," a New Orpheum Theater reviewer exclaimed.[30] Tucker was able not just to sing southern songs—"Negro melodies"—as "fine as the native," but in mastering the art of racial disguise as an inviting endeavor, she endeared herself to a wider number of spectators who marveled in their own deception.[31]

Indeed, this was a great trick for audiences to see: Tucker proving her real identity by removing one glove at the end of her show, wiggling her white fingers at the crowd. Later when she wore a costume with very long sleeves, she took off her wig at the end of her numbers to show her blonde hair. As part of the ruse, audiences also had to believe that they were hearing a specific kind of music that could only be produced by black men and women, and Tucker was part of a larger group of performers who could deliver a particular style of singing. In his observations of "coon shouters," composer and folk ballad pioneer John Niles explained that despite the modern popularization of the form, coon shouting was an ancient, global practice. "In every singing nation on earth it happens," he remarked. "Some native Southern Negro blues are perhaps the best musical vehicles for shouters, but the method of putting over a song with energy and noise and voice-breaks is universally understood."[32] Chicago reporter Amy Leslie described Tucker's voice as "big, resonant, and brassy like an E flat horn" even when she later performed without burnt cork makeup.[33]

While most reporters declared Tucker to be an unusually gifted coon shouter, not all their remarks were positive. Critics sometimes expressed distaste for songs of a different genre, such as "Yiddisher Rag," which was described as a "rag in more ways than one, unworthy in Miss Tucker's repertoire."[34] It is unclear whether this objection was based on the style or the substance of the song, but expectations were evident that Tucker would remain in the minstrel style, faithful to "Southern-style" ballads. Anything too loud, rowdy, or out of character was looked upon unfavorably. This is not surprising given the central role of racial stereotypes in popular culture at the time. From Aunt Jemima to the Gold Dust Twins, grotesque ideas about black people drove commercial culture and allowed white Americans to imagine themselves as superior. Tucker's signature songs, such as "Rosie, My Dusky Georgia Rose," "Why Was I Ever Born Lazy," and "Nothin' Ever Troubles Me," captured the essence of romantic ideas about the South while embodying white assumptions that black women were domestic and passive. Sung slowly, with a heavy drawl, Tucker's melodies entertained northern audiences who fantasized about a world apart from the ugliness of urbanization. Watching the singer in blackface as an "attractive looking young wench" situated theatergoers right in a moment of pleasant reassurance in which black people were properly subservient.[35]

Tucker's popularity extended beyond capturing the essence of coon shouting. Her tone was rich and flowing. She dramatized songs such as "Pick Me Up and Lay Me Down Dear Dixieland" with a knowing sense of nostalgia. She knew when to hold the big notes and when to be much more colloquial, as in the case of the folkish "Missouri Joe." Her sound was filled with texture, and her lyrical delivery placed audiences at the center of the action, whether through the playful criticism of "My Husband's in the City" or the passion of "That Lovin' Soul Kiss." Her personality seeped into the pauses, the laughs, and the spoken parts of her songs. What critics regarded as special, even "refined," was her method of providing more than just a song, but an irresistible story. Tucker had a way of updating traditional ragtime melodies, fusing a northeastern Jewish shtick into tales of the most popular racial stereotypes in the South, with loyal mammies and "happy darkies" dotting the landscape. The paucity of primary sources makes it very difficult to re-create a clear vision of Tucker's live performances, but newspaper accounts describe a woman who endeared herself to the public in a completely new fashion. Initially it was her sound that seemed so distinctive, but over time her movements and mannerisms would become part of her trademark.

White coon shouters like Tucker did not go unnoticed by the black actors who also performed on the vaudeville stage. Famed African-American vaudeville actor Ernest Hogan, dubbed the "unbleached American," admitted that white actors carefully studied the movements and singing techniques of their black counterparts and contorted what they saw. Hogan was optimistic that others could follow in the footsteps of George Walker and Bert Williams, the most successful and highly paid African-American vaudevillians at the time, but he urged others to tap into their creativity and produce acts that would be more difficult to replicate. Black women received far fewer opportunities than black men, but in general Hogan felt that the African-American performer had not "competed with his white brother to the extent that he should." Hogan's article, published in the entertainment industry's most prominent periodical, *Variety*, speaks volumes about the role racial issues played on the stage. Hogan indicated that black performers had more opportunities in vaudeville, with "no so-called color-line," than they did elsewhere. This may not have been a completely accurate reflection of reality, yet it indicates that even as racial stereotyping remained one of the most common forms of vaudeville entertainment, black actors entered the field more easily than they could access other areas of employment.[36]

In our contemporary mindset, it might be difficult to understand how African Americans could have written about coon shouting in a straightforward manner. It is even more startling that Hogan penned the highly popular Tin Pan Alley song "All Coons Look Alike." While many African Americans would increasingly organize against the predominance of demeaning stereotypes, most notably in the black press and through organizations such as the National Association for the Advancement of Colored People (NAACP), entertainment remained a relatively flexible entryway for those whose other options were often the lowest manual labor or domestic service. On the one hand, African-American entertainers faced segregation on the road, received little if any credit as songwriters in published recordings, and encountered numerous other obstacles. On the other hand, black actors were recognized for their talent, were rewarded financially, and were provided some spaces were they could present their own material in an original, perhaps less demeaning manner. Black organizations would discuss and debate the role of African Americans in entertainment over the course of the twentieth century; there was not one uniform opinion within the black community.[37]

Tucker was performing in cities across the northeast, and at one point she had the chance to visit her family in Hartford. She was shocked to see how her parents had aged and how Albert clung to Annie rather than to her. She remembered that before she left for New York the community had embraced her singing in the restaurant and her talents at amateur nights, but it was unclear how receptive her parents were to her visit or to her work on the vaudeville circuit.

However, neighbors and friends now shunned her. Many who were once close to her stayed away, and some called her a whore to her mother's face. The Abuza family had been ostracized for their daughter's actions, and the shame brought on them was apparent when she walked along the streets and children shouted about the "paint on her face," which was a sign of dishonor. The singer was not alone in facing this kind of shame. The stigma of acting as a low profession was still pervasive among middle-class families, and it was difficult for entertainers, especially women, to prove themselves worthy and respectable. Tucker's contemporaries Cantor and Berlin encountered serious opposition from future in-laws on the basis of their profession when they wanted to marry. Tucker quickly left town, swearing not to return until she had reached the pinnacle of success. But she promised to buy her parents a new home and to pay for her brother Moe's college education, so the pressure was on for her to find lucrative engagements.[38]

Back on the road, Tucker's work in blackface began to lead to engagements at higher-profile theaters. When she convinced legendary showman Tony Pastor to book her at his theater in 1908, she could hardly believe that she would stand on the stage she had dreamed about as a young girl in Abuza's restaurant. Pastor's proved to be a major coup for Tucker; one reporter wrote that the show "made her a solid hit, and the house was unwilling to let her go." Tucker performed alongside Leonzo, a "Juggling Dutch Butcher," and Mademoiselle Zoar, a "novelty wire walker"; the range of acts was truly staggering.[39] Tucker's success at Pastor's led to a more long-term role as part of the Manchester and Hill burlesque wheel, for their show the Gay Masqueraders. Burlesque had historically been a place for working-class men to view women's bodies and take in sexual humor, but the rise of vaudeville led to a change in the shows. By the time Tucker entered, much of burlesque had been cleaned up, and managers were trying to appeal to "the better classes," as with the productions of Joe Weber and Lew Fields. Yet competition with vaudeville would always make it difficult to attract audiences, and the genre never divorced from its bawdy reputation; women were still often on sexual display, by way of revealing costumes and suggestive movement.[40]

As part of the company, Tucker had to perform an acting role as well as sing her usual blackface routine in the beginning act of the show. Twentieth-century burlesque included an opening number by the company followed by variety performance. It then ended with a skit, usually some form of satire. Memorizing lines worried Tucker, who also wondered whether she could assume a different character. Yet she came to realize that burlesque was particularly useful for those beginning in the entertainment industry, and the burlesque experience allowed her to create several different kinds of performance personalities.

Traveling across the country for several months with the Gay Masqueraders, Tucker began to form friendships with members of the company that she had been unable to forge in the past. She endeared herself to people in the theaters and in the towns the troupe frequented. All of this paid off: Tucker earned rave reviews for her work in the Gay Masqueraders, with a large demand for encores. Deemed the "hit of the Gay New York company" when the burlesque troupe visited the Majestic Theater, she was stealing the show everywhere they traveled. *Billboard* reported that Tucker was "climbing the ladder of success at a merry pace."[41] She still made sure to visit the offices of important songwriters, finding new material to perform to set her apart from other acts. "Don't make your act a carbon copy of someone else's," she recalled telling herself.[42]

It was on the burlesque wheel that Tucker first encountered Fanny Brice. Another child of Jewish immigrants who began as a coon shouter, Brice shared with Tucker a determination to succeed on the stage. Tucker reminisced about first seeing Brice as a "tall, lanky, funny-faced kid with rubber legs."[43] Though Brice spoke no Yiddish, whereas Tucker was fluent, ironically Brice would become known for her Yiddish accent and musical inflections. According to Tucker, the meeting in burlesque was the beginning of a thirty-year friendship. The two would share stories as entertainers and as women who had made poor choices with men. Both women saw themselves as outsiders and, over time, used their talents to create appealing comic characters.[44]

Tucker's time on the burlesque wheel proved particularly advantageous when Mark Klaw, one of the major New York talent agents, traveled to see Tucker in a Holyoke engagement and offered her a spot in the Ziegfeld Follies. Tucker felt as if she were dreaming. She begged to perform as herself, but Klaw insisted that she remain in blackface. Still, this was Broadway, and the Follies were the biggest, most elaborate productions in New York, featuring all the most famous stars of the day. Tucker agreed to continue with the Gay Masqueraders until her Follies engagement began. In the meantime something happened that would provide her with even more courage to join the Follies. When she got off the train for an upcoming Boston show, she realized she had no way to go on in her blackface costume because her luggage had mistakenly been sent to another city. She was in her street clothes, with no makeup, no wig, and none of the other elements she had become so accustomed to over the years. "I had never yet walked out on the stage without some sort of disguise," she recalled. "In tights and a G-string I wouldn't have felt more stripped."[45]

Tucker was ready to prove that her success had nothing to do with the makeup, and she hoped that the "great Ziegfeld" might hear that she could still shine without blackface. When the matinee audience saw that the blackface performer they expected looked very different, confusion set in, but Tucker explained what had happened. She not only disclosed that her luggage had been lost but also told them that she was Jewish and had been doing the blackface act for years. Finally she could truly be herself, and she grasped the chance to be seen. This was a shining moment for the woman who longed to perform without a mask but could not completely forget the harsh words from her first encounter with Chris Brown—that she was too ugly for the stage.

She tore into one of her signature songs, "That Lovin' Rag," and the audience loved her performance for seven more numbers. She may not have sounded different from when she was in disguise, but she felt as if she were a new woman, coming into her own for the first time. Filled with a renewed sense of possibility after the matinee in Boston, Tucker went on stage that evening performing again as a white woman, in a borrowed evening gown with stylish hair and makeup. The signature facial expressions, mannerisms, and glamour that would eventually become quintessential Sophie Tucker were beginning to emerge.

The singer later recalled, "It was the end of blackface for me and the start of something new and grand and glamorous."[46] After this experience, she believed she could be the kind of headliner people would return to see again and again, and the evening audience's applause gave her no reason to doubt herself. Tucker was ready for the Follies—for the lights, fancy costumes, marquis signs, and wide publicity. Nothing, especially not the racial disguise she wore to establish herself, would get in her way. Tucker envisioned the world of big-time show business and its fame and fortune, and she couldn't wait to arrive.[47]

3

⬦——⬦——⬦

ACCEPTANCE AS
A RISING STAR

*T*ucker came to the *Follies* of 1909 with the highest of hopes. Tired of performing in second-tier houses, frustrated by the lack of big-time recognition, she hoped the *Follies* would cement her place as a show business headliner. In the next few years she would reach the level of success she desired, but the path to stardom was not easy, and the politics of the *Follies* were more complicated than she could have imagined. Impresario Florenz Ziegfeld had already produced two elaborate, well-received shows, and he aimed to top each one with something more dazzling and intricate. By 1909 he was well positioned to feature the biggest stars and to work with directors, writers, and stage designers who were at the height of the industry. Anyone who was anyone hoped to work with him.

As a young boy, Ziegfeld parted from the classical music his father taught formally in Chicago, instead delving into the world of popular culture. Ziegfeld worked a stint in Buffalo Bill's Wild West Show as a sharpshooter, and by the time of the 1893 World's Fair, he was exhibiting a famous strongman, the Great Sandow. In the tradition of P. T. Barnum before him, Ziegfeld had a passion for orchestrating spectacle, and he understood public desires. When he was traveling with Sandow, he made connections with Broadway entrepreneurs, particularly those who hoped to import some of the latest European fads. When Ziegfeld encountered Warsaw-born French star Anna Held in London, he knew he had found something special. A petite, dark-haired woman whose risqué singing captured audiences, Held was the first object of Ziegfeld's longtime quest to bring beautiful women to the stage and to market them as embodiments of desire and sensuality. Ziegfeld became romantically involved with Held, and although her first US performance, in 1896, predated the *Follies*, the Ziegfeld publicity machine that fueled Held's career allowed him to understand the appeal and advertising power of a single body type.[1]

Then Ziegfeld's tastes in women shifted. Still in a relationship with Held, he took on tall and slender performer Lillian Lorraine as a mistress and modeled the Ziegfeld girl after her. Svelte, leggy "American" women were apparently better suited to *Follies* costumes, as well as to the Anglicized theme of the shows. As the *Follies* became an American institution known for high production values, glamour, and more dazzle than any other Broadway production, the expectations for exceptional white chorus girls only escalated. With their long limbs, perfectly coiffed hair, and sensational costumes, Ziegfeld women promoted a new aesthetic that others in both the fashion industry and Broadway would try to emulate. By the time Tucker joined the cast of the *Follies*, playing on the roof of the New York Theater, the production was noted foremost for its display of beautiful women, crafted and staged according to Ziegfeld's preferences.[2]

Overweight and brassy, Tucker stood out, and this heightened her anxiety. Previously she had accepted her size as an attribute in routines, but now her weight consumed her thoughts when lithe dancers in rehearsals surrounded her. She had very little contact with Ziegfeld himself and doubted whether she was actually going to perform in the show. Star Nora Bayes, who like Tucker had changed her Jewish name, Goldberg, to something more ethnically neutral, was one of the biggest vaudeville personalities at the time. She was famous for incredible delivery of songs such as "Shine on Harvest Moon," but notorious for her diva-like behavior.[3] Naturally Bayes was front and center at rehearsals, and while Tucker was happy to take in all the intricacies of a big-time production, she was increasingly disappointed to play a lesser role.

Amid her anxiety, Tucker tried to remember that Ziegfeld saw something special in her. The impresario had told the press about his incredible "discovery" in the singer, even boasting that he had a picture of the theater where he first saw her performing.[4] According to the show program, Tucker was slated to perform some of the classic Tin Pan Alley standards she had perfected over the years. She would wear a stunning gold lamé gown, the most glamorous dress she had ever worn on stage. When Ziegfeld realized that the show was missing a song and dance number centering on President Roosevelt's recent jungle expeditions, he felt Tucker was up for the task: the new act, "Moving Day in Jungle Town," would feature a blacked-up Tucker surrounded by scantily clad girls in animal prints. Although she explained that she was no longer blacking up in her burlesque routine, the singer had little choice but to follow Ziegfeld's instructions. This last-minute change meant she could not rehearse adequately; she was hastily given a jungle costume and told to learn the music for the act.[5]

The Atlantic City opening of the *Follies* on June 7, 1909, was the biggest event of the season, with a star-studded crowd including all of the major stars of early film and stage. Lillian Russell, George Cohan, Weber and Fields, and many others entered with excitement, and critics from the leading newspapers came to report on who would become the next show business up-and-comers. Tucker was in a panic. Perhaps she couldn't deliver the kind of talent that this caliber of patrons expected. She knew that she had Tin Pan Alley songwriters in her corner; by this time Irving Berlin was becoming a close friend, and she was representing Tin Pan Alley music with frequency. Still, Tucker felt a great deal of self-doubt watching stunning women such as Lillian

Lorraine effortlessly dazzle the crowd. When it came time for her to perform the jungle routine, Tucker felt that the distracting animal costumes and background dancers did little to allow her to stand out as a vocalist. It was "no sensation," as she remembered—all the audience took away from that number was that she was a "big gal with a big voice." She felt that she hadn't made any kind of impression.[6]

Tucker was determined to shine in her solo performance. Shedding the animal costume for her gold gown, matching golden slippers, and a glossy, intricate hairdo, she knew that if she did not pour everything she had into the performance, the audience would miss her. Tucker watched as Bayes and dancer Bessie Clayton received encore after encore before it came time for her, a nobody, to take the stage.

Tucker began her performance planning to sing three songs, but as the roars of the audience rolled in, she kept going, three times as long as she had been scheduled to sing. Applause for Tucker lasted into the next performance. She felt as if she had finally achieved the kind of success she had always hoped for, the recognition that would justify all the mistakes she had made by leaving her family in Hartford. She went downstairs to her dressing room and sighed with relief.[7]

Yet things were far from secure for the overnight *Follies* sensation. When Bayes heard the crowds cheering for Tucker, she could not accept being upstaged by a newcomer. Berlin reassured Tucker that her act was so successful she could perform anywhere, no matter what happened with Bayes, but Tucker was not convinced. She feared being thrown out of the *Follies*, and when she later learned from Ziegfeld that she would no longer be performing her solo act—just the silly jungle routine—her heart sank. Nevertheless, she was relieved that she would continue to earn a paycheck and help her family. By this time she was contributing to her son Bert's education in boarding school and helping to pay for her brother Moe's law school tuition. She dreamed that her parents could move into a nicer house.

Even though her role in the *Follies* was small, she was able to deliver; one critic had singled out the jungle number as a "bright spot" in an otherwise disjointed and disappointing show.[8] For about nine weeks during the summer of 1909, Tucker continued in the New

York production of the *Follies*, which the *New York Times* gave a glowing review. The *Times* reporter listed Tucker as having one of the best of the "women parts" alongside more experienced stars.[9] But Tucker's stint in the *Follies* would be short-lived due to personal conflicts between others in the production. Bayes and Ziegfeld argued constantly over the details of Bayes's number, and Bayes's anger was perhaps fueled by Ziegfeld's fondness for Lorraine. To alleviate this tension, Eva Tanguay came to replace Nora Bayes and took Tucker's jungle routine for herself.

Apparently Ziegfeld later regretted dismissing Tucker, and others noted that it was a mistake. At Tucker's Golden Jubilee in 1953, Gene Buck, lead writer and assistant to Ziegfeld for over a dozen *Follies* shows, claimed that there was no doubt that the "chubby, talented girl from Hartford was a threat." Emphasizing his great respect for Ziegfeld and his ability to recognize talent, Buck declared, "I still claim that Ziggy made a great mistake in 1909 when he failed to glorify a great little gal, Sophie Tucker."[10] Though Ziegfeld missed out on working more with Tucker, he was a pioneer in providing opportunities for other performers who might have been overlooked due to their ethnic or racial background, most notably Fanny Brice, Eddie Cantor, and especially Bert Williams.

Although Tucker regretted that her experience in the *Follies* was not what she had wished for, she admitted learning more than she could ever imagine from Bayes. Initially angry and hurt that Bayes had pushed her out, Tucker later took this as an important lesson about how to succeed in show business—to develop a thick skin and refrain from holding grudges. She also noticed that Bayes and other headliners treated secondary performers in a disparaging manner, and Tucker vowed to view them as equals. She recalled embracing those around her: "In every show I have been in, as the star, or headlining the bill, I have known every single person in the cast. I've made it like one big family."[11] Because her relationship with her real family was strained, she shifted focus to ensuring that her stage community would always be welcoming and accepting. Tucker also deeply empathized with those behind the scenes because her years on the bottom rungs of the business had been formative and essential to how she perfected her craft.

Along with life lessons from Bayes, the *Follies* provided Tucker one of her most life-altering moments when she met Mollie Elkins, an African-American woman who would become her closest friend and confidant for the next two decades. Elkins worked as a maid for Lillian Lorraine but had performed in vaudeville with Bert Williams and George Walker, in one of the most renowned black troupes. With their beginnings on the New York stage in 1896, Williams, Walker, and their growing team of dancers, writers, and actors had at least a decade of experience before Tucker began touring in burlesque. Just as the "coon song" allowed many white performers to become famous impersonating African Americans, it also provided the means for more African Americans to work in the entertainment industry. Williams and Walker perfected their craft when ragtime was the rage, creating much of their own music and supervising their own shows. Large casts widened employment opportunities for entertainers like Elkins, and although the shows were often in the stereotypical minstrel tradition, the two men worked to express themselves with humanity and creativity as much as they could.[12]

Although little is known about the specifics of Elkins's career before she met Tucker, she had witnessed enough in the world of minstrelsy and other forms of entertainment to provide the *Follies* newcomer with sound advice on the business. Tucker first encountered Elkins sitting alone in Lorraine's dressing room, with Tucker feeling low and marginalized by the bigger players during rehearsal. Tucker longed for someone to talk to, and a light conversation between the two women turned into the singer pouring her heart out to the show business veteran, who proved knowing, calm, and sensible. That conversation restored Tucker's confidence and gave her the courage to shed some of her insecurities. She later remembered that she was forever changed by her initial interaction with Elkins: "That friendly, wholesome talk, that promise to root for me, the feeling that there was now at least more than one person in the theater to whom Sophie Tucker was more than just a name on the program, sent my blues flying."[13]

After the debacle with the *Follies*, Tucker lived briefly with her brother Moe while she was ill with what may have been a serious case of laryngitis. Tucker's friendship with Elkins had grown strong, and Elkins paid for her doctor visits when money ran out. Elkins and her husband took care of their ailing friend, providing encouragement that she would recover despite the loss of her voice. Eventually, Tucker began to heal, so when she received notice from her old friend Harry Cooper of the Empire City Quartet that there was room for her in a show at a hotel in Arverne, Long Island, she jumped at the opportunity. Tucker recalled that Elkins offered to work as her maid when the singer could not afford it: "I'll make you look important," her friend declared.[14] Both women recognized that having a maid rendered a performer more important in the eyes of others. When Tucker became more successful in later years, Elkins traveled with her as her personal maid, but she was much more of a personal assistant— telling Tucker when to eat and what to wear and boosting her confidence. Elkins would even help Tucker during her act when she forgot a prop, and the singer realized that this kind of improvisation won the audience over. The two women forged the kind of relationship that Tucker had been longing for since she entered show business. Elkins understood her in ways that her mother and sister could not, largely due to her own experience with the ups and downs of a performer's life.

Tucker's relationship with Elkins was a genuine friendship at a time when African Americans were oppressed while white performers appreciated and borrowed from their talents. Tucker would take part in musical exchange with other African-American performers as her career evolved; however, Elkins was her closest friend for many years. The singer's descriptions of Elkins focused on her friend's generosity, wisdom, and overall philosophy rather than on the tasks Elkins undertook for the her. Tucker reminisced, "For true greatness of spirit I have never met anyone who outmatched Mollie." These were strong words coming from a daughter of Jewish immigrants who had encountered many people who had fought to make a life for themselves in America. Although Tucker was not at this point a public promoter of African-American equality, her autobiography does not indicate that she viewed Elkins in a different light from her white friends. Records providing a sense of Elkins's voice are unfortunately absent, but articles in the black press upon Elkins's death indicate that the friendship was as Tucker described it. After she met Elkins, the singer thought more seriously about the rights of black performers and worked to help them through many different avenues.[15]

The public friendship between the two women is all the more significant because racial conditions were particularly precarious at the time Tucker and Elkins became close with one another. Rioting in Springfield, Illinois, in the summer of 1908 left black homes and businesses destroyed, and black residents fled the city in fear. With segregation and disenfranchisement firmly intact in the South, white activists such as Moorfield Storey and Mary White Ovington joined black leaders to protest horrific conditions, forming the NAACP in 1909. Newly emergent black political organizations signaled a major, organized response to discrimination, and many white men and women, particularly Jews, were sympathetic to the plight of their African-American counterparts. Yet there was a great deal of scrutiny toward those who championed black causes, and as the escalation of lynchings attests, many people were concerned about intimate relationships between blacks and whites. In particular, anxiety about romantic liaisons between black men and white women proliferated.[16]

Less public discomfort was expressed about intimacy between black and white women, largely because sexual threats were removed. The underlying assumption was that black women in such relationships served as domestics because historically this had most often been the case. Even when black and white women tended to the most private activities together—childbirth, nursing, dressing, and bathing—public objections were not raised because black women were seemingly subservient. In the case of Tucker and Elkins, this general perception may have allowed for the two women to mask the true nature of their relationship, one which began with Elkins providing financially for Tucker, then later receiving a great deal of respect and reciprocity from Tucker when the latter made it big.

As Tucker prepared to perform at a hotel in Arverne, Long Island, it may have seemed like a small-time gig on the heels of the *Follies*, but it would prove to be one of the biggest moments in her career. During Tucker's routine, Ed Bloom, who worked for talent agent and vaudeville entrepreneur William Morris, was seated in the audience. Bloom was confident enough in Tucker's abilities that he booked her to play the next week at William Morris's signature house, the American Music Hall, located in the heart of Broadway. Tucker could never have imagined how this encounter with Morris and his staff would forever change her. She recalled of the Arverne gig, "I turned a corner that day, perhaps one of the most important corners in my life."[17] Tucker and Elkins reveled in the excitement of her securing a more high-profile job, with a salary that would bring Tucker out of the doldrums.

Morris was a natural friend for Tucker. He had been born Zelman Moses only a decade before her in the eastern part of the German Empire. His family emigrated to the United States when Morris was nine. They changed their name to assimilate and managed to scrape by on New York's Lower East Side, with Morris working various jobs while attending public school. He was a quick study, but he was drawn to the world of entertainment in the theaters owned by Tony Pastor, and he dropped out of school. Moving from a job in bookkeeping to clerking for theatrical agent George Liman, Morris realized that he excelled in managing talent and was adept at marketing. By the time he was twenty-five, Morris was an independent agent working on commission, booking acts for major theaters such as Poli's, Proctor's, and the Keith-Albee circuit. Suffering from tuberculosis at the age of thirty, Morris took respite in the Adirondacks to escape the congested conditions of the city. By this time he was married with two children. He left behind his business and spent almost three years trying to prevent what was at the time a likely death.[18]

When Morris returned to New York, vaudeville was in a battle among savvy competitors. B. F. Keith and his right-hand man, Edward Albee, had created an oligarchy on circuits and booking, joining forces with Morris Meyerfield and Martin Beck, owners of the West Coast Orpheum circuit. This arrangement, with regions of the country designated for the Keith/Orpheum vaudeville empires, made it increasingly difficult for others to operate in the profession. Keith and Albee immediately challenged any independent owners who stood in their way, either by opening rival houses in the same city or by blacklisting acts that dared to join another booking agency. Morris was one of the toughest rivals for the vaudeville giants because he, unlike many others in the business, refused to succumb to their pressures and intimidation.[19]

Although Morris was vaudeville's most successful independent booking agent by 1905, he realized that the only way he could continue in the profession and compete with Keith-Albee would be to control his own theaters. By the summer of 1908, he had received enough financial backing to start his own vaudeville circuit, the William Morris Amusement Company, with eventual plans to visit cities frequented less often by the larger vaudeville companies. His main theater was the American Music Hall in New York City, a lavish, 2,500-seat structure that rivaled the best in the business. For several months Morris scouted talent in Europe and began to lease theaters across the country, from Chicago to New Orleans, and across the West. By 1909 he was looking for stars to headline his theaters and build his reputation as a gifted agent. He would always be more interested in the talent than in the business side of the enterprise, and his initial encounters with stars such as Will Rogers, Harry Lauder, Charlie Chaplin, and of course Sophie Tucker proved his acumen for identifying great entertainers.

There would be several downturns for the agency as Morris competed with Keith and struggled through lean times. His ailing health always plagued his success, and he was often forced to take time away from the city. Yet in a world of competitive, cut-throat showmen, entertainers viewed him as their advocate. As one of his oldest clients, Tucker would remain loyal to the William Morris Agency through thick and thin, and she credited Morris with all of her success.[20]

Morris's belief in the value of vaudeville and the talent of his performers was manifest in his granting of large salaries and thoughtful but candid opinions. Weekly salaries for big-name headliners reached into the thousands, even in the earliest years of the American Music Hall. By the time Tucker had played several engagements, her salary increased from forty to a hundred dollars a week. Newspaper articles heralded Tucker's debut as one of the greatest singing sensations audiences had ever witnessed, giving Morris incentive to book her for return engagements.[21] Still billed as "America's Greatest Coon Shouter" in 1909, but this time without blackface, Tucker was eighth on the Morris vaudeville track but was documented to have the greatest appeal with the audience even on a program with violin virtuoso Violinsky and ventriloquist Arthur Prince.[22] She moved quickly to the sixth position on the bill, and the press urged patrons not to miss this newfound star, who had a delivery as inviting as her presence. One critic proclaimed with certainty, "There have been carloads of 'Coon Shouters' but there is only one Sophie Tucker, and it will probably be a long time before we hear her equal."[23]

Hoping to fill the most space in the entertainment section of the country's newspapers, the Morris Agency carefully orchestrated press reports about Tucker and other performers. By the time Tucker performed in Morris's theater in Chicago, Morris's publicity agent and former *Dramatic Mirror* editor Jack Lait had critics in a frenzy to hear his new star. Lait's enthusiasm resounded among the Chicago press as he gushed over Tucker's talents. Even on a bill with recognized performers such as the amazing hypnotist Pauline and female impersonator Julian Eltinge, it was Tucker who endeared herself to Chicago critics.

Tucker formed long-lasting relationships with established critics, such as Ashton Stevens and Amy Leslie, that would prove vital to the longevity of her career. After reading each review, Tucker wrote personal notes to journalists, "thanking them for their criticism and promising to benefit from it." She also began to keep articles, postcards, fan letters, and other items related to her career and paste them into scrapbooks she bought at local five-and-dime stores. The pages in the scrapbooks grew thicker as Tucker took long train rides to Morris houses in Boston, New Orleans, Indianapolis, and Cincinnati in the fall and winter of 1909.[24]

In compiling the scrapbooks, Tucker made sure that every relationship, program, and accolade was documented and preserved for return engagements, where she could greet supporters with the same fresh smile and kind words she imparted the last time they saw her. The singer knew that Morris was not a permanent ticket to lasting stardom and that she would have to work to maintain headliner status. More than most female stars of the time, Tucker understood the importance of laying a solid foundation with her core supporters—the press, audiences, bookers, and others behind the scenes who never received the kind of public recognition she did, but who were responsible for her success. The individuals who played a large role at the beginning of her career would be faithful to her for decades, largely because she never dismissed them or forgot their contributions.

The scrapbooks were also proof of Tucker's success, tangible evidence that she had accomplished what had seemed both outrageous and impossible in the eyes of her family. The more representations of public acceptance that Tucker could collect, perhaps the more easily she could justify the choices she had made to leave her husband and son. The family Tucker chose to create on the basis of relationships within the entertainment industry was often stronger than that she shared with her parents and siblings, and Tucker's devotion to needs of her fans and managers was her highest priority. This may have kept Tucker in business longer than most of her contemporaries, but it also isolated her from more meaningful connections in her personal life.

Tucker was becoming acutely aware that although her star was rising, she could not yet afford to pay Elkins to permanently accompany her on tour. Elkins had a family of her own to care for and needed steady work. When she was in New York, Tucker visited with her dear friend, and she sent money to Elkins when she could. Upon seeing Tucker's name in lights at an Atlantic City theater during the tour of Morris houses, Elkins stood by her side and relished with her the moment she had longed for as a child. Tucker continued to send money to her mother every week, and to her brother Moe to help with his full-time study of law at New York University. The relative financial and professional security of the Morris agency alleviated the anxiety Tucker often felt when she wondered whether each performance would be her last, and she focused more on the quality of her voice.

Tucker was no longer singing in blackface, and it is unlikely that she was impersonating African Americans in the same way she did when she first started her career. Yet "coon songs" such as "That Lovin' Rag," one of Tucker's first hits, and "My Southern Rose" were still crowd pleasers. Tucker continued to be billed as a coon shouter, probably because of the quality of her voice, which was similar to the voices of African-American women, and because the rags she sang had originated within the black community. In addition, songs with content about black life could be called either coon songs or ragtime, and syncopated rhythms fit both genres in the eyes of music journalists. As one critic noted, "She has the voice of a brass band and a teasing, ragtime tempo in which she uses her eyes, her hands and vocal chords with astonishing vigor."[25] The singer's physical delivery—her expressive face, constant movement, and attention to form—were increasingly becoming as remarkable as her sound and would later define her as a "Red Hot Mama."

It also appears that Tucker adapted her mannerisms and delivery on the basis of location; according to press reports, during performances in New Orleans, she spoke in dialect and offered stories of a "black wench" who was in love with a "yaller coon." New Orleans audiences hooted and shouted for Tucker to perform encores, reveling in the fact that she had offered characters right out of the "black Darktown Conservatory."[26] In Indianapolis it was reported that she had "the negro's choicest dronings and shouts reduced to an art."[27]

Always focused on the security of her career, Tucker gave people what they wanted even though her friendship with Elkins and her attention to black songwriters such as Shelton Brooks suggests a much more progressive racial mindset. Her relationship with Elkins was making her more aware of racial discrimination; later she professed that Elkins gave her an "understanding of her [Elkins's] people."[28] Yet Tucker did not feel that she was in a position to move away from the caricatures that fueled much of American popular culture; perhaps she thought she could do more for her black counterparts once she achieved a higher degree of fame.

Ironically, as she rose to fame as a coon shouter, Tucker was able to take more risks and perform new types of songs. She knew that audiences demanded fresh material and that her career required a vast repertoire. At the beginning of her engagement with the Morris houses, Tucker delivered a Tin Pan Alley standard, "My Husband's in the City," and it quickly became one of her signatures. A reply to Berlin's 1910 ditty "My Wife's Gone to the Country," the song depicted the joy of being away from a lousy husband, except on the weekends, and prioritized the fun a woman could have independently. Bemoaning the fact that her husband had come back from the city on Friday, "for what I do not know," Tucker laughed and happily shouted in a higher register that "he only stays till Sunday, hooray, horrah, horo!"[29] At a time when conventional, even arranged marriages were very common, this song was quite progressive. When Tucker later recorded the song, she had a group of men cheering "hooray" with her in the background, validating her desire to live outside of traditional marriage as well as the sense that she recognized her own needs more than any man could.[30]

In addition to offering playful commentaries on relationships, Tucker moved a step further by singing about sex. She began to study the art of the double entendre. Tucker recalled that in her early days in the German Village, songwriter Fred Fisher had urged her to sing racier numbers: "Big and gawky and entirely lacking in what the fashion writers nowadays call 'allure,' I made a song such as that, funny but not salacious."[31] During the chaste Progressive Era, reformers tried to curb vice and to censor materials depicting anything about female sexuality. Distribution through the mail of writings on birth control was banned after the 1873 Comstock Laws were passed, and open discussion of reproductive freedom was risky. Other white women in vaudeville, particularly Tanguay and later Mae West, were known for bawdy entertainment and sexually suggestive movements, and both Tanguay and West were notorious among peers and reporters. However, Tucker realized that she possessed assets that made her different from some of her contemporaries. She was not a conventionally sexy starlet, and with time she learned to straddle the very fine line between comedy and crassness. Having left one husband and living on her own for years, Tucker was anything but a conformist. Her kind of performance style seemed like a natural fit.[32]

In her second week at the Chicago Music Hall, Tucker introduced a song Fisher had written called "There's Company in the Parlor, Girls, Come on Down," which she considered her first foray into "hot songs." There were brothels in every major metropolitan city, and the song was a subtle reference to women's sexual empowerment. Minna and Ada Everleigh, owners of Chicago's famous Everleigh Club, earned thousands each week catering to elite customers, and the women of the Everleigh house gleefully flocked to see Tucker. From that point on, Tucker was determined to include a song with sexual overtones in her act—in fact, she made it a rule. Even when theater managers were wary about offending audiences, Tucker insisted that she was singing about sex in a way that spoke truths that people were afraid to utter out loud. There was a difference between smut and sex, as she recalled in her initial contemplations about this career move. By always delivering hot songs in the first person, she provided a comfort level by centering sexual encounters and mishaps around her own experiences. Tucker was never afraid to make fun of herself, and it was that daring quality that audiences loved most about her.

Without direct access to Tucker's live work and her repertoire of hundreds of songs, it is difficult to describe the particularities of any given performance. The vast repertoire was her strategy for staying relevant: she recalled, "I very seldom sang numbers for the audience to sing with me."[33] Still, it is clear that she banked on songs that emphasized female strength and intuition, and even in cases where she recommended romance, as with "You've Got to Be Loved to Be Healthy," her material always urged women to consider their own needs and preferences. Confidence anthems such as "She Knows It" secured Tucker's romance expertise, which included pride in her body. When she boasted that she had the "loveliest form just like September morn," she let audiences know that women could be attractive in all shapes and sizes, and that romance should include humor. Announcing "I've got the cutest ways, put you all in a daze, and I know it," Tucker basked in a kind of frankness that told her audiences who was boss.[34] In a style similar to that of present-day divas, she spoke of her unique fabulousness with total confidence.[35]

In 1910 Tucker was not yet branded primarily as a transmitter of hot songs, but her manner of delivery, particularly her talky, straightforward elocution, made it easy for her to move in and out of material, from traditional rags to ballads to saucier melodies. By the spring, Tucker was booked with the Pantages chain, a West Coast operation that would introduce her to new cities as she crisscrossed the country from the Pacific Northwest to Chicago. Developed by Greek immigrant Alexander Pantages, the circuit featured theaters that were cheaper than rival Orpheum theaters but still lavish, and that seated close to three thousand people. The Pantages circuit did not procure top headliners in the fashion of the Morris houses, largely because the pay was less and the performance schedule more demanding. But for entertainers like Tucker, who were still establishing themselves in vaudeville, it was a smart choice, especially as the novelty of Tucker's act was highly dependent on new audiences. Morris was keen to position his rising client on a broader national level. It is also likely that due to her close association with Morris, Tucker was blacklisted from the more prestigious Orpheum circuit. Threatened by Morris's success and western aspirations, Keith-Albee and Orpheum leaders were creating a list of over eight hundred acts that had performed for Morris by 1909 and were refusing to book them. Tucker could only entertain western audiences through the Pantages tour.[36]

The tour widened Tucker's personal horizons. It was a thrill to explore this part of the country—to make new friends, to take in the beauty of the Pacific landscape, and most of all to know that her fame was extending beyond eastern cosmopolitan centers. Tucker not only visited large cities such as San Francisco, she moved through towns reminiscent of her native Hartford. Smaller theaters and less competition allowed the headliner to build a following in ways that were more difficult in New York City, and she prepared to add contact information for new audience members to her scrapbooks. "Do I like the West? The question is, Will the West like me?" Tucker told a Spokane reporter. After multiple performances, the answer was emphatically positive. Newspapers heralded her amazing stage presence, unique voice, and glamorous gowns; during interviews reporters commented that she was as alluring in person as she was on stage. Some found her less pleasing to the ear—one reporter described her voice as "a cross between a foghorn and a calliope"—but overall Tucker was a hit.[37]

Morris's publicity agent Jack Lait had labeled Tucker the "Mary Garden of Ragtime" after seeing her in Chicago, and this new branding followed her across the Pantages circuit. A Scottish opera singer with a considerable vocal range, Garden had built a career in France before coming to America around the time Tucker was performing in the American Music Halls. Garden's personal life was scandalous, and her performances were often outrageous, with highly sexual movements that in some cities caused great uproar.[38] However, Garden was a household name, and the billing gave Tucker some anxiety about meeting public expectations for a "gorgeous looking prima donna." Still, Tucker recalled, this branding inspired audiences to come see what the fuss was about. She would have to up her game.[39]

New branding also moved Tucker away from her designation as a world-renowned coon shouter, which focused more on the songs she would deliver than on her personality, which was now associated with Garden. Coon songs were still very much part of her routine, but in an interview with a Portland reporter, she acknowledged that she was no longer reliant on this method of performing to sustain her livelihood, and she talked more about helping to make the stage a "playground for grownups." With coon shouting in the past as a "bread and butter matter," Tucker could offer songs of that genre when she wished, but having reached the "topmost pinnacle"—as the reporter described her career—she could venture into other kinds of material.[40]

Yet she was far from detached from her reputation as a coon shouter. During a Portland matinee performance of songs such as "Lord How He Could Love," "Grizzly Bear," and the "Angle Worm Wiggle" Tucker angered a woman named Lola Baldwin, who served as the superintendent of the department of safety for young women. Baldwin felt that Tucker's performance was immoral and demanded that the manager shut the show down. Tucker recalled that it was the way she performed—running her hands up and down her body while she sang—rather than the lyrics that gave the songs a "naughty" effect.[41] The Portland police apparently found nothing offensive about the show, but Baldwin pressured them to arrest the star anyway. Accounts conflict; although it seems Tucker was arrested and then released on bail to perform again the next day, it is unclear whether the police in Portland arrested her again when she performed the same offending songs in her return engagement. In any case, when Tucker left Portland the manager of the theater was profusely apologetic to her and promised that she would always be welcome. Baldwin's outrage was a rare incident on the Pantages tour, but it illustrates the sensitivity many had toward what they considered indecent songs. Tucker fared better than many of her female peers in dodging censorship and frequent arrest, but the potentially threatening nature of performances of popular music, with sexual movements and provocative delivery, would for years be a topic of public scrutiny.[42]

In January of 1910, Tucker's career was reaching new heights as she made her first two recordings with Edison Records. Her first album featured "That Lovin' Rag," and "My Husband's in the City," offering her trademark coon song with a flippant commentary on marital woes. She was featured on the cover of the *Edison Photography Monthly* in July as part of a quartet of stars who were Edison artists, along with Stella Mayhew, Marie Dressler, and Marie Narelle. Tucker had secured her status as a viable commercial artist.[43] With the exception of Australian-born Narelle, who was famous for Irish melodies, the women on the cover were known for their girth and their ability to poke fun at themselves. Tucker received one hundred dollars for each recording and one penny in royalties for every record sold, which represented a considerable financial and professional achievement. Edison Records later released eight more of Tucker's recordings, through July of 1911.[44]

Still, the process was unsettling. "My God, I sound like a foghorn," Tucker recalled about her first foray into recording, convinced that her records wouldn't sell because she sounded dreadful. For a live performer who molded her act in sync with audience responses, this was a natural reaction to the new technology of recorded sound. By 1910, phonographs were on the rise, and prominent recording companies depended on the most famous singers to sell not only music, but also the phonographs that played either Edison's cylinders or the flat discs offered by others in the industry. Originally conceived in the late nineteenth century as experimental mechanisms to record and play a host of sounds, phonographs had become associated with music by the time Tucker recorded. Until radio they existed as the primary means by which Americans heard the greatest singers and musicians of their time. By 1929, the phonograph and record business was a hundred-million-dollar industry in the United States.[45]

Like vaudeville and the many other enjoyments fueled by industrialization during the Progressive Era, recorded sound moved through stages of experimentation. Manufacturers such as Edison, Edward Easton, Emile Berliner, and most successfully Eldridge Johnson's Victor Talking Machine Company competed to deliver the best-quality product. Individual artists entered at a time when they had the power to shape the industry, as the success of one type of performer fueled demands for more of a particular genre. Satisfaction of public desire to hear a recording artist depended on access to and purchase of a phonograph.

Beyond driving the business of listening machines, artists were able to separate their voice from their physical appearance in recordings. For larger women such as those on the cover of the *Edison Photography Monthly*, records had the potential to be even more profitable than live engagements, as artists were freed from the expectations of their physicality and, in some cases, their race. Yet Tucker always preferred live performance to recorded sound, even when the technology improved. She banked on her body type as a hallmark of originality and part of the act of self-effacement. Because she recorded relatively infrequently for an artist of her stature, many of her songs are sadly inaccessible to present-day listeners.[46]

After her tour with the Pantages, Morris booked Tucker at his American Music Hall in Chicago, then brought her back to New York by January 1911.[47] One of the most significant elements of her act at this time was the introduction of a new song, "Some of These Days," which would become her theme song and later the title of her autobiography. Penned by then-unknown African-American songwriter Shelton Brooks, the song was sought after by many artists, but Tucker made it famous. The song was published by leading sheet music entrepreneur Will Rossiter, who, according to Armond Fields, negotiated a deal for Tucker to perform it exclusively. "Some of These Days" advanced not only Tucker's career, but also that of songwriter Brooks. Ontario-born Brooks had spent his youth playing piano in Detroit before working in vaudeville and writing the music and lyrics to "Some of These Days" at the age of twenty-two. Afterward, he penned several other successful songs, which Tucker performed as well. One critic declared that during her December performance in Chicago, Tucker "outsang anyone who has attempted the Rossiter hit [Some of These Days] before her."[48]

Tucker's recollections tell a completely different tale about how she came upon "Some of These Days." She made no mention of Will Rossiter and instead credited Mollie Elkins with bringing Brooks to her attention. "Since when are you so important that you can't hear a song by a colored writer?" Tucker remembered Elkins asking her when she was in the heyday of success. Elkins told Tucker that Brooks was waiting around "like a dog with his tongue hanging out" hoping that the vaudeville star would give him the time of day. It is unclear whether Elkins actually made this introduction, but either way, Tucker was credited not only with making the song famous, but also with giving a black writer a unique chance to be heard. The black press published several stories about the relationship between Tucker and Brooks, and at her golden jubilee celebration many decades later, civil rights leader Ralph Bunche told the story of Tucker's generosity toward Brooks as a representation of her overall attitude toward African Americans and racial equality.[49]

By the summer of 1911, Tucker's career had taken a hit when Morris fell on hard times. Morris's attorney, George Leventritt, who had handled all of the financial operations of the American Music Hall enterprises, died suddenly of a heart attack. Unfortunately, he had never put anything in writing, and this left most of the details on theater ownership and the rest of the circuit unknown. Morris was forced to seek support from other vaudeville owners. Marcus Loew, who had entered the industry running penny arcades and nickelodeons, took over the Morris agency for a while. Despondent at the demise of his circuit, Morris declared that he would retire in the Adirondacks, to which he often retreated because of his ailing health. Tucker was deeply saddened to lose the guidance of the man she now affectionately referred to as "The Boss," and she took to managing her own career.[50]

In this more uncertain climate, Tucker decided to move away from the comfort of vaudeville when she accepted a part in *Merry Mary*, a musical at the Whitney Opera House in Chicago. Tucker was earning enough money to bring Elkins on as her maid, and she felt that a musical would bring her even greater acclaim. To her disappointment, critics panned the show, claiming that she could not act or "dance the simplest steps." Ashton Stevens, one of the most prominent Chicago drama critics, revealed that Tucker was still funny, but that the songs and choreography of the show were lacking in appeal.[51]

Others echoed that Tucker had done her best to entertain, but that the silliness of the musical and other "rakish proceedings" prevented the show from serving as an effective vehicle for the star.[52] They also complained of the untrained actors in the musical, which could not stay afloat even after a series of script changes. The show's program featured leads Earl Flynn and Eddie Martyn, but Stevens wailed, "for the honor of their families, let's hope they aren't the real names."[53]

Tucker agreed with this consensus after some time passed. "I know now that I was pretty terrible," she confessed in her memoir.[54] Fortunately, she had the courage to take on another dramatic part in a Chicago production of *Louisiana Lou* six months after *Merry Mary* flopped. *Louisiana Lou* featured much more experienced actors, such as Alexander Carr and Bernard Granville, and Tucker received only third billing with a limited amount of stage time. She was cast as Jennie, the nanny of the central character Lou; the plot centered on Lou's romantic entanglements with two men. Tucker was given three songs, only one of which was a solo. Playing a maid, Tucker returned to her coon shouting roots, perhaps even in blackface: after the failure of *Merry Mary*, she was determined to stay on stage at any cost. In rehearsals Tucker had trouble remembering her lines and feared that she would become the laughing stock of the Chicago theater community. In contrast to years of live shows in vaudeville based on her own routine and songs, this musical was a new challenge, involving a different kind of performance style and esteemed theatrical actors as colleagues. The pressure to stay at the top was rising.[55]

Tucker did not disappoint audiences when *Louisiana Lou* premiered on September 3, 1911. The show was a huge hit at the La Salle Theater. One critic described her "astounding vocalisms," and another professed that she "brought cheer with her every time she came on the stage."[56] The show remained a bona fide success for months, with sold-out performances and eventual plans to travel across the country. After a year in Chicago, the cast of *Louisiana Lou* traveled from the Pacific Northwest and Canada all the way to northeastern cities; by then, Tucker shared top billing with her male castmates and was earning $350 a week. She played some nightclub dates and made solo appearances at other theaters when a hiatus occurred, but Tucker devoted over two years to the show, performing 512 times by February 1913. She was firmly associated with the success of *Louisiana Lou* in the press and was positioned to maintain headliner status at the show's conclusion.

Louisiana Lou was bringing in steady money for the star, and Tucker started to live in the fast lane, with late-night parties and frequent gambling. Like her father, Tucker loved cards and would always have to watch herself, as debt from poker was not unfamiliar. She bought expensive jewelry and started to back shows that bombed, leaving Tucker in the red. Financial woes led the singer to realize that although she was living more like a headliner, she needed to keep better track of her investments. Without Morris's guidance, Elkins was the only one telling her to curb her spending. After many months on the road with the show, Tucker eventually did stop gambling and associating with a "fast crowd." She knew she had to save money no matter how wealthy she may have felt, and although she would always have very expensive tastes, she mostly refrained from risky endeavors.[57]

After two years in the musical, Tucker was determined to get back into vaudeville. She told one reporter that although she was proud of the success of *Louisiana Lou*, it bore "no relation to vaudeville." Critics had drawn attention to Tucker's difficulties acting and had emphasized that the strength of her role lay in her singing. Tucker would come to thrive telling her own stories and creating a character based on her own life. Performing in scripted shows never quite suited her, either on the stage or in film.[58]

Tucker ached to return to the kinds of venues she had played under Morris's agency. She secured new management under booking agent Max Hart, who was primarily associated with the Keith circuit. With Morris out of the picture, major players like Hart were less concerned about Tucker's association with their former competitor and were willing to take her on, especially after her successful tour in a hit show. Under Hart's direction, Tucker was scheduled to play at major vaudeville houses. Knowing that she would need to refresh her act, she learned new songs and employed famed Broadway dressmaker

Madame Francis. By this time Tucker knew that a performer's wardrobe, both on and off stage, was very important to staying on top, and she developed a sense of how to wear fine clothing, particularly clothing that flattered her larger physique. The press commented on her tailored suits, crepe dresses, and matching hats in elaborate detail, noting that Tucker's style was fashion forward, especially as some of her wardrobe emulated the lines of men's suits. Tucker claimed that these clothes brought both comfort and "a feeling of freedom."[59] "In show business clothes matter," Tucker remembered, because audiences and the press commented on a headliner's wardrobe as much as on anything they did in their routine.[60]

By October of 1913, Tucker was scheduled to headline at Poli's theater in her hometown of Hartford, something she had dreamed about since she left seven years before. It appears that she had seen her son, Bert, very little since she began touring. Her sister and mother had brought him to New York, and she had made a short trip to see her family in Hartford during her time in *Louisiana Lou*. Bert was enrolled in a military academy, and her brother Moe had established himself as an attorney. Her brother Phil had married, and Annie was still single and quite attached to young Bert. Tucker was determined to buy her parents a new house and to relieve her aging mother, who still worked in Abuza's Restaurant. With a bigger paycheck from *Louisiana Lou* and the success of Max Hart's bookings, it seems she was able to make good on that promise. By 1920, the family would move to another home on Barker Street, which was a more prestigious area within the Jewish community.[61]

Tucker's return to Hartford as a major star rather than Charles and Jennie's shunned daughter was one of the most important moments in her life. She felt that those seven days in her hometown compensated for "all the effort and the disappointment and sorrow that have gone over the dam."[62] As the train pulled into the depot, Tucker saw her name plastered all over the city as "The Pride of Hartford"—a billing she had longed for but perhaps doubted she would ever see in her early days in New York. The embraces of her family reassured her that the decision to leave was finally understood, and that she had achieved the kind of stardom she had promised her parents she would when she was a teenager. The *Hartford Courant* anticipated Tucker's return as an unmatched coup for Poli's theater, emphasizing that she was the most famous Hartford girl to ever grace the American stage.[63] People who had shunned her years before now packed in to see the native daughter sing her famous ragtime melodies, with encore after encore and to thundering applause. Tucker thanked audiences again and again for their gracious reception. She was overcome with powerful emotions and was prepared to sing all night if Hartford residents desired more from her.[64] She knew that she had made it in vaudeville and musicals, but she understood now that she was accepted as a legitimate entertainer by the people who mattered most to her.

Tucker's time with her family reminded her of the strict rules of the Abuza home. Although she was a star, she was still treated the same as she was when she was a girl, expected to defer to her mother and father. Her financial contributions to her family's improved status did not matter; she would always be secondary to her mother when it came to household matters. While she was home, Tucker witnessed her mother working with other Jewish women to collect money for a Jewish home for the aged in the community, which raised her awareness about the importance of providing for others. Tucker knew how most of these women had scraped to survive when they first came to America, and now they were giving to elderly residents who had no family. Tucker would later become one of the most charitable entertainers; Jennie Abuza's strong feelings about providing for those in need undoubtedly influenced her daughter.[65]

The visit also encouraged Tucker to place her finances in the hands of her brother Phil, who was concerned about her money management as well as her proclivity to gamble with her earnings. Until this point, Tucker had not invited her siblings or parents to take a major role in her career, but the time she spent in Hartford changed this dramatically. Since she had started in the business, she had been completely alone—certainly cared for well by friends such as Elkins and Morris—but not accompanied by any family. Phil's position brought the Abuzas closer to Tucker's professional life, and she no longer wondered if she could fit back into the community that had raised her.

As the train left Hartford and Tucker's mind moved to her next engagement, she felt a surge of relief that the sacrifices she made were worth the pain she had endured. And after years of feeling lonely, Tucker was also embarking on a new relationship with a man, Frank Westphal, that would test the compatibility of a life in show business with a romantic connection. National fame was a new reality with professional possibilities that Tucker had never imagined for herself, but also limitations that would shape her ability to find love. Once everyone knew her name and cheered for the onstage persona she was brilliantly perfecting, she wanted to find someone who could understand the real Sophie Tucker. Time would tell whether this could ever become attainable for the woman who craved acceptance from all corners but let ambition take the lead.

4

THE HAZARDS OF BECOMING A JAZZ QUEEN

ophie Tucker could rest easy, knowing that her finances were secure as she became more and more of a household name, and as she continued to book engagements into the foreseeable future. Ragtime was the rage, and American cities exuded a new energy, filled with people pursuing the latest entertainment crazes. Tucker's messages about female empowerment became even more resonant during a period that witnessed contentious debates over the passage of an amendment granting woman suffrage. Showing producers, theater owners, and the public that she could stick to her staple songs while always moving with the musical trends of the times, Tucker sprinkled in her own brand of spice. She exceeded the hopes of vaudeville's managers by packing in the masses and performing on an almost twice-daily basis in theaters all over the country.

Success was much easier to attain in her professional life than her personal one, however. As Tucker became one of the greatest stars and was dubbed the "Queen of Jazz," her private world would be significantly affected by her rise to the top. She had hoped for love and marriage, recognizing that her union with Louis Tuck had been a mistake based on youthful foolishness. Now in her late twenties and seemingly wiser, she imagined that she could build a meaningful relationship outside of the expectations of her parents and the larger Jewish community. She envisioned that life would be infinitely more satisfying with a man by her side. She later wrote that she knew she needed to marry "because that's the way I'm made."[1]

Yet as Tucker became more successful, she began to realize how difficult it would be for most men to accept an independent, financially secure woman. She reflected, "Once you start carrying your own suitcase, paying your own bills . . . you've done something to yourself that makes you one of those women men may like and call a 'pal.' . . . But you've cut yourself off from the orchids and the diamond bracelets, except those you buy yourself."[2] Therefore, when Tucker met Frank Westphal a few months before she played her triumphant gig in Hartford, she was delighted to mesh with someone who seemed like an equal. A piano player who could riff back and forth with the singer, Westphal had a wonderful sense of humor and a knowledge of show business that impressed her. Seven years her junior and Gentile, Westphal was quite different from what her family would have envisioned for their daughter. As for so many of her male, Jewish friends in the industry, Tucker's religion did not dictate her romantic decisions.

In March 1913, Tucker was granted a divorce from Tuck on the grounds of "cruelty."[3] It seems that before she met Westphal, Tucker had not considered severing herself legally from Tuck even though she had been separated from him for over five years. In the press Tucker claimed that Tuck had been verbally abusive and that his actions had forced her to live with her mother and petition for custody of their child. Tucker did not disclose the fact that she had left for New York when her son was an infant. The revelation that Tucker was divorced and the mother of an eight-year-old child was apparently less scandalous because of the "extreme and repeated cruelty"

Tuck had allegedly inflicted on his wife. Divorce was still highly frowned upon, and it would have been inexcusable for a woman to separate a son from his father unless there were justifiable grounds.

Interestingly, Tucker's autobiography makes no mention of this kind of poor treatment. She claimed that Tuck was dead by the time she married Westphal.[4] By the time she published the autobiography in 1945, she had already divorced two more times; perhaps an admission of three divorces was too much.

Tucker and Westphal were linked both romantically and professionally, performing alongside one another almost every day. Tucker was the main attraction, and at the time Westphal seemed content to accompany her. By the beginning of 1916, when Tucker was transforming herself into the "[Sarah] Bernhardt of Ragtime" in Brooklyn theaters, Westphal was becoming less comfortable with the singer's hefty earnings compared to his own.[5] Tucker felt it was best for him to have his own business. Westphal's interest in automobiles and former stint as a racecar driver led Tucker to purchase the Sophie Tucker Garage for her man to run. She later realized that it was a disastrous idea to put her name on Westphal's business, hammering in the fact that he needed the publicity to succeed. Nevertheless, even as he ran the garage beginning in the summer of 1916, Westphal did not give up on performing, and he branched out as a solo act, refusing to be known as "Mr. Sophie Tucker."[6] He was simply not satisfied to stay out of show business, and Tucker could not ameliorate his insecurities.

As he tried to establish himself on his own, Westphal was still often billed along with Tucker. The two had a volatile, uneven relationship. Tucker loved Westphal's sense of humor, recalling that it was most likely what kept her sane on the road for so long. The two played off each other's strengths in developing their acts and thrived on stage together. Still, Tucker's larger salary and independent lifestyle nagged at Westphal. The singer recalled that on paydays he would "cringe and slink off." The garage was not elevating Westphal's ego, and working with Tucker was also emotionally defeating. It was very unusual in the 1910s for a woman to earn so much more than a man and not to require his financial protection. This "inferiority complex," as Tucker called it, weighed on Westphal for the entirety of their relationship.[7]

Even though there were troubles, by 1917, after the couple had been together for about four years, Westphal decided to propose marriage. Perhaps he believed that having legal status as a husband would alleviate his anxieties about Tucker resembling the head of the household. When their tour across Canada and the Midwest provided a short break, the two were married in October 1917 in a private ceremony in a Cook County clerk's office in Chicago. Fearing that her mother would discourage her from marrying outside the faith, Tucker did not notify her family until after the wedding.[8] Tucker told the press that becoming Mrs. Sophie Tucker Westphal was a good "compromise" that suited both her and her husband. She even commented that her domestic life would be forever changed because she had to change the monograms in her home from an S to a W.[9]

Westphal's constant jealousy is understandable. Although he was often part of the act, she had become the top headliner and was unveiling a bevy of new numbers. Song pluggers and music publishers flocked to her dressing room after each performance. Entertainment chronicler *Billboard* claimed that any endorsement from Tucker would turn a song into a hit. In particular, the press reveled in Tucker's role as "the most representative interpreter of ragtime that the stage has ever known," with an act that differed from all others. Her knowledge of hundreds of songs, coupled with her enormous vocal range, placed her in an enviable position.[10] A darling of Chicago audiences in particular, Tucker had enough clout to walk away from an engagement at the Windy City's McVicker's Theater when she was mistakenly not listed on the top of the bill. As she told the press, "I am the noted headliner of my road shows. . . . And any act publishing anything different is a pure amateur."[11]

Tucker was part of a larger revolution featuring women on stage. From the turn of the century to 1920, a growing number of women had joined the theatrical profession, with almost 20,000 working as performers in circuses, as chorus girls, and in numerous other venues. Within this group, only a small number were headliners, and most did not have the kind of artistic control that Tucker did; still, women occupied a significant proportion of the theatrical workforce.[12]

Among Tucker's contemporaries was Eva Tanguay, who Tucker recalled was "the most publicized and highest paid performer." Overweight and lacking conventional beauty, Tanguay captured audiences as the "Cyclonic One," with an enormous amount of energy and personality in her performances. Also in the vaudeville headlines was Belle Baker, a child of New York's Lower East Side, who shared Tucker's singing talent and Fanny Brice's comic delivery. Born to Russian immigrant parents, Baker rose to fame in the same years as Tucker, debuting in 1913 and becoming a major box-office-breaking star. Tucker recalled giving Baker advice about both men and show business, as someone who had also "come up the hard way."[13] Baker's unconventional ethnic looks—she was short with dark features—drew comments from the press in a similar fashion to Tucker's. The two performed together in 1916, and the press commented on the absence of "professional jealousy" between the women, who shared a mutual respect for one another.[14]

Tucker's growing fame paralleled major political developments for women. Given the swelling movement for women's suffrage in the first decades of the twentieth century, it is not surprising that more women wanted to express themselves, whether in labor unions, at home, or on stage. Angered and frustrated that women were not given the right to vote along with black men in the Fifteenth Amendment, which was ratified in 1870, suffragists such as Susan B. Anthony, Elizabeth Cady Stanton, Carrie Chapman Catt, and millions of organized women devoted themselves to securing this fundamental right. While some female performers publicly attached themselves to the movement, including actress Mary Shaw and opera performer Lillian Russell, others shied away from what was still a very controversial and potentially alienating cause. Entertainers participated in suffrage rallies to increase their own publicity and described their roles in suffrage-themed plays as artistic opportunities. Undoubtedly the relationship between suffrage and the stage was deeply intertwined, as leading suffragists would sometimes occupy slots on the vaudeville bill, while performers moved in and out of rallies and forums. Although Tucker advocated for female independence and even sexual freedom in her stage shows, she did not connect herself formally to the suffrage movement. In fact, in an article where Tucker described the "feeling of freedom" she had when wearing suits that resembled menswear, she jokingly made a point that she had not "become a suffragette."[15]

Tucker seemed unstoppable. The singer was now managed by Keith-Albee pal Max Hart and could finally work within the Keith circuit. Here she sang along with performers such as the Three Keatons, Mae West, and Evelyn Nesbit at large New York venues such as Hammerstein's, the Alhambra, and the Royal. In summer 1914, at $1,000 a week, she finally booked an engagement at New York's Palace Theater, the most prestigious venue for any performer. To think that Tucker was playing at the same place that Nora Bayes was booked—a star who only a few years before had demoted her to a smaller part in the Follies—was almost unimaginable. Feeling elated, Tucker purchased an automobile and happily worked alongside Westphal, who himself received praise as "a master of syncopated piano music."[16]

After her triumphant return to Hartford in 1913, as her parents incrementally came to accept her profession, her relationship with her family became smoother. She recalled that she enjoyed showing Albert around New York City when she played there, although she still never expressed a desire to care for him in a more permanent sense, even as a wealthy woman. She spent Jewish holidays with her family in Hartford when her schedule permitted, and she knew that when she was home she had to "stop being a headliner and the boss, and remember I was just a daughter, who had to sit back and let the men of the family take the lead."[17] This passivity was quite different from her relationships on the road and something she could only tolerate in stints. Still, she enjoyed having her family all together and seeing her brothers and sister around the dinner table as she had when she was young. Married and feeling better about her place in the Hartford community, Tucker recalled she "hadn't anything left to wish for."[18]

This feeling of peace and satisfaction would abruptly be halted when Tucker, while playing in Chicago, received a telegram from her sister, Annie, saying that her father was gravely ill. Charles Abuza had had a stroke that had left him paralyzed; in Tucker's recollection he had passed by the time she reached Hartford. Abuza died on May 24, 1915, and was buried at Zion Hill cemetery. Friends of the family and Tucker's closest companions, including William Morris, came to the house for comfort. Although her current agent, Hart, hoped that Tucker would return to the stage immediately, Morris convinced him that her father's death had taken quite a toll on the singer and that she should allow herself to grieve for a month before returning to show business. Although she was close to both of her parents, her father had supported her work on a much different level than her mother did, sometimes visiting her performances on his own. He had a fondness for entertainers dating back to his early years running Abuza's Restaurant, and he had come to accept Tucker's professional choices perhaps more quickly than others. Her desire to overlook religious tradition may have been less appalling for Charles than it was for Jennie Abuza. Tucker felt a particular kinship with her father, who more readily embraced American values and ultimately his daughter's role in shaping American culture.[19]

Tucker recalled feeling despondent singing after her father's death. She began to deliver more ballads, such as her lyricist friend Jack Yellen's "I'm Waiting for Ships that Never Come In," tapping into her sadness and allowing audiences to connect with her on a different level. It is unclear when Tucker first met Yellen, but when she did, she immediately recognized that his music would suit her style and personality. The two became fast friends and worked together for more than twenty years. Like Tucker, Yellen was born in Eastern Europe to Jewish parents before his family emigrated to the United States. Composer of treasured songs such as "Ain't She Sweet" and "Happy Days Are Here Again," Yellen was on Tucker's payroll as a songwriter who would compose exclusively for her, and he created one of her most famous ballads, "My Yiddishe Momme." Tucker stated that after Morris, Yellen was her best friend, and her 1945 autobiography was dedicated to him over anyone else.[20]

Yellen's ballad "I'm Waiting for Ships that Never Come In" was depressing and hopeless. The song must have been quite a tearjerker for audiences listening to Tucker bellow about life as a game of poker that she could "never win."[21] After a while Tucker had to put her personal life aside and move back to more of her usual repertoire. Yet the ballads taught her about singing with more dramatic force and with a wider diversity of orchestral accompaniment, opening up the range she exhibited over the next few years.

Ironically, it was the death of Tucker's parents—particularly that of her mother years later—that led to some of the biggest shifts in her style, allowing her to explore slower, more emotional songs. Known primarily as a comedian, Tucker became able to move in and out of her self-deprecating framework to other styles that had universal appeal. As Tucker told one reporter, sorrow was a high price to pay for the stylistic change. She wrote, "Eventually my father's death had the effect of softening me and softening my work," and her mother's death deepened the delivery of her most famous ballad, "My Yiddishe Momme," in the 1920s.[22] From then on, audiences and reporters would regard Tucker as a purveyor of both hot material and heartfelt lamentations.

Tucker wanted to continue her professional relationship with "The Boss," Morris, but she still was not able to. Morris could not offer her the advantages of the Keith circuit and was still crippled by its dominance, but he continued to be involved in Tucker's career informally and remained a dear friend. When B. F. Keith died in 1914, his partner, Edward Albee, inherited the Keith-Albee empire, and Morris acts remained subject to a Keith circuit blacklist. By 1916, however, motion pictures were becoming popular, and vaudeville was under the threat of becoming stale. Morris always had a fresh list of clients eager to work with him, and the show business weekly *Variety*, which advocated for the rights of performers, always touted him as a prince among lions. Albee, who was more of a money handler than a talent man, realized he had been fighting against Morris long enough. He decided to eliminate the blacklist and work with Morris in managing clients. The new relationship between Morris and the Keith-Albee circuit allowed for the William Morris Agency to grow quickly.

Tucker was eager to join Morris's agency once he was reestablished, with his faithful friend and longtime employee Abe Lastfogel as his right-hand man. Over the next few years, Morris acquired entertainers such as Noble Sissle, Eubie Blake, Eddie Cantor, and the Marx Brothers and could boast that the agency was "In Daily Contact with Every Branch of Show Business," as he did in one advertisement.[23] The agency would soon play an active role in orchestrating the exposure of clients in London, and by 1925, Tucker would join a large cohort, including Blake, Sissle, Ted Lewis, and Gilda Gray, that traveled across the Atlantic.[24]

Popular tastes were changing, and interest was growing in a new form of music: jazz, whose origins are a matter of great debate. Some claim that New Orleans–born Creole cornetist Buddy Bolden may have originated the form at the turn of the century, playing more syncopated music with a heavy blues resonance. Early jazz in the wartime years bore similarities to ragtime, and the two were often conflated, although jazz featured a larger emphasis on brass instruments in addition to, or in place of, the piano. One important milestone in the development of early jazz was the formation of the Original Dixieland Jazz Band, a group of white New Orleans musicians—a cornetist, clarinetist, trombonist, drummer, and pianist—who were frequently credited with introducing jazz to the larger public. In 1917 the group made what is considered the first jazz recording, and copies were consumed by millions. The Dixieland Band also became a staple at premier cabarets such as New York's Reisenweber's Cafe, where Tucker would later perform.[25]

Although jazz originated as an African-American art form, segregation and lack of access to recording facilities relegated the genre primarily to white audiences before the 1920s. Both black and white musicians performed jazz during the war years, but the nature of the music varied greatly, depending on where it was performed and the racial makeup of the audience. With the migration of a half million African Americans during the war years, cities such as Chicago, Cleveland, and Philadelphia witnessed tremendous population increases, fueling wide-scale access to jazz for growing black audiences in the North and Midwest. Chicago in particular became a hotbed of jazz for black artists. Eager audiences on the South Side clamored to hear the New Orleans sound of Joe "King" Oliver, who was soon followed in popularity by his student, Louis Armstrong. African-American greats such as Oliver, Armstrong, and Jelly Roll Morton did not have access to broad audiences until the 1920s; before that time, recording was primarily reserved for white entertainers.

Jazz meant many things to many people during World War I and the 1920s; there was a great deal of overlap between definitions of jazz and those of other forms of music, such as ragtime, Tin Pan Alley, and vaudeville melodies. Because African Americans were still highly segregated, with all but the most famous musicians playing in black clubs for black audiences, jazz was delivered to other audiences by white performers playing at theaters such as the Palace and at prestigious cabarets. Yet the African-American origins of the music did not go without notice; one of the first descriptions of jazz in a 1915 issue of the *Chicago Tribune* discussed how jazz was a form of the blues, only more compatible with dancing. The blues "started in the South half a century ago and are the interpolations of darkies originally," the writer remarked, "The trade name for them is 'jazz.'"[26]

With pressures mounting for Tucker to distinguish herself vocally and from other female artists who performed solo, she and Morris discussed potential options. They arrived at the conclusion that Tucker should perform jazz with a band of young men who would serve as backup. After auditioning young men from vaudeville and nightclubs, Morris, Tucker, and—Armond Fields suggests—even Westphal selected a group of individuals who would become the Five Kings of Syncopation. The first to play in the band were pianist Slim Pressler, violinist Sam Green, drummer Ralph Herz, saxophonist Phil Saxe, and cellist and clarinetist Peter Quinn. Tucker recalled that moving from being the Mary Garden of Ragtime to being the Queen of Jazz marked the end of an era in her career. The new billing—Sophie Tucker and her Five Kings of Syncopation—was a completely new concept for a female entertainer at the time.[27]

In June 1916, Tucker and her Five Kings debuted at New York's Royal Theater and were quickly embraced by the public. Commenting on the difficulty of moving with the changes in vaudeville, the press announced that Tucker's act was "the best she had ever been identified with." Merging new songs such as "Oh, Daddy Come Home," and "Walkin' the Dog," with instrumental elements that updated ragtime melodies, the band allowed Tucker to move into a new form of music. With her band standing behind her, she delivered a powerful visual of a woman in charge while playfully bantering with her boys in between songs. This reboot could not have done more for Tucker's career. After this initial success, Morris arranged for Tucker and the group to play the West Coast Orpheum circuit for twenty-four weeks.[28]

Over the next five years, Tucker moved between cabarets and larger theaters with the Five Kings in an incredibly successful tour. Cabarets first took off as an entertainment venue in the 1910s, increasing in popularity during the war years as more theatergoers took part in public dancing and audiences longed to be closer to performers. Many who had enjoyed vaudeville as a family-friendly environment sought out the adult company cabarets provided, and proximity to performers afforded audiences a much more intimate experience. Patrons dined and drank while watching famous dancers such as Irene and Vernon Castle, who demonstrated all of the current ballroom fads, from the fox trot and the one-step to the more classic tango. This shift from the formal structure of the theater to a looser exchange between performer and audiences greatly benefitted entertainers like Tucker, who thrived on her closeness with her fans. With a Parisian flair, and with the stigma of debauchery overcome by luxury, cabarets flourished as another attractive leisure option. Particularly in the years before Prohibition, with alcohol permitted during performances, audiences often opted for cabarets over larger theaters, and the terms *cabaret, café,* and *nightclub* became increasingly interchangeable.[29]

The press revealed that in addition to her talent, Tucker's attitude was truly exceptional; one critic claimed that her success was a product of "square dealing and gratitude." Songwriters scrambled to write songs for Tucker and her band, who were immediately credited with turning tunes such as "Ev'ry Day" and "The Jazz-Dance" into hits.[30] Playing the West Coast, Canada, and her usual hot spots in Chicago and along the Northeast corridor, Tucker made new friends while gaining more respect from people in the industry. Al Jolson watched Tucker's performances in Chicago, and as she played in the same towns as Belle Baker and actress and singer Trixie Friganza, Tucker began to cement professional ties. At the Majestic in Chicago, Tucker and the band performed with the Marx Brothers, whose hijinks with the Five Kings and their instruments brought the house down. More than her own relationship with the Marx Brothers, Tucker recalled the determination of their mother, Minnie Palmer, who watched and critiqued her sons' every move in a way that she admired. Tucker's mother had longtime reservations about her career choice; Palmer's management and celebration of her sons' career was perhaps something she would have wanted from her own parents.[31]

Tucker was asked to define jazz, which she claimed was "only a fad" developed to accompany particular dance styles that required not just the feet but the "entire body." The singer's 1918 conjecture would prove wrong, but as a performer who had seen many kinds of acts come and go, she was less likely to believe in jazz's potential for longevity, especially before it became a defining cultural development of the 1920s. Highlighting the difficulty of playing jazz for any musician, Tucker emphasized her band's role as a forerunner within the genre. She was proud to bring the kind of music that could restore to the public "a lost art of rhythm," and Tucker and the Kings became an important vehicle for delivering jazz to mass audiences. Songwriter Maceo Pinkard, who had previously composed songs such as "Just Give Me Ragtime Please," dedicated his tune "The Blue Melody" to Tucker and the Kings, calling them the "1917 Jazz Band Sensation." By January 1918, one newspaper claimed that Tucker had "done as much as anybody to popularize this style of entertainment." With shows at highly prestigious theaters such as the Orpheum, Palace, and Hippodrome, she was at the top of the profession, thanks to her trademark wit and musical variety. She also flaunted an ability to distinguish herself from others who were less able to change with the times.[32] She later referred to her 1915 rendition of "I'm Sorry I Made You Cry" as a major moment in music history, "the first time any singer went into a fast tempo which later became the style used by all the bands." Although she may have been overstating her role among her peers, Tucker wanted to be known as a jazz pioneer.[33]

Tucker also claimed she was the first to introduce jazz on the stage by doing the shimmy while performing songs in the ragtime tradition.[34] The shimmy, a dance craze of the period, saw people shaking only their chest and shoulders while keeping the rest of the body still. While some at the time may have thought Tucker was exaggerating— as others, including Mae West, claimed the shimmy as their original move—Tucker played a central part within the open, fluid nature of the jazz category. This is precisely what allowed her to align herself with self-described jazz artists. Though Tucker's impact is forgotten in most histories of early jazz, she grasped this opportunity to reinvent herself and reached one of the high points of her career.

It is important to recognize the significance of Tucker's designation as "Jazzbo" amid a largely male cadre. Tucker's role as an arbiter of jazz distinguished her from other female performers, who remained at the top of the bill as vaudevillians but did not play as noted a role in shaping the hottest musical development. Described by *Variety* as "progressive" in her field, with a "unique and almost incomparable style of work," Tucker was a forerunner among musicians and a hit with fans.[35] Walter Kingsley, who was described as one of the most "profound authorities on jazz" in 1919, testified to Tucker's relevance in an article about important benchmarks in the history of the genre, calling her an "innovator in jazz music." For Kingsley, Tucker's performances with her band of such numbers as "Shimmy Blues" and "Another Good Man Done Wrong" turned the tunes into instant classics.[36]

The emergence of jazz paralleled other dramatic changes as the United States entered World War I in April 1917. Part of the effort to become ready for war involved the heavy policing of individuals by both the state and local communities, out of concern about any behavior that could affect morale. This involved federal encouragement for citizens to report anyone who seemed suspicious, but also broader campaigns against "deviant" sexuality, labor militancy, and any other seemingly radical actions. The values of democracy, white American normalcy, and political consensus were a central part of war propaganda under the newly formed Committee on Public Information. Mass culture was inherently suspect, and the government quickly censored anything potentially seditious or unpatriotic.[37]

Musical themes that had previously been fixtures among Tin Pan Alley writers, emphasizing ethnic distinctions, gave way to those that united Americans more homogenously. Irving Berlin, who had built his career on Yiddish-inflected, immigrant songs shifted gears to writing Americana. He enlisted in the army and he found new material that many in the military found appealing. Berlin's "Oh! How I Hate to Get Up in the Morning" was beloved by his fellow service members, and by 1918, Berlin had organized soldiers to perform in a musical review called *Yip! Yip! Yaphank!*, which poked fun at the routines of military life. Berlin successfully performed the show at the Century Theater with the support of the army. These experiences during wartime bolstered Berlin's career as a producer as well as a composer.[38]

Vaudeville was one of the areas that was under the watchful eye of the federal government because it was considered potentially salacious. When Tucker was on the Orpheum circuit at the beginning of 1918 she had no intention of stopping.[39] She defended the institution of vaudeville in *Variety* as "part of the backbone of the nation" and praised Albee for leading the charge. Albee's direction in "real work at the front" was an embodiment of patriotism, and vaudeville's actors were engaging in appeals for war bonds, tobacco funds, and the Red Cross. With his status perhaps a bit threatened, Albee noted that Tucker's words could significantly alert the public to vaudeville's "improved conditions." He felt that vaudeville was moral, worthy, and important during wartime, as was well conveyed by Tucker, one of its most admired spokespeople.[40] This kind of assertion was typical for performers when they wanted to advertise an upcoming performance or make a personal statement, and many of Tucker's contemporaries also filled *Variety* with their personal musings.

Inspired by her mother's charity work in Hartford and the Jewish mandate of *tikkun olam* (performing good deeds to improve the world), Tucker dove into the war effort with vigor. She scrambled to raise money for the tobacco fund—a drive to send cigarettes to soldiers. By the winter of 1918, the press was reporting that Tucker was one of the most dedicated of celebrities, working tirelessly on behalf of soldiers and sailors in an effort "not duplicated by any vaudeville star in this country."[41] Among her many activities were performances for soldiers at Camp Upton, alongside stars such as singer Blanche Ring and fellow vaudevillian Anna Chandler, as well as a benefit hosted by Albee for the United War Work Campaign. Here, she volunteered with friends such as Jolson, Berlin, Friganza, and Baker. Praising her efforts for the mobilization of war resources, the press called her the "irrepressible Sophie Tucker."[42]

Tucker also participated in the wide-scale effort to help Jews in Europe and Palestine who endured suffering in war zones. With the Joint Distribution Committee of the American Funds for Jewish War Sufferers, established in 1914, prominent American Jews such as Louis Brandeis, Louis Marshall, and Julius Rosenwald led the charge to alert American citizens to the need for relief. Between 1914 and 1918 over 3 million Jews raised approximately $20 million globally.[43] Several benefits at New York's Palace Theater and other venues sent proceeds to Jewish war victims, and along with Berlin and Brice, Tucker worked continuously.[44] On a local level, Tucker donated funds from some of her appearances to Jewish inmates at the Clinton prison in

Dannemora, New York, so they could observe the High Holidays of Rosh Hashanah and Yom Kippur with proper meals.[45]

By 1919, she had also become involved in aiding Zionist groups, participating in an open-air concert to support the Zionist organization the Maccabaeans, and was corresponding with the Zionist Organization of America, which included prominent officers such as Brandeis and Rabbi Stephen Wise. She helped to secure contributions for the Palestine Restoration Fund and was on the radar of high-ranking Jewish leaders as someone who could be counted on for support. This was the beginning of Tucker's long campaign to raise and donate money for people in need; it was something she learned from her mother and would grow to a much larger scale as her fame and wealth increased.[46]

As much as she displayed generosity toward those who were fighting the war, Tucker was quite particular about her song choices during wartime. She expressed strong distaste for anyone who tried to dictate the kinds of material she could perform. Her repertoire at the time included standards such as "It Took the Sunshine of Old Dixieland to Make You a Wonderful Girl" and Shelton Brooks's new song "I Want you Every Day," in addition to war-related music like "Mammy's Chocolate Soldier."[47] This last piece, issued at some point in 1918, revealed the continued commodification of racial stereotypes. Tucker appeared on the cover of the sheet music, indicating that she was still comfortable with profiting from this genre. However, by August of the same year, she announced that she was no longer willing to sing "darky lullabys" [sic] and "Southern blue songs." Tucker attributed the change in her repertoire to a desire for newer, fresher material and a desire to break from the label of "white coon shouter." The singer was perhaps feeling more and more uncomfortable promoting the kind of racism inherent in this music. With Mollie Elkins accompanying her to many of her performances and still an important confidant, Tucker was more determined to shed associations with demeaning characters.[48]

Although one Chicago vaudeville periodical spoke of Tucker's perfection of "comedy war songs," Tucker expressed a change of heart about the genre.[49] Again, in a half-page statement in *Variety*, she expressed her feelings about the place of mass culture during wartime. She begged publishers to stop sending her comedic warrelated material, claiming that she had no desire to "exploit an unusual deplorable situation." Urging publishers to send her only "natural hits on their own merit," Tucker still emphasized her patriotism, drawing attention to the thousands of dollars for war relief she raised through tobacco funds. Yet politics and entertainment were very separate in her mind; she explained that audiences did not come to her shows for her to "inspire their patriotism to teach them to be good Americans."[50]

Although she was fully enmeshed in celebrity culture, Tucker's personal life was in a state of upheaval in the fall of 1918. Reports of a separation from Westphal surfaced in the Chicago press. Tucker was performing at the Edelweiss Gardens there, and the problems the couple had faced since the beginning of their relationship were now seemingly insurmountable.[51] Tucker recollected swearing off men in show business. Elkins was there to comfort Tucker during these hard times, and Tucker remembered still believing that "somewhere in the world there was a man for me, . . . not only when I was in the big money, but through years to come."[52] Tucker was again single; for the second time, she had been unable to sustain a marriage with a man who chafed at her ambitions. When she and the band recorded the unusually downbeat "Learning" and "It's All Over Now," in which Tucker sang "I used to love you but it's all over," she had a great deal of personal material to draw on.[53]

For the next two years, Westphal and Tucker remained separated, though from time to time he would appear on the bill with her and the band. It seemed the couple coexisted best when they were performing. The press was still reporting on Tucker's marriage to Westphal in January 1920, and in October Tucker filed for divorce in Chicago's Cook County Superior Court. She recalled that Elkins was the one who provided her with the courage to sever ties with Westphal after years of unhappiness. Tucker charged Westphal with desertion—a common claim for divorce at the time—stating that her public life starkly contrasted with her private one, which left her "broke down." The divorce was covered widely in the press, including the Yiddish *Forward*, which explained that Tucker's husband did not know how to "appreciate her talent."[54] Westphal received no financial gain in the settlement; nor did he ask for alimony. Staying at Chicago's Hotel Sherman until the divorce decree was granted, Tucker had the support of her many friends in town while still playing in vaudeville houses. The singer recalled her deep devastation; she blamed herself for marrying another performer but was still hopeful that another man would come along to give her "companionship and love," no matter whether she was successful or not. However, with two failed marriages in less than two decades, Tucker was understandably wondering whether this would ever be possible. She reminisced, "The greatest obstacle to my success as a woman is my success as an entertainer," but it was not likely that after all she had sacrificed, she would ever dream of giving up her stardom.[55]

Her relationship with the other men in her life was still fairly reliable. Tucker continued to play with the Five Kings of Syncopation, although the musicians often changed, and because they were often new to the business, they could bring Tucker a great deal of aggravation. The singer recalled that rehearsals were sometimes "trying" and that she would reprimand the band when they got "out of hand." Still, Tucker tried to instill her work ethic in these young men, along with tips about saving money and the financial roller coaster ride of the entertainment industry.[56] The band members' frustration with their salaries, in addition to their sometimes rambunctious off-stage behavior, sometimes caused a rift between them and the headliner. At one point, Tucker replaced her band entirely because they refused to perform unpaid for war benefits.[57] Nevertheless, Tucker's reputation as a motherly figure—later famously captured in "My Yiddishe Momme"—emerged with her mentorship of the Kings, and although she would not be associated with a formal band in the rest of her career, the press and industry leaders spoke of her as an entertainer who embraced newcomers.

In December 1918, Tucker and Morris strove to repackage the singer in a way that would keep her in sync with the growing trend of nightclubs. Tucker appeared at Reisenweber's with her Five Kings of Syncopation and exceeded all expectations at the Columbus Circle establishment, with two performances per day. Providing more intimacy between the performer and the audience, the nightclub format suited Tucker perfectly, allowing her to give her audience even more of what they demanded. Moving around the room, talking to guests, and encouraging dancing, Tucker could shine in her element while ensuring that every performance would be unique.[58] Earning $2,000 a week in the same nightclub that had hosted the Original Dixieland Jazz Band in its initial years of popularity, Tucker was accruing a great deal of cultural capital and matching Eva Tanguay's vaudeville salary at the same time.[59] Tucker commanded her own band in the posh 400 Club Room, supposedly named for the four hundred wealthiest, most important citizens who would come to the site. By November 1919 Tucker was deemed "the girl who made Reisenweber's famous"; the press started to call the 400 Club Room Sophie Tucker's Room after she had performed only a few weeks at the establishment, and after a year, the space was formally renamed the Sophie Tucker Room in her honor.[60]

The first year at Reisenweber's was a shaky one, however, as the outbreak of the influenza pandemic in January 1918 affected all public spaces, requiring many theaters to close their doors. In New York City alone, eight thousand cases were reported in the first nine months of the outbreak, although it appears that New York residents did not suffer as greatly as people in other American cities, including Philadelphia and Boston.[61] Orders from the health department caused a depression that affected all associated with the theater industry, as well as the large number of people who had purchased nonrefundable tickets. Although not all theaters abided by this directive, and cabarets, due to their smaller size, still operated as long as audiences came in, fears of contagion kept many at home. Reisenweber's closed for a short period during the spring and summer of 1918, but it opened again by the fall, with Tucker and the band back in action. Tucker fared better than many in the industry, particularly managers who depended on operating at a regular pace. For two years, the health department maintained strict regulations for retail stores, offices, and theaters. By January 1920, theaters were able to run afternoon shows, but new regulations ordered that they close by 8:00 or 9:00 in the evening, depending on the venue.[62] These were serious precautions taken for a deadly virus. At 50 million worldwide, the number of deaths from the flu exceeded the number of people killed in World War I.

From December 1918 to October 1919, Tucker made several recordings with the Five Kings under the auspices of Vocalion Records. Hits like "I'm Glad that My Daddy's in a Uniform," "Don't Put a Tax on Beautiful Girls," and "Everybody Shimmies Now" were available for all to purchase, and Tucker demonstrated her continuing willingness to work with new technologies. Although she always preferred performing live, she had already recorded nine songs with Edison Records, and after 1920 she continued recording fairly regularly. The discography of Tucker's records, however, presents a skewed sample of her repertoire; she knew hundreds of songs and never performed in the same fashion twice. Her recorded collection is merely a fraction of the music she gave to the public and does not capture the physical movements that often defined her. Furthermore, a large part of Tucker's act was her verbal interplay with the band and the audience; the essence of this dynamic is lost in recordings.[63]

During Tucker's time with her band, she placed more emphasis on jazz and less on hot music, largely due to the political climate. By the spring of 1919 much of the industry, including managers and theater owners, were cracking down on what were considered indecent songs and movements, due to a Federal Trade Commission investigation into vaudeville. As it had during during World War I, the government was cracking down on immoral activity, but this time it was to suppress radicalism rather than to secure morale. The postwar era ushered in the Red Scare in the United States, brought on by the Bolshevik Revolution in Russia and spreading fear of political dissent by the fall of 1919. Attorney General A. Mitchell Palmer authorized raids of many allegedly subversive organizations and investigations of individuals suspected of radicalism. Immigrants with alternative political views were major targets; they were often arrested and threatened with deportation.

A xenophobic celebration of white American pride coupled with a new era of big business replaced many of the progressive values that had dominated the period when Tucker first became a headliner. Reisenweber's also instituted a ban against "cheek to cheek dancing and improper dancing embraces." This had more bearing on patrons than performers, and Tucker was still permitted to sing songs about the shimmy, but it is unclear whether they were accompanied by her usual physical movements—shaking her body and running her hands over her curvy figure.[64] In general, anything seen as un-American, whether labor activism or sexually provocative lyrics, was quickly squashed. Because it was "dangerous" for any singer in "legitimate or vaudeville houses" to use double entendre or sexually suggestive messages, content became much more sanitized and continued to express patriotic themes.[65]

Even under these tightened rules, audiences packed in to see Tucker at Reisenweber's for the next several years, during which she also appeared in larger theaters between her performances at the cabaret. Whichever musicians were performing as the Five Kings, they were a hit; at one point she may even have had a few African-American women backing up her vocals.[66] She worked alongside Jolson at the Winter Garden Theater and on the same bill with Helen Keller at the Palace. She also appeared at the 44th Street Theater with Mae West.[67] Under the auspices of the Shubert Brothers, the largest theatrical giants, she performed in musical reviews such as *Hello, Alexander* and *Gaieties of 1919*, with varying degrees of success. Some critics charged that Tucker lacked the class required for Broadway, and others fired back, claiming that the popular songs she had perfected and the personality she owned ("she doesn't pretend to be an opera singer") were suited to Broadway when the play demanded it. One critic was annoyed at any charge against Tucker, listing her extensive contributions to the war effort, her leadership role in organizing other performers, and her personal donations. "If she were good enough for that," the article claimed, "she's Good Enough for Broadway."[68]

Even as she moved from venue to venue, Reisenweber's was a constant source of fulfillment, and even a short time away from the cabaret gave the press reason to hype her return.[69] Reporting that business had doubled since Tucker came to the cabaret, which allowed her to work on a percentage basis, the *Dramatic Mirror* exclaimed, "Pretty good for a Jewish girl who started in balancing a grub tray."[70] Tucker remembered her postwar years, spent largely in New York, as some of the happiest of times, during which she felt settled after so many years on the road. She also continued to adore Chicago for its loving audiences and even more supportive critics, describing it as her "second home." Travel to Chicago included entertaining at theaters such as the Marigold, Edelweiss Gardens, and the Majestic, where she was deemed the "master showwoman of the times."[71] As the world changed dramatically around her, Tucker was becoming more central in the cohort that included the greatest entertainers in America.

Tucker's passion for Jewish causes continued as she contributed to charities for Jewish war veterans through the Jewish Welfare Board.[72] Tucker also took part in benefit shows supporting the construction of new synagogues in Harlem and Washington Heights.[73] Her aid to Jewish inmates became more publicly known, and she was approached by the Hebrew Committee of Auburn prison to contribute funds for a Passover Seder. When the Jewish chaplain at Clinton prison asked her for similar help, he profusely thanked Tucker for the aid she had already provided, stating, "The boys ask me to tell you that they will never forget Sophie Tucker—long may she live."[74] This kind of grateful expression would become more frequent over the years as Tucker donated much of her time and money to philanthropy.

Tucker's awareness of the often difficult plight of her fellow actors also intensified. The Actors' Equity Association, the central actors union, went on strike in August 1919, protesting the unfair, exploitative practices of managers. Forced to rehearse an unspecified number of hours by a consolidation of theater owners and booking agents who had the power to fire anyone at will, hundreds of actors sought improved conditions in the form of more reasonable work hours and pay schedules. As a union member, Tucker worked to help her fellow performers. With the Actors' Equity Association backed by the American Federation of Labor, the strike resulted in a halt of almost all rehearsals and productions in New York and other cities. This caused theater managers to lose hundreds of thousands of dollars per week. Tucker joined one of the most fantastic protest parades, with two thousand actors walking down Broadway on August 16, witnessed by over twenty thousand spectators. Over the course of a month, the loss of profits became too much for managers to take, and a settlement was reached that met actors' demands. After the strike ended, Tucker remained committed to the cause of equitable treatment for performers. For years she had been under the wonderful care of Morris, who arranged for optimal booking conditions; however, in her early days Tucker had gained enough experience with the whims and demands of managers to make her extremely empathetic to others.[75]

The year 1920 brought one of the most significant events in the life of anyone with a career in the nightlife business: the advent of Prohibition. Many relished the celebratory, probusiness atmosphere accompanying the election of President Warren Harding, but there was an underside to the new commercial culture. During the Jazz Age many people had to scramble to make a new kind of living, or instead to profit from the illegal distribution of alcohol. Vaudevillians had to regroup under the threat of widely popular motion pictures, while Hollywood moguls sought out new talent to advertise as major celebrities. With both Reisenweber's and vaudeville under siege, the 1920s would once again reshape Tucker's billing and style. She continued to rise in an atmosphere where many of her peers fell into obscurity, but not without failure and, most significantly, not without incredible heartbreak. Ironically, the woman who rarely identified herself as anyone's mother would universally become a "Mama" by the end of the decade.

5

EVERYBODY'S MAMA

or Tucker, the 1920s were a high point. No decade in American history celebrated mass culture with such intensity, as millions flocked to the movies, dance halls, and other tantalizing leisure sites. Tucker's talents were in high demand; she was regarded as one of the biggest acts both in the United States and internationally, on the vaudeville stage, in cabarets, and in musical reviews.

In fact, Tucker's impact on the 1920s is still captured in popular culture. The fictional world of HBO's *Boardwalk Empire* series features the songs and likeness of Tucker in its tale of mobsters and bootlegging in corrupt Atlantic City. The Broadway smash hit *Chicago* sends its lead, Roxie Hart, onto the stage at the top of her notoriety, wailing, "Sophie Tucker will shit, I know / to see her name get billed below Roxie Hart." Like the character of Roxie, who capitalized on new forms of publicity to bill herself as the most scandalous woman on the stage, Tucker knew she had to hold the often fleeting interest of the public. With vaudeville facing stiff competition from motion pictures and so many Hollywood starlets splashed across industry newspapers, Tucker had to run with the needs of growing audiences or get lost in the shuffle.[1]

For Tucker, as for many other entertainers, an often repressive social and political climate dictated their career moves. When Prohibition went into effect in January 1920, it signaled the culmination of a longer battle of rural versus urban, wets versus dries, and supposedly authentic citizens versus so-called imposters. Beginning with nineteenth-century organizations such as the Woman's Christian Temperance Union and later the Anti-Saloon League, the movement to abolish the sale and distribution of liquor most often targeted the behavior of immigrants, whether Germans who controlled many breweries or a more homogenous concept of others who could not be productive citizens. Promoted for decades by Progressive reformers and then later as an element of necessary sacrifice during wartime, abstinence from alcohol became part of the overall effort to clean up America's cities, accompanying factory inspections, labor legislation, and investigations into political corruption.

Unsurprisingly, Prohibition had a tremendous effect on night-clubs, hotels, and restaurants, forcing the closure of some of the oldest landmarks, such as New York's Hotel Knickerbocker. Many establishments that were dependent on liquor revenues chose to go out of business rather than to serve imitation cocktails. The press speculated that movie theaters, amusement parks, carnivals, and other dry sites would witness a boost in attendance and that vaudeville profits would increase significantly. These profits never surfaced; it seems that instead of attending dry amusements more frequently, more Americans chose to stay home. The rise of organized crime and the frequency of bribery among Prohibition agents made the rising profits at dry sites a pipe dream.[2]

The ineffectual, understaffed Bureau of Prohibition made a good-faith effort to stamp out the liquor trade by enforcing the Volstead Act, the legal apparatus for carrying out the intent of the Eighteenth

Amendment. Yet poor training for agents and financial incentives for agents to look the other way damaged their ability to uphold the law from the onset. In one raid on Atlantic City establishments, not unlike a scene from *Boardwalk Empire*, Tucker was caught with liquor in the room she was occupying at the Café de Paris, yet there seemed to be little consequence for the performer. Like many, Tucker openly defied Prohibition, and she bemoaned its effect on entertainment. "Gloomy ratholes" that offered alcohol competed with luxurious legitimate theaters, and audiences often flocked to the less appealing venues. As Tucker remembered, "Entertainment was reduced to a bottle on the hip. . . . Trying to compete with that bottle was hell."[3] Liquor flowed more than ever during Prohibition, forcing performers to move to sites they would have otherwise chosen to avoid. When Prohibition forced the shutdown of cabarets and restaurants, new ones quickly sprung up in their place, with the main focus on alcohol rather than atmosphere or entertainment.[4]

Tucker encountered other problems during this time. Trouble that had been brewing between the singer and her band led to an ultimatum in the winter of 1921. As she recalled, the band refused to go on with her for a performance at New York's Palace Theater unless their pay increased significantly, and after years of struggling with them on a variety of issues, she had had enough. Tucker was earning at least $1,200 to $1,500 a week by this time, and although she felt that her band was earning "top money," they apparently disagreed because they did not all earn the same salary. It is difficult to know how their salaries compared with those of musicians playing for other entertainers, and perhaps those who had played with Tucker for a longer time were at the higher end of the salary bracket.[5] Regardless, the Five Kings were unsatisfied enough to leave the headliner and perform as their own act. Tucker used the breakup to her advantage, singing about their disappearance and mocking their behavior. *Variety* critic Sime Silverman claimed, "The boys may regret not having stayed away from New York until after Miss Tucker left"; her comedic routines about how her band left her performances were hardly a positive endorsement.[6]

Earlier on in her relationship with the band, Tucker had gone to great lengths to protect the value of her name. In 1918, during a spat with the Five Kings, Tucker took out a page in *Variety* to proclaim that the "Five Kings of Syncopation" were not to be billed in connection with her name unless she was present: using "formerly with Sophie Tucker" was out of the question for the young men. After the 1921 break, Tucker never again performed with a band. Once again, she experienced a sense of disgust toward men who tried to capitalize on her fame, and she knew she had the most control as a solo act.[7]

Between the troubles that cabarets were having due to Prohibition and the departure of the Five Kings, William Morris felt that it was time his client entertain British audiences. It seemed that all of England was calling for American vaudevillians, ranging from singers and dancers to skaters, caricaturists, and dramatists like Harry Green, who presented "sketches of Hebrew life." American headliners such as Nora Bayes and Ethel Levey had performed in London with success; press reports expressed admiration for their versatility. Yet not all entertainers translated to British tastes, and many flopped on the other side of the Atlantic. This was a risk that Tucker was willing to take.[8]

In March 1922, Tucker and her sister Annie set sail aboard the *Homeric* for London, and the press eagerly anticipated how the singer would be received. Although Mollie Elkins had traveled with Tucker for many of her engagements, Tucker decided not to bring her to London this time. Also traveling to London were two new pianists, Ted Shapiro and Jack Carroll. This trip would be particularly important for Shapiro, a Tin Pan Alley songwriter and sometime accompanist for Eva Tanguay. He was a last-minute add-on to the act, and Tucker was not impressed with Shapiro's talents when they first met, but he came to be her sole accompanist and stage partner for the rest of her career. Undoubtedly, Shapiro was critical to her London debut, and that experience was just one of the reasons Tucker depended on him to help shape her act. At the time, having two pianists at once was a novel concept that would distinguish Tucker from other singers.

In her memoirs, Tucker recalled the trip as being particularly meaningful. It reminded her of just how far she had come from the time her mother first came to America with two children, traveling in steerage. "It was going to be up to me to show the British what America can do for an immigrant girl," Tucker remarked wistfully, knowing that there was a great deal of pressure on her to satisfy an unfamiliar, and potentially hostile audience.[9] Tucker was a ball of nerves when she arrived in London because everything seemed different.

After visiting British vaudeville houses—termed music halls in London—she understood that her repertoire would seem unfamiliar and worried that her show would not translate well. She took some comfort in knowing that her lavish gowns would dazzle theatergoers compared to the plain costumes performers wore in London, but she would have to rework her songs to deliver much more universal messages. Tucker recalled working with the best songwriter in London, Eric Valentine, to change American words to those used by the British. She slowed the tempo of her songs to match those she heard in London's music halls so audiences would understand her more clearly. Visiting theater after theater with Morris, who eventually came to help his client in London, Tucker knew that British audiences made up their mind very quickly about an act, and when it was a flop, no one would give the performers the time of day.

Morris was extremely familiar with Britain, having spent his early days in the business promoting British singer and comedian Harry Lauder for American audiences and sending many of his clients to London for a change of pace. Tucker's memoirs reveal Morris's patience with the anxious star. He worked closely with her to examine exactly how her talents could best be used on the British stage. From finding a songwriter who would adjust her lyrics to booking her in smaller venues before her major opening, Morris knew how to reassure Tucker and to give her the confidence to perform with gusto. Morris's attention to the needs of his clients is one of the reasons so many loved him, and Tucker's reputation in London was important to Morris's firm because he was building a growing reputation for overseas success.

After she learned of her first scheduled performance at the grand Finsbury Park Empire Theater, Tucker felt she had to test her new act for a smaller audience. When she performed at the working-class Stratford Empire Hotel, her hard work in revamping her show proved worthwhile. Audiences loved her comedy numbers, and she realized that she could present much more of her racier content in Britain, where audiences "love a good bawdy joke," as she remembered. She also wanted to get reassurance by singing for her "own people." Morris found a Jewish benefit at the Palladium Theater, where Tucker came in as a featured American star. With both of her Jewish pianists on stage accompanying her—"We are among our own Yiddisher kinder," she told them—Tucker sang the ballad "Bluebird, Where Are You?" first as a standard ballad and then, as she fondly remembered, like a *chazan* (cantor). This straightforward delivery of traditional Jewish music was not part of Tucker's American repertoire because she feared alienating her broader audiences. London's Jews provided her with an opportunity to truly come into her own, and she knew that she could handle whatever new engagements came her way. Tucker's willingness to move back to her Jewish roots also marks a turning point toward more frequent use of cantorial melodies, Yiddish, and Jewish-inflected humor.[10]

Tucker performed all over Britain: in Glasgow, Nottingham, Manchester, and many other cities. *Variety* reported that Tucker was initially nervous, tinkering with new material, but in the end won over audiences.[11] She thoroughly enjoyed meeting new people—from the Cohen family, who owned Harrods department store, to British actors and actresses. Learning about British culture in the provinces allowed Tucker to enmesh herself in the customs of her audiences, something she had loved doing since her early days on the burlesque wheel. Tucker reminisced about being reunited with the Marx Brothers in Manchester, at a dinner with Harpo on one side of her and Groucho on the other, and enjoying the British scene with other American performers touring abroad. Tucker was settling into a groove when she learned that she would perform in the musical review *Round in Fifty* at the Hippodrome Theater with famed British music hall entertainer George Robey. Morris had also booked her for a standing engagement at the fancy Hotel Metropole, so it was back to London for another new venture.[12]

Tucker's temporary feeling of comfort did not prevent her from experiencing an overwhelming sense of dread as she prepared for *Round in Fifty*. In a journal she kept while she was in London, she indicated how intimidated she was to perform with "England's greatest comedian," with her name in lights below his on the marquis. Regarding the first matinee show she wrote, "I, so nervous, so frightened I nearly died. Everything black in front and in back of me." Although she felt that she did a fine job, she recalled that she just wasn't herself—that nerves had got the best of her. By the evening show, however, she had calmed down and was able to win over the audience. She expressed a sense of relief and fulfillment, declaring, "I just put my heart and soul in my work and I put over the bit of my life. God, but it was wonderful."[13] The American press indicated that Tucker had a "secure" position among London audiences and was earning $2,500 a week between her engagements at the Hippodrome and the Hotel Metropole.[14] Although the initial foray at the Hippodrome produced jitters, Tucker felt very relaxed at the Metropole, with its well-dressed patrons and inviting atmosphere, which reminded her of Reisenweber's in New York. Living at the Metropole while she performed at the two London venues, Tucker was over the moon, and she took her sister Annie and pianist Shapiro to dinners and benefits throughout the city.

British newspapers adored the American star. Audiences particularly admired her for laughing at herself, turning her own "limitations" into powerful comedy. Press comments related that Sophie Tucker was one of the best American comedians; British journalists wrote about her "originality" and "style."[15] It was clear that the American "Jazz Queen" was something new and that the British wanted more of the woman who made America "Sophie Tucker Crazy."[16] As she thrived in her craft, Tucker found herself fitting in well. She spent time with American Ethel Levey and with British actors such as Heather Thatcher and Barry Lupino. She also dazzled the British lords and ladies who frequented the Metropole, a hot spot for high society. She sang for Prince Henry, later to become the Duke of Gloucester, and although the American press reported that some of Tucker's lines were censored (she told the prince to come back and see her when he became king), the incident did not affect Tucker's tremendous popularity in Britain.[17]

Writing in the *Vaudeville News* to urge others to perform abroad, Tucker described the amazing experience of entertaining in London: "My success has been phenomenal. My American friends and English artists were very loyal and it's been a pleasure."[18] Without the pressure to conform to new American fads or the constraints imposed by Prohibition, Tucker could grow in ways that would perhaps have been more difficult in America. At this point, most Americans could conjure in their minds an image of Tucker and the songs and mannerisms that had become her trademark. For the British she was a brand-new item, someone who had gone from being a complete unknown to someone who was as "fashionable as the fashions themselves."[19]

As Tucker wrapped up her last week in London, she performed in the East End's Rivoli Theater for primarily Jewish audiences. They gave Tucker, billed as a "Jewish actress," perhaps the biggest reception she had yet received. When it was time to leave, she felt deep sadness about departing from a place that had made her feel so welcome and friends who had become meaningful. Yet she knew that her time in London would only heighten the anticipation of American audiences, and Morris publicized Tucker's return at a frenzied pace. A full page in *Variety* taken out by the British "singing violinist" Tucker (no relation to Sophie) told American audiences that she was in constant demand among the British social set, who delighted in the opportunity to socialize with the singer.[20] With the Jazz Age in full swing and Americans obsessed with new versions of the kind of music Tucker had initially performed in the war years, she was more popular than ever. Everywhere she went after her return to United States, she received standing ovations that, as one critic asserted, "Babe Ruth or a presidential candidate would well be proud of."[21]

Tucker continued to perform intermittently at Reisenweber's through 1922, but the restaurant was struggling to stay afloat. Prohibition agents had tightened their grip on the nightlife scene, and by the fall, when bureau agents discovered that liquor was being sold in the cabaret, Reisenweber's was granted one year of parole so it was able to remain open. Yet parole violations were discovered, and the US District Court for the Southeastern District of New York ordered the restaurant to close. By February 1923 Reisenweber's was no longer Tucker's home turf and a guaranteed venue for her success. The shutdown of this beloved New York institution was a blow to customers, who had relied on the restaurant for witnessing performances from the best in the business. For Tucker, the closing of Reisenweber's demanded that she find another venue that could bring her the same degree of recognition and audience interaction. The sense of stability and consistency Tucker had felt during her time at the New York cabaret would never quite be replicated after she was forced to return to her more itinerant life.[22]

For the next two years Tucker performed in vaudeville houses across the country, joining the Orpheum circuit and enjoying top-notch billing in the Midwest and on the West Coast. Tucker's West Coast tour in 1923 was a huge success. She took out a page in *Variety* to say that the eight months she had spent on the Orpheum circuit were filled with "wonderful appreciation and ovations."[23] Everywhere she went, the singer seemed to hit her stride; one Cleveland reporter declared that to be "Tuckered" meant to have "laughed until your sides ache."[24] Tucker's good friend film idol Rudolph Valentino was enamored with the singer, expressing in a telegram to her that although she could overpower him with her girth, he still longed to "hold you in my loving arms."[25] Tucker and Valentino never had more than a platonic relationship, but this telegram is representative of the general feelings most in the industry—and in the audience—had for her. She was indeed "everybody's pal," as she was commonly described in the press.

Tucker always expressed grief about her personal woes during performances, playing for laughs wherever she could get them. During one Palace appearance, during a song about men who "keep her broke," Tucker bemoaned the fact that both of her pianists and even her maid had more active love lives than she did.[26] "Aggravatin' Papa," which she recorded with Okeh Records in 1923, urged men to be faithful to their wives, while "Papa, Better Watch Your Step" warned that hot-tempered women would come after cheating men with an unmatched fury.

In interviews Tucker let female readers know that they should find a path toward self-acceptance, no matter what their shape or size. Discussing the dresses she had brought back with her from Europe, Tucker told one reporter that although she wished to look as slender as possible in her stage gowns, she felt that more "stout" women should learn how to dress for their physique rather than emulating silly trends. Particular choices in dress color, hem length, and waist lines all mattered in accentuating the positive features of larger-figured women, and Tucker expressed dismay that many women could not claim their own curvy bodies as proudly as she had. Tucker went further than giving advice: she declared that she was organizing a "Fat Women's Club" to help others stop "being forever in misery and dodging food." Tucker's group would promote self-acceptance and solidarity among those who took an oath "only to see the beauty of the double chin." While the idea was mostly described in jest, it came from Tucker's real frustration with dieting and with media comments about her weight.[27]

At a time when the iconic flapper—slim, boyish, and athletic—was the reigning image for women to emulate, Tucker's comments about including larger bodies in discussions of clothing and diet were quite progressive. Although the corset had been abandoned and the flowing, shapeless dresses popularized in the 1920s were more for-giving for fuller figures, women were still being given the message that petite was preferred. Clara Bow, the It girl of the period, stood in stark contrast to Tucker and the women she spoke to for her "Fat Club." Having an alternate model of womanhood undoubtedly influenced many women in Tucker's audiences who were older and larger than the starlets of the day. Though the notion of plus-size beauty was not emphasized in public discussions or advertisements within the fashion industry, Tucker was anticipating a different way to understand the female form. As much as any other celebrity, she loved clothing, jewelry, and looking beautiful; however, Tucker tried to frame beauty as a broader concept.

It was also publicly recognized that Tucker was one of only a few celebrity women who dared to be funny. As one article proclaimed, women were "desperately concerned about beauty and poise" and therefore could not risk poking fun at themselves or positioning themselves in an awkward manner. There were no female humor columnists, no female cartoonists, and aside from Tucker, Tanguay, and Belle Baker, who attempted to make people laugh on stage, humor was left to men. According to the article, Tucker had "no beauty or sex attraction," there was nothing at stake, and she could sacrifice her dignity. The article omits the long history of women like Fanny Brice and the Elinore Sisters, who were brilliant comedians; the perception at the time was that women could not be both funny and conventionally beautiful. As a woman who talked about herself as a sexual object and spoke of her own unique kind of beauty, Tucker claimed humor as her own. Eddie Cantor said of his friend, "Sophie's style and material are hardly what you'd want at a Holy Name Break-fast. . . . She sings the words we used to write on the sidewalks of New York."[28] Humor was a critical part of who she was as a performer and essential in her friendships and romantic life. Performers from Lucille Ball to Tina Fey would continue to struggle with this misconception about funny women over the course of the twentieth century and beyond, but Tucker was among the first to truly redefine the idea of a female comedian.[29]

It seems Mollie Elkins joined Tucker on the Orpheum tour but grew ill and was unable to continue traveling with her. Elkins's departure and the knowledge that her friend would not be able to work alongside her in the future was quite painful for Tucker. She replaced Elkins with African-American dancer Ida Forsyne, who worked as Tucker's maid for two years and sometimes performed at the end of her act. Born in Chicago in 1883, Forsyne was a gifted artist with an incredible range; in particular, she displayed a talent for Russian dancing. Forsyne had worked with black dancing troupes such as Black Patti's Troubadours and had traveled from London to Moscow in the 1910s. Approaching forty in 1922, Forsyne was having more trouble finding work, as parts for black performers were difficult to come by and usually reserved for younger women.

Working with Tucker was, in Forsyne's opinion, a good opportunity, with earnings of fifty dollars a week. Forsyne considered her boss a "wonderful performer" and emphasized that Tucker was her advocate on stage and off. When rules dictated that black performers were not allowed to watch the show when working backstage, Tucker insisted that Forsyne be permitted to do as she pleased. Furthermore, Tucker refused to allow Forsyne to perform in blackface, which management encouraged all black performers to do. Tucker described Forsyne's facial expressions as quite remarkable, making her dancing even more magnificent. Although it seems the two parted in 1924, when Forsyne joined singer Mamie Smith as part of the Theater Owners Booking Association—a segregated vaudeville circuit that was among the only venues for black audiences in the South—Tucker's relationship with Forsyne was only one example of her growing connection with black artists. The widely circulating black newspaper the *Chicago Defender* wrote of Forsyne's travels with Tucker as a "great step" for the dancer, giving her exposure in *Variety* and other press outlets.[30]

Even before she employed Forsyne, Tucker was receiving praise in the black press for working with black songwriters and performers, most notably Shelton Brooks. Much had already been said about her popularization of "Some of These Days," and "Darktown Strutters' Ball," which gave Brooks a chance to later work with other white stars, such as Nora Bayes and Al Jolson, and to establish himself as a performer in his own right.[31] Tucker never stopped crediting Brooks with much of her success. She stated that "Some of These Days" captured her life philosophy as well as being her most successful hit; she wanted it to be played at her funeral.[32] Songwriter and noted pianist Eubie Blake also credited Tucker with putting him and singer Noble

Sissle "on the map" by agreeing to sing their first collaboration, "It's All Your Fault" in 1915. Blake's obituary made a central point of the help that Tucker provided him during his formative years.[33] Sissle and Blake joined the prestigious James Reese Europe Society Orchestra as a songwriting team, and by 1922, the team would compose the first all-black musical *Shuffle Along*, meant to portray African Americans in a way that refuted the racial stereotypes of the day.

Although still rare for most white performers of the time, these kinds of collaborations were not uncommon for Tucker, who felt more and more strongly over time about providing black entertainers equal rights in the industry. In the fall of 1924 she toured with a black orchestra, Leroy Smith and his "ten classy musicians," at popular venues such as B. F. Keith's Orpheum Theater in Brooklyn and the Hippodrome. Both the *Chicago Defender* and another central African-American newspaper, the *Pittsburgh Courier*, featured this collaboration in their theater pages, and overall Tucker was becoming a subject of interest among black readers.[34] She also appeared in an act with dance impresario Bill "Bojangles" Robinson at Cleveland's Palace Theater, and the two maintained a relationship in the following decades, with Tucker committed to black charitable causes and benefits that Robinson supported.[35]

Prominent black blueswomen such as Bessie Smith, Alberta Hunter, and Ethel Waters were great inspirations for Tucker. Like Tucker, these women had left their childhood homes for a life on the stage. They faced racism and often horrific violence and degradation, and their talent was a source of salvation.

Born in 1884 in Chattanooga in a dilapidated cabin to a family with six siblings, Smith longed to get out of the oppressive South. Talent she discovered by singing in church translated to a job in traveling vaudeville and tent-show circuits by the time she was eighteen. In the 1920s, Smith was performing in Eastern cities such as Philadelphia and especially New York, where she embraced the thriving movement for artistic freedom in Harlem.

Hunter, born in 1895 in Memphis, left the South for Chicago by 1907 around age eleven, with both the push of segregation and the pull of a career in show business driving her. After a few years she managed to disguise her age and perform in some of Chicago's most prestigious cabarets, which featured black talent for white audiences. Unlike many of her peers, Hunter composed most of her own songs. Tucker, Jolson, and Cantor would frequent the fashionable Dreamland Café, where Hunter was often featured.

Waters was born in utter squalor in Chester, Pennsylvania, in 1897 and sought music as her only refuge from a tumultuous environment. She joined a black vaudeville circuit at seventeen, billed as "sweet mama stringbean," and recorded her first song by 1920. Over the next decade she would sign a contract with Columbia Records and make a remarkable crossover to white vaudeville, performing at the Palace Theater in 1927. With a career on the stage and in film, Waters became one of the most successful black performers of the century, challenging racial stereotypes perhaps more than any other woman of her era.[36]

Tucker would have done anything to learn more from African-American artists. She hoped to enrich her act by studying her black contemporaries, and she identified with these women as outsiders like her. After watching Waters perform, she paid her to sing for her in private company, hoping to learn Waters's unique "style of delivery."[37] She asked the same of Hunter, who refused to go to Tucker's dressing room and teach her songs but recalled that Tucker's piano player would come to Hunter's rehearsals and "get everything down." Although this may sound like Tucker was taking advantage of her fellow artists or, in the worst case, ripping off their music and style, the dynamics between Tucker and these performers was not entirely one-sided. Undoubtedly, black women did not have the advantages or opportunities of their white counterparts; however, some black women found studying Tucker's act and her gift of self-promotion very useful. Tucker's amazing stage presence and the manner in which she skirted the boundaries of acceptable sexuality were important for blues performers to internalize, and Tucker had a reputation as a racial progressive who was sensitive to social injustice.[38]

Mention of Tucker in the black press was frequent. As early as 1923 the *Pittsburgh Courier* termed blues singer Sara Martin the "Colored Sophie Tucker," which seems odd, given the popularity of African-American blueswomen who might have served as better points of comparison.[39] This would not be the first time African-American reporters used Tucker to describe successful African-American acts or as a yardstick of their success. Tucker's relationship with female black artists was complex, as was her delivery of race music that appealed across the color line. On the one hand, Tucker genuinely respected black women in the industry who were creating some of the most innovative music of the day; on the other hand, her access to much broader audiences and her freedom from the barriers of racism and discrimination gave her a platform that women like Smith and Hunter could never fully attain.

Still, Tucker did not escape criticism from the black press, which questioned why she received more opportunities than black singers who were perhaps more talented. Speaking of jazz as an "establishment of a brand of entertainment" that African Americans had created, one critic wondered why entertainers such as Tucker and Jolson had been able to "specialize in some kind of jazz offering" without crediting those who had invented the genre.[40] The black press also derided industry heads for rewarding white performers financially when African Americans displayed equal or greater abilities. Some believed those on the black vaudeville circuit could outsing both Jolson and Tucker, and they did not "pull a fabulous salary." There was deep resentment among some African Americans, who justifiably felt that their artistry had been co-opted. White appropriation of black sound is a longstanding theme in the history of American music. Discussion of Tucker's fortunes would not be the first or last time that African Americans would express intense frustration about their marginalization, whether during the Jazz Age or in the early years of rock and roll.[41]

Tucker was not oblivious to these charges, nor were her contemporaries such as Jolson and Cantor, who had long profited from either performing in blackface or building on African-American art forms.

Tucker, however, seemed to resonate more deeply within the black community, perhaps because her performances were similar to those of black women like Hunter and Bessie Smith. The first-ever black blues recording, "Crazy Blues," was initially supposed to be made by Tucker, but instead was sung by Mamie Smith in August 1920. Tucker could not attend the recording session, so Okeh Records, a relatively new label, took a risk on black vaudevillian Smith, and it paid off well. "Crazy Blues" not only sold 75,000 copies in Harlem in its first few weeks, it proved the commercial viability of black female artists, who had previously been barred from recording. Other labels scrambled to hire their own counterparts of Smith, and more black women finally entered the recording business.[42]

Tucker's sound would become affected by a more diverse recording community. The recording industry experienced significant changes once the work of African-American artists proved lucrative, and race records—discs made by black performers—became part of a niche market for major recording labels by the early 1920s. Okeh was the first to begin this trend, with "Crazy Blues," but larger labels such as Columbia and Victor soon adapted the practice. Race records extended not only to the blues, but also to religious sermons, string bands, and many other sounds produced by African-American voices. Although Smith's hit demonstrated the purchasing power of African-American consumers, race records were also sold to southern whites, most often in a separate, designated section of the store. Minstrel images on the covers maintained the notion that African Americans were still less than civilized, and black performers' success in the industry did not translate to white acceptance. Southern retailers had to assess their clientele and decide whether to sell these race records. For the black community, it was a major moment to finally hear their own recorded voices.[43]

Tucker was recording in the midst of this phenomenon, working with Okeh Records from 1922 to 1928. The songs she put out during this period reflected the open sense of her personality in her stage shows, also influenced by the blues. Songs such as "You've Got to See Mama Ev'ry Night" established her as an authority on relationships, usually with the upper hand over silly, bumbling men. Although the delivery and musical elements sometimes sounded similar to performances by African-American women, Tucker's lyrics contrasted with those of black blueswomen who wailed about heartbreak. Bessie Smith's 1923 standard "Any Woman's Blues" includes the phrase, "I love my man better than I love myself," something that Tucker would never have uttered.[44] The combination of sexual aggression and Tucker's self-effacing ways offered a more comic take than the delivery of Bessie Smith or Alberta Hunter. Tucker had perfected the art of speaking many of her lyrics rather than singing them, always exaggerating her sense of humor. When Okeh released a Yiddish version of "Mama Goes Where Papa Goes," Tucker offered an unusual blend of Jewish and African-American cultures. Ballads such as "After You've Gone" and "Blue Bird, Where Are You?" demonstrated Tucker's wide range, which could satisfy more old-fashioned listeners as well as those who begged for current trends.

As much as the industry tried to segregate black and white voices, exchanges across the color line were common as blues and jazz floated between artists and many recorded versions of the same song. Tucker sang "St. Louis Blues" in vaudeville shows, and Bessie Smith recorded it in 1925; the two also recorded "Aggravatin' Papa", "After You've Gone," and "I Ain't Got Nobody." Waters later recorded Tucker's theme song, "Some of These Days," and no one woman held a monopoly on "The Man I Love," which Tucker recorded in 1928. The creation of jazz and blues was fluid and porous, and although African-American origins were undeniable, Tucker put her own spin on the material. Tucker's sound became ambiguous when she was advertised in the race record category. A Pittsburgh store billing itself as the "Headquarters of Race Records" listed Tucker's recording on the same list with Waters, Bessie Smith, Charlie Jackson, and the Reverend J. C. Burnett.[45] Given this kind of advertisement in the black press, it is not surprising that one *Chicago Defender* reader asked the paper whether Tucker was black.[46]

Even as Tucker was recording more frequently, her primary domain was still live performance, and through 1925 she continued to perform in vaudeville houses across the country. Tucker embraced becoming a "Red Hot Mama" by the middle of the decade, recording the song "Red Hot Mama" in 1924 and frequently performing the playful melody during shows thereafter. The song presented her as an object of male affection, with lyrics such as: "I could make a Texas farmer forget his hay / I could make the devil throw his fork away." In this case, "Mama" was a woman with irresistible sex appeal whose feistiness manifested in a hot, sometimes uncontrollable temper. Written by Bud Cooper, Fred Rose, and Gilbert Wells, the song was an instant hit, and the press embraced Tucker's new label.[47] She was still, to many, the Queen of Jazz, but the Red Hot Mama introduction provided her with something she had never had before: a formal acknowledgement of her sexuality. This phrase, soon to become revised as the "Last of the Red Hot Mamas," would follow her for the rest of her career.

Tucker was not only a hot mama. In the spring of 1925, during a Palace engagement that *Variety* boasted would include all new songs, Tucker encountered a turning point in her career when she introduced Jack Yellen's new ballad written with Lew Pollack, "My Yiddishe Momme." As she ended the performance with this piece, delivering the song in both English and Yiddish, she received the loudest applause of the night. She was apparently brought back on stage to make a speech about the song's meaning.[48] Hundreds of people reportedly wept, including the "hard-boiled song pluggers."[49] Although Tucker spoke of her own feelings toward her mother after the audience demanded more from her, the song was about more than one performer's personal experiences. It offered a powerful commentary on so many themes facing Americans in the 1920s. For second-generation Jewish immigrants, the song spoke to the Yiddish mama's Old World ways, which were diminishing in a modernizing society. For a more general audience, the song expressed a reverence for motherhood more generally, referring to sadness about growing older and recognizing how much a mother sacrificed for her children. As Tucker sang of needing her mother "more than ever now," she told audiences that even as she approached forty, there would always be a need for the kind of love and acceptance that her mother could provide. Others sang the song, most notably Belle Baker, but it was mainly associated with Tucker, becoming one of her most requested and frequently performed ballads. Recorded in both English and Yiddish in 1928 by Columbia records, "My Yiddishe Momme" was a best-seller.[50]

Tucker recalled that "Gentiles have loved the song."[51] This was ironic at a time when anti-Semitism was manifesting itself in American immigration policy, which placed tight quotas on those coming from Eastern Europe. Henry Ford's vitriolic rants about the Jewish "menace" in his conspiratorial publication *The International Jew* represented a high-water mark of religious intolerance. Public appreciation of "My Yiddishe Momme" did not necessarily mean that anti-Semitism was receding; rather, the song, whether sung in English or Yiddish, transcended religion and ethnicity. Even before Tucker sang "My Yiddishe Momme," prominent author and playwright Jack Lait had commented on the contributions of Jews to the world of entertainment and the positive popular reception that had proliferated. Successful entrepreneurs such as Marcus Loew, Adolph Zukor, and the Shuberts were investing not merely in productions for other Jews, but in programs that would entertain the masses. Rather than demonizing Jews as a "menace and a shame," as Henry Ford had done, Lait offered another perspective: that Jews were the "most sincere stage uplifter" and that the world at large had "hugged to its bosom" many talented Jewish entertainers.[52]

Lait's words rang true in terms of the public response to "My Yiddishe Momme"; it seemed that everyone expressed their deep gratitude for the song. One patron who had already seen Tucker perform it begged her to sing it again at the next show because it reminded him and his wife "so much of our own mothers."[53] For Jerry Koslow, a Jewish veteran of World War I recovering in a veteran's hospital away from his home, the song connected him with a culture he felt was absent in his current life.[54] Others requested the sheet music and repeat performances, commenting on Tucker's amazing delivery. Whether listeners emphasized the Yiddish version or the English one, or the fact that it could evoke an "awakening" of "Jewish hearts," the song would forever be connected to Tucker.[55]

The singer was steadfast in her explanation that the song was meant for all listeners. She told one San Francisco reporter, "I'm not singing it for the people who understand Yiddish, but for everyone. And 'everyone' gets the loveliness of this cry of reverence." Tucker presented the "Yiddishe Momme" type of ballad as a solution to the problem that, in her opinion, the more racy "red hot papa and mama stuff" was becoming tired. Always afraid of becoming stale, Tucker promoted herself as embarking on a new trend, claiming, "I know at heart I'm not a jazz singer—but a Yiddisher mama!"[56]

Tucker tried to present herself as maternal. She gave an alternative version of the story of her first marriage and Albert's birth in an interview with *San Francisco Call and Post* reporter Evelyn Wells. She claimed that her marriage to Louis Tuck was arranged and that after she gave birth, she was left a widow.[57] Therefore, she had no choice but to leave her son with her mother and move to New York. Her autobiography, published years later, would counter this narrative; she was never consistent in explaining the events of her early life. Trying to embody two types of mama figures—the sexpot and the keeper of the home—Tucker moved back and forth between these identities and often aligned them in her routines. Hot songs were intertwined with renditions of "My Yiddishe Momme," and audiences were delighted by all of it. This would become one of her most unique abilities for the rest of her career, allowing her more flexibility than most other female performers.

As the song took the United States by storm, Tucker wondered about its possibilities overseas. She decided that it was time to travel back to London, and in August 1925 she boarded the *Aquitania* with her sister Annie and pianist Ted Shapiro. Although Jack Carroll had been performing with Shapiro and Tucker since they first united, he had gotten married and decided to stay in the States.

Tucker performed at the Kit-Cat Club, a popular members-only cabaret, earning $2,000 a week for two performances per day. After about a month there, Tucker moved on to the Alhambra, a vaudeville house that apparently required her to sing for longer stretches, straining her voice. British audiences continued to delight in Tucker's show. One patron who could not afford a ticket begged the star to let him and his wife attend her Alhambra performance as her guest. They had fallen on "hard times," and the man said that seeing Tucker would allow them to forget their troubles temporarily, being in the presence of "the biggest star that has visited Britain."[58] This kind of appeal was not uncommon; the personal attention Tucker paid to her fans encouraged them to believe she could help them in times of need. Her charitable work—with religious organizations, prisons, and hospitals—was widely publicized. The *London Star* also commented about Tucker's positive attitude and the kind accolades she gave to others.[59]

The American press had been talking about the number of entertainers flocking to Europe, such as Ethel Barrymore and Doris Keane. Morris's other clients performing in London, many at the Kit-Cat Club, included Paul Whiteman, Ted Lewis, and Vincent Lopez.[60] But Tucker's success was unrivaled; Chicago critic Amy Leslie described Tucker's popularity among royals and aristocracy, suggesting that the singer influenced British attitudes toward America by offering the best in "jazz and red-headed mama ballads."[61] William Morris received word that Tucker was the "biggest hit England has had in years," and news of Tucker's smashing debut at the Kit-Cat Club even reached French newspapers, which described elated British audiences— among them, the well-dressed aristocracy.[62]

During her visit, Tucker also visited a Jewish shelter housing Ukrainian refugees. American quotas restricted the immigration of these individuals, so they did not have the chance to live in the nation that she and her family embraced. Tucker heard their stories and related to their sadness. The singer threw a banquet for over ninety people celebrating the Jewish holiday of Sukkot, giving those in the shelter a night of happiness. Journalists for the *London Jewish Times*, still written in Yiddish, were particularly impressed with the singer's generosity, explaining that Tucker provided a ray of hope during trying times. The five months she was spending in London were delightful, and the singer was thrilled to both perform and take on the charitable causes she pursued in the United States.[63]

Yet just as things could not have been better for Tucker, in early December she received devastating news that her mother was very ill. Annie left quickly, while Tucker continued to honor her professional commitments. By Christmas she received word that she should take the first boat home, as her mother's health was quickly failing. She made plans to leave in January. Her performances over the next few weeks were under great duress, although she was comforted by all of the American and British performers who came to support her. January 18, the night before she left, Irving Berlin showed up at the Kit-Cat Club, and the two performed together. Berlin had recently married socialite Ellin Mackay. The protestations of Ellin's father, New York scion Clarence Mackay, had created a flurry in the press, when Berlin, the son of Jewish immigrants, eloped with his Catholic daughter, one of the richest debutantes in the country. The scandal in the United States had caused the couple to flee to Europe to seek privacy. Berlin was happy to see his friend Tucker, commenting, "She says I made her a success but I guess it is truer that she made mine."[64] Berlin's sentiments marked a high note during an incredibly painful moment. Tucker boarded the *Leviathan* on January 19 to return to Hartford, and time was of the essence.

Unfortunately, storms were particularly rough and the landing of the *Leviathan* was delayed for days. Tucker was keeping her mind off her sadness by entertaining passengers, and Shapiro and her friend Rudolph Valentino, who happened to be traveling back to the United States, were doing their best to lift her spirits. When Tucker received a telegram that her mother had passed, she was devastated, and she was even more despondent that she might not see her mother's body before burial, due to the Orthodox Jewish custom of burying the dead no more than two days after death. The press caught the story that Tucker had been in a race against time to see her dying mother and documented the journey with intense interest.[65] When she landed in America on January 25, she discovered that her mother had made the rabbi promise not to bury her until Tucker could see her one last time. The singer recalled the meaning of this gesture for a woman who was always guided by faith, and her mother's love was never more apparent. Tucker reminisced, "She was willing to set aside her Orthodox beliefs. There was nothing that she could have done that would have showed me how much she loved me and how well she understood my love for her."[66]

Jennie Abuza's death marked the end of her daughter's ongoing search for acceptance from her family. Even though she knew her mother was proud of her accomplishments, she was never quite reconciled to her mother's anger over her abandonment of Albert. Abuza's will indicated that Tucker "gave her everything," most likely referring to the money she always sent for her mother to buy a nicer home, clothes, and other extravagances. While she was comforted to know that Abuza appreciated all that she had done for her, most significant to Tucker was her mother's willingness to move outside the framework of Orthodox Judaism. True love for her daughter, as she finally demonstrated, meant having to go against tradition and adapt to the circumstances of modern life.

It took months for Tucker to even think about performing again. Her friend Cantor described Abuza as a remarkable woman, relating that he "cried as I have not cried in years" when he learned that Tucker was in Europe instead of by her mother's bedside.[67] Rabbi Ernest Trattner, of Temple Emanuel, Hollywood's central synagogue, sent sincere condolences as well, reminding Tucker of her large heart, her compassion for others, and her place in the California community.[68] Perhaps one of the most prized treasures she saved in her scrapbooks was a birthday card from her mother, sent only weeks before Abuza passed.[69]

Tucker eventually found the strength to work in early spring, but she didn't feel like herself. Her delivery seemed "mechanical," and inside she was just empty. She hoped that Morris could find her something new and exciting that would reenergize her after so much heartache. At a low point, she questioned whether she could ever again provide the kind of dynamism that her audiences expected. "I had a feeling I was done for as a performer," she recalled.[70]

Morris felt that the best setting for Tucker would be in a café similar to Reisenweber's, where she would feel comfortable relating to audiences on a personal level. New York had been her most stable home for many years, and performing at one venue, without the more chaotic schedule of moving around from theater to theater, seemed a good idea to Morris. Even more important, Morris wanted to assure Tucker that her star had not fallen and that she could still attract the kind of crowds she had in London only months before. To this end, Morris found the Trocadero nightclub, formerly owned by the mob but up for sale, and suggested it as a smart venue for show-casing his client. Always following her agent's advice, Tucker pur-chased the club in the heart of Broadway. It was renamed the Sophie Tucker Playground and scheduled to open in March.[71]

Tucker's ownership of the nightclub was quite remarkable in 1926, when women still occupied only a small fraction of the workforce and were almost unseen at higher executive levels. Female film stars and vaudeville players were earning hefty incomes, but few had the kind of entrepreneurial instincts that Tucker did. By this point, Tucker had become a brand, both in the United States and interna-tionally, and she could count on audiences coming to see her exclu-sively. The concept that Tucker would serve as both hostess and entertainer highlighted her amazing ability to connect with her fans, and as motion pictures rose in popularity, with stars seen on screen but not in the flesh, the café format was still quite appealing. With room for four hundred patrons, Sophie Tucker's Playground was much more comfortable than smaller speakeasies. The fluidity of nightlife in New York, with venues coming and going amid the thriving trade in illegal liquor, made the opening of the Tucker café a highly antic-ipated event. As Tucker had been away from "floor work" for some time, devoting herself to vaudeville and her London shows and then to grieving her mother's death, there was much talk in the press about her return to a cabaret venue, where she excelled at putting herself on the map.[72]

Variety hailed March 16, 1926, as the date of the "greatest cabaret premiere ever." Tucker's phenomenal opening attracted six hundred people. It seemed everyone in the celebrity world was there, from the Duncan Girls, Belle Baker, and Tex Guinan to multiple music publishers and song pluggers. Tucker's set of her "best songs" sent her audience cheering, and at one point she came out in "high yellow" makeup—a kind of blackface—to do an impersonation of film star Lenore Ulric, who played a prostitute in the film *Lulu Belle*. As much as Tucker's opening was applauded as an incredible success, the *Variety* journalist wondered how long the cabaret would maintain elite status, especially among intense competition. "Soph is about the only one trying it single handed," the reporter declared.[73]

A month after the opening, the cabaret was a proven "gold mine" and was set to remain open over the summer months.[74] Tucker recalled that the club was frequented by her British celebrity friends as well as the bootleggers who controlled the underground liquor racket. She also remembered the courtesy of these gangsters, who always checked their guns before entering the club. "On most nights you could count as many as fifteen guns in the coat pockets of our customers," she joked. While liquor may have flowed at the tables of patrons who brought it into the club, Tucker claimed that she never attempted to sell it during the time she owned the Playground. Until the heat of August settled in, things seemed comfortable for the star, who felt back in her element amid fans and other entertainers.

As new cafés sprung up in the neighborhood and threatened the cabaret, Tucker was becoming uncomfortable about keeping it going. It seems the summer weather led many to avoid sites that lacked the recent invention of "air cooling," and business was slowly becoming affected. Tucker decided to get out before her finances were severely harmed, taking the advice of Morris, who felt that the club had succeeded even though liquor was never sold. In her own recollection, the club had served its primary purpose of getting her "back into shape for work" after her mother's death, building her confidence while surrounding her with the people she cared for most.[75] It was never intended to be a long-term endeavor, and the singer felt good about closing its doors, knowing she could now move on to new opportunities. After the closing of her Playground, Tucker began performing in *Le Maire's Affairs*, a musical review produced by Rufus Le Maire and starring Ted Lewis and Lester Allen.

Before Tucker debuted on a national radio station in 1931, in 1927, she appeared on a Yiddish radio show in Chicago, recorded in front of a live audience. As one Yiddish newspaper reported, this was the first time that Tucker would perform on a Yiddish radio program as a guest of the Jewish West Side. It touted her appearance as quite a coup for the Jewish community, relating that she was the "most well paid vaudeville star of the English stage." Although Tucker did not frequently perform exclusively in Yiddish for these kinds of smaller, ethnic media, she knew that her presence meant a great deal to Jewish Americans, who interpreted her success with community pride. She was also used in ethnic advertising. One Yiddish ad for Lucky Strike cigarettes presented a photo of the singer with her explanation that Lucky Strikes was the only brand that did not hurt her throat, but preserved her voice through all of her vaudeville acts. These documents illustrate Tucker's resonance among those for whom English was not a first language. The Yiddish press maintained their interest in the singer even into the 1950s.[76]

As Tucker rose to the height of success in the 1920s, her relationship with her son, Albert, became more complicated. Bert was in his early twenties and for some time had expressed a desire to perform on stage like his mother, primarily as a dancer. It seems that Bert wanted to join his mother at a Palace Theater engagement in January 1925, but she discouraged the joint act, and Bert did not appear in vaudeville at the time. He waited for his mother to leave for England before he officially trained for the theater. He learned dancing from Ned Wayburn and then obsessed with learning all of his mother's songs. In front of a mirror, he "rehearsed the expressions and the business he had watched her do so often."[77] This practice paid off: by February 1926 Bert was performing at New York's Publix Theater, working as a singer and dancer with partner Sam Stone. The press noted that "Alfred," as they mistakenly called him, had not used any of the "family fame" or his mother's connections to get ahead, although he had worked with songwriters and song pluggers to learn her material.[78] Tucker declared that her son gave "the best impersonation of me I ever saw anyone do."[79]

When Tucker began working in Le Maire's Affairs, Bert got a job in the show as part of the dancing wing, as well as holding signs and undertaking other backstage tasks. Billboard reported that when he was not performing he was studying in a local law office, preparing to enter Harvard Law School.[80] This may have reflected high hopes of Albert's—he never went near the legal profession; however, he remained determined to stick with a career in entertainment. Bert did not remain in the back lines for long. After a few weeks in his mother's show, the young man had signed with Chicago producer Paul Ash. One newspaper commented that if Ash did not "make a musician" out of Bert Tucker, his mother would have something to say about it.[81] Billings for Albert still advertised him as "Sophie Tucker's son," and Tucker appeared in photos with him. She had never appeared in images with any family members in previous years, and this gesture proved her support for Albert.[82]

Tucker and friend Amy Leslie, one of the most prominent Chicago theater critics, went to see Bert perform as a solo act, and Tucker was quite nervous about whether her son would prove to be a hit. Yet Bert's impersonation of his mother's performance of the "Turkish Towel" song won over audiences, especially once they discovered that Tucker was in the audience. Mother and son embraced on the stage, and Tucker recalled telling the audience how grateful she was for their approval. Variety indicated that Bert's stage debut was indeed a success, and his mother wired the newspaper to say that she could not be more proud.[83] She recalled her son telling her that he wanted to focus on his own career and would not continue dancing in Le Maire's Affairs. She advised him to continue honing his dancing skills while taking good care of his health. "If you don't, I give you less than two years and you are finished," she recollected telling him.[84]

For reasons that are not quite clear, the two met up again a few months later when Sophie was performing in motion picture houses. Moving from straight vaudeville to singing in movie theaters was a growing trend for many entertainers, with big stars earning salaries as much as $5,000 a week, and Morris thought that Tucker should take part in this phenomenon.[85] In November 1927, Bert and his mother performed on the same bill for a week in a Chicago motion picture house, with the press noting that this was the first time they had done a "mother and son act."[86] A month later, at Chicago's Oriental Theater, the two drew especially large crowds with a joint performance, with patrons lining up at nine o'clock in the morning in the pouring rain.[87] Yet by early 1928, Tucker was reconsidering the effect of her performances with Bert, particularly during an engagement at the Paramount Theater in New York, where it seems she almost refused to go on with her son. She had never fully accepted others sharing her spotlight, and she was concerned about Bert upstaging her and about the age difference between the two of them. Apparently, Morris tried to dissuade the manager of the Paramount from booking the two together but was not successful.

Tucker went on with Bert, but afterward reports from *Variety* stressed that audiences need not be so explicitly reminded that the star had a grown son. Audience members would naturally ask about her age, perhaps thinking "singers of hot stuff should look it and not be chilled by a grown-up child alongside."[88] After this performance, Tucker and Albert did not appear together, and it seems Albert moved on as a solo act, though his time in show business was short-lived. Tucker would continue to help him financially in various entrepreneurial efforts for years to come, but she never let her child compromise her stardom.[89] The two remained in contact but were never as close as they were in those few performances together.

As the decade drew to an end, Tucker would shift to a more unstable position in a precarious climate. Pressure to join the ranks of stars who had transitioned from vaudeville to motion pictures overwhelmed the singer, and as the world witnessed the greatest economic crash in modern history, entertainment was in decline. Tucker would be cemented as "The Last of the Red Hot Mamas," and that branding perhaps pigeonholed her in ways she could not anticipate. With her team of Morris, Shapiro, and her siblings supporting her, she moved into unfamiliar territory, unwilling to slow down her career at midlife. Tucker planned to remain on top as long as audiences would have her, and the next years would test whether she had the staying power to achieve her goal of longevity. They would also test her ability to maintain personal relationships and to achieve the kind of romantic love she had always hoped for.

Tucker and her mother, Jennie Abuza, undated.

Tucker and her sister Annie
Abuza Aronson, undated.

Bert Tucker, undated.

Left: William Morris, undated.

Bottom: Tucker and Belle Baker, circa 1916–1917.

Tucker and the
Five Kings of
Syncopation,
undated.

British audiences
welcome Tucker,
1925.

Tucker, Jennie Abuza, Moe Abuza, and Annie Abuza Aronson
in New London, Connecticut, 1925.

Annie Abuza Aronson and Jules Aronson, undated.

Tucker portrait, 1927.

Tucker at *Honky Tonk* opening night, 1929.

Tucker in Los Angeles broadcasting RKO Program, 1929.

Ted Shapiro and Tucker while performing in *Follow a Star* in London, 1930–1931.

Tucker at Chicago's Edgewater Beach, 1932.

Tucker and Ted Shapiro, 1936.

Tucker in menswear, circa 1937.

Left: Tucker with Judy Garland at MGM Studios, 1937.

Bottom: Tucker greets crowds as president of the American Federation of Actors in Los Angeles, 1937.

Tucker on the beach in Atlantic City with son, Bert, and daughter-in-law, Lillian, 1938.

Tucker and Margaret Chung, circa 1944.

SOPHIE TUCKER'S PLATFORM
More Affection & Better Loving Conditions
A Hilarious And Spicy Material Song On Mercury
Records By The Queen Of Them All...Sophie Tucker
LISTEN TO
"SOPHIE TUCKER FOR PRESIDENT"
COUPLED WITH
"MAX FROM THE INCOME TAX"
MERCURY 5839 · 5839X45

FOR PRESIDENT

SOPHIE TUCKER

AT THE MARAMOR

CAST YOUR VOTE ☐

MONDAY, OCTOBER 19

BALLOTS CLOSE 8:30 P.M.

BALLOTS CLOSE 11:00 P.M.

Top: Mercury Records advertisement, Sophie Tucker for President, circa 1952.

Left: Ballot for Tucker for President, circa 1952.

Top: Tucker singing with gusto, undated.

Bottom left: Mourners arrive at Tucker's funeral, 1966.

Bottom right: One of Tucker's many scrapbooks at Brandeis University.

6

GRASPING FOR
RECOGNITION

The year 1928 began in the happiest fashion for Sophie Tucker when she learned of her sister's engagement to businessperson Julius Aronson. Although Tucker had plans to travel to London for the spring and summer seasons, she immediately made it a priority to ensure that her sister could have "the grandest wedding any girl ever had." Tucker had promised her mother that she would take care of Annie when the time came for her to marry and that she would provide her sister with a lavish Jewish wedding. She undoubtedly felt a sense of duty to her parents, but Tucker was also deeply devoted to Annie, who had raised Albert, had traveled with her for years, and had been a constant presence in her life. This event would also ensure that one of the Abuza girls would have a traditional Jewish wedding and a kosher reception with all the trimmings. It would be a vast departure from Tucker's weddings to Louis Tuck, which was more of a formality, and to Frank Westphal, from which her family was absent. Two hundred guests were invited from across the East Coast to attend the celebration at New York's Chalif's Rooms. As the bride stood under the *chuppah* (marriage canopy) wearing a beautiful white lace dress, Tucker felt overwhelming emotion. She reminisced, "I was taking the place that Ma, if she were alive, would have had."[1]

The newlywed Annie Aronson was not the only one with a man. Tucker had entered into a relationship with Jewish merchant Al Lackey of New York, whom she had met at Reisenweber's sometime in the first years of her booking. Lackey enthralled her with his charm and persisted in courting the singer after her nightly shows were over. The two began frequenting New York nightspots, and once the relationship became more serious he followed her to London. He was younger than Tucker and without a job that was identifiable while he was with the singer. She had her reservations about him and certainly about marriage. Still, Lackey was a constant companion for the next several years, providing a great source of comfort after Tucker's mother's death. The relationship seemed quieter than the one with Westphal, and Tucker revealed less about Lackey than about her first two husbands in her autobiography. Although Lackey was a source of emotional support for Tucker during various critical moments, he was similar to Tuck and Westphal in his lack of a source of income. Tucker recalled her instinct to avoid another man who would be dependent on her. "I'd had one experience of being married to a man who made less money than I made. . . . I wasn't going to repeat it, no matter how much I was in love."[2]

Over time this conviction seemed to matter less and less to Tucker. In 1928 she made a dramatic and surprising choice to marry Lackey at the end of December in a Newport, Kentucky, courthouse. Although Tucker recalled that Lackey never founded a business of his own, he had been serving as her personal manager and was "smart about show business." Tucker admitted that marrying him was not consistent with her "better judgment," but her love for Lackey seemed to triumph over potential adversity.[3] Upon discovering the singer's marriage, the press related that Lackey was a thirty-eight-year-old "bond salesman and son of a Philadelphia merchant" who had met Tucker when she was appearing at Reisenweber's. Mentioning that this was Lackey's first marriage and Tucker's third, one journalist expressed surprise that the singer was willing to make another attempt at matrimony.[4]

As she had planned, Tucker traveled back to reliable England after Annie's wedding, returning to perform at the Kit-Cat Club and other familiar venues, such as the Alhambra and the Palladium. Tucker was not shy about her admiration for the Brits. She was impressed by the "democratic clientele" of British cafés, which were patronized by people of various class backgrounds, and by British fashions, which were "positively courageous" in comparison with those in the United States. "I love English audiences because they love me," Tucker admitted.[5]

One of the significant moments for Tucker was when she introduced to London audiences the song "I'm the Last of the Red-Hot Mamas," which she claimed to have first sung at the Palace months before. Although she was already a red hot mama, the phrase "Last of the Red Hot Mamas" would become her most famous introduction, and she would receive this billing for the rest of her life on stage. Tucker delighted in the branding and touted Jack Yellen's song as one of her new signatures. At the Kit-Cat she reminded audiences that "modern flappers" were nothing compared to her. The printed lyrics of "I'm the Last of the Red-Hot Mamas" appeared in a *Variety* story about Tucker's British success, and her claim to be a relic of a bygone age only bolstered her appeal.[6]

The song highlighted Tucker's more sexually provocative lyrics. Describing younger women as inexperienced and prudish, Tucker bragged that her kisses made men "feel like they've had their tonsils out." She promised that she was "getting hotter, hotter all the time" and that she had as much stamina as ever and possessed a lover's know-how that others could only learn from, but not match.[7] Tucker was over forty by this time, but she never saw that as a reason to diminish her feistiness. Instead her weight, and increasingly her age, allowed her to express ideas that censors would target in other, more overtly provocative performers. In one interview Tucker described the much more sensual Mae West singing "My Pleasure Man" and getting arrested, while Tucker went on to deliver the same tune without interference, although she confined her performance of the song to large cities because "they wouldn't get it in other places."[8]

Some of Tucker's fans cautioned her that she was being too "sentimental" in calling herself the last of anything. Other talent still possessed "red hot mama" billing, such as West, Helen Morgan, and up-and-comers whose names were not yet on marquees.[9] This reminder about new stars only proved that an era was fading, and Tucker would have to seriously consider the growing success of motion pictures. By 1928, the movie industry had come a long way from its beginnings at the turn of the century, when nickelodeon patrons paid a few cents to see a few reels of film. Located primarily in working-class, immigrant neighborhoods, nickelodeons had a reputation as seamy and undesirable. Yet with more advanced technology, film transitioned from a medium people watched for fleeting delights to full-feature, star-based picture shows. From 1908 to 1914 nickelodeons were gradually replaced by larger, more elaborate theaters solely dedicated to film. The initial, working-class audiences who supported nickelodeons also included middle-class viewers who enjoyed motion pictures as much as the kind of entertainment Tucker provided on stage.

It is easy to understand why Tucker and other women in vaudeville were threatened by film. Women made up a large proportion of the motion picture audience, propelling the creation of fan magazines, celebrity-based advertising, and plots based on romance. With more theaters located in urban than rural areas, mass culture took off in new ways for those who worked in office buildings, department stores, and other urban locales and could catch a matinee on a lunch break or to unwind after work. By 1928 there were 28,000 theaters in the United States, over half of them in major cities. Poster girls like Mary Pickford and Greta Garbo, who shaped fashion, makeup, and ideas about youthful vitality, also influenced expectations for female beauty.

The growth of the film industry was largely thanks to the work of savvy producers—many of them Jewish immigrants like Tucker who had started with nickelodeons or other small businesses. These producers expanded the industry in ways that were unimaginable a decade before. Facing less anti-Semitism in newer media, men like Adolph Zukor (Paramount), Samuel Goldwyn and Louis B. Mayer (MGM), and Sam, Harry, and Jack Warner (Warner Brothers) went on to create the most successful film studios of the era, often working as families. Studying the reactions of audiences as Tucker had done, these moguls provided innovative, new pictures that could change the nature and expectations of filmgoers. The major studio heads combined theater ownership, film distribution, and star contracts, mastering the art of the vertically integrated business as Andrew Carnegie had done with the steel industry in the nineteenth century. With independent filmmakers edged out by the 1920s, the largest eight firms controlled 90 percent of films made each year.[10]

Vaudeville had already been threatened by Prohibition; motion pictures hastened its demise. Many of the central figures in developing the studio system—Zukor, Marcus Loew, William Fox—had backgrounds in running vaudeville houses and sharply understood how the transition from one medium to another meant larger profits. As motion pictures became more elaborate and the content grew richer, the film itself became more than enough entertainment. Little by little, vaudeville theaters were converted to film houses, some with a few performers like Tucker appearing before or after the movie. By the beginning of the 1920s, a quarter of theaters that combined film and vaudeville had ceased offering the latter; by 1926, *Variety*, the leading entertainment periodical, had shifted its main focus to movies. Film palaces housed thousands of seats and offered all the luxuries of live entertainment. With the establishment of the much-hyped system of stars, plotlines, and concessions, it is no wonder that New York's Palace Theater was the single remaining vaudeville-only house by 1932.[11]

Since a permanent move to England was out of the question for Tucker—she loved the United States, American audiences, and her cohort of American performers—she was forced, like so many other vaudeville stars, to aggressively pursue feature films. Yet she was not confident that her talents would translate well to the silver screen. Self-effacing humor and an unconventional body type might be awkward in films filled with young, lithe starlets. Was there room for a heavy older woman to play a love interest, and would the Red Hot Mama even want to play a more subdued role? For Tucker age wasn't an issue, but it might be to studio heads. She articulated in one interview that she had real objections to aging: "When a woman realizes how old she is, she is a dead one. Never do I expect to lose the enthusiasm of youth if I live to be a hundred." These issues would come to the fore as she entertained her first dalliance with the movies.[12]

In September 1928, Tucker signed a contract with Warner Brothers to play a leading role in the film *Honky Tonk*. The press immediately reported on this development. Tucker joined a host of stars, including Al Jolson and Ted Lewis, under Warner Brothers contracts.[13] According to one estimate, Tucker was getting between $85,000 and $120,000 to sign with the studio for one picture, with the option to make three more films, although it is unlikely that Tucker received this amount. It is difficult to know how much she actually earned; Armond Fields suggests the star was paid closer to $6,000 for *Honky Tonk*.[14] In any case, filming would begin in January and would require a several weeks' stay in Los Angeles.

Although she said that age did not matter, Tucker had a desire to appear younger. Reporters described plastic surgery she had to lift "a little fat and loose skin off the face." Tucker insisted that these cosmetic alterations had nothing to do with her recent marriage to Lackey and were part of the business, particularly if she was headed for motion pictures.[15] Months later she denied having cosmetic surgery, even showing one reporter that her face lacked the scars that would be seen on her ears and forehead if she had. "I haven't had any lifting done and I don't intend to," she professed. Although she had earlier corresponded with the Chicago doctor who reporters alleged had performed the surgery, Henry Schireson, their exchange was not about cosmetic surgery, but about her performances and even her mother's health.[16] Regardless of her inconsistencies on this topic, she was noticeably nervous about how she would appear on screen, fretting that her face might not be as photogenic as she wished.[17]

Yet when she began filming, her physical appearance was the least of her problems. In her autobiography, Tucker skipped the years she made *Honky Tonk*, moving out of chronological order to save her ordeal of "crashing Hollywood" for the end of the memoir. Her experience in feature films was perhaps too disappointing to include among tales of devoted nightclub audiences and success abroad. In her recollection, Tucker entered the filming of *Honky Tonk* with the greatest of hopes; she was fresh from success in London and was welcomed with open arms by the Warner Brothers staff. Yet the script was far from what she had imagined; her character did not resemble her own personality, and in a panic she called William Morris to get out of the film. "I must not make this picture," she remembered telling Morris, fearful that it would completely ruin her. Her agent assured her that Warner Brothers would put her at ease, making the kinds of changes that would suit her. Tucker was a nervous wreck as she waited for her meeting with the studio heads.[18]

Tucker knew the Warner brothers from her early days as a performer. Sam, Harry, and Jack were also part of an Eastern European Jewish family. She had spent time in their family's Youngstown, Ohio, home when she traveled, and she believed that Jack, who had taken over the company after Sam died in 1927, would listen to her as a friend. But her meeting with Warner producer Darryl Zanuck, director Lloyd Bacon, and others did not go as she had planned. Her contract did not provide any allowance for script changes, and even worse, she felt as if the men in the meeting treated her like a diva from vaudeville with no experience in the film world. As she prepared for *Honky Tonk*, she bemoaned the lack of rehearsals and her inability to put more of a personal touch on her character. Although she was happy that some of the original songs were replaced with new ones written by her team of Jack Yellen and Milton Ager, she knew that the picture was completely out of her control. It irked her that the publicity department was selling a manufactured product rather than genuine talent. As she remembered, "I asked myself can the studio fool the public?" In addition to being discontented with the process, Tucker felt isolated from the other actors. She was a world away from the home she had made for herself in vaudeville and cabarets.[19]

Always savvy about her own publicity, however, Tucker revealed no hint of her frustrations when describing to the press her experience making the film before it premiered. Boasting of the look and feel of *Honky Tonk*, Tucker indicated that her time working on the movie had been amazing. Not only did she refrain from mentioning her protestations to Warner, she went a step further to claim that the film's producers had adapted to her wishes. She particularly highlighted their willingness to accept her look in the makeup room, emphasizing the potential for success outside the traditional starlet model: "I told 'em the folks expected Sophie, not Greta Garbo." She bragged, "The story looks great and I think it fits me." There was good reason for her to hype the production. She indicated that after *Honky Tonk*, she would be making two other pictures with Warner Brothers, one depicting the life of a singer in New York's German Village with humble beginnings echoing her own. She also mentioned that Ager and Yellen had written eight new songs for *Honky Tonk*, giving it the signature Sophie Tucker sound. She pitched the movie as a vehicle for her stardom that had a "mother angle" to it, but she let her audiences know the film would mostly center on her comic flair.[20]

Tucker's friend, Chicago critic Amy Leslie, also promoted the star in a way that distinguished image from reality. Leslie claimed that the woman who was characterized as "fat, rough, reckless in speech and a man destroyer," was far from the Tucker she had gotten to know, who was "wholesomely tender and motherly." Part of Leslie's intention may have been to associate filmgoing audiences with a softer version of her friend, similar to the character in *Honky Tonk*. But Leslie also touted Tucker's marketing genius, claiming that her friend was not as fat as she led on and that the notion that Tucker could "crush any less ponderous human being" was just an advertising ploy. This portrait of a polite woman who refrained from gambling, alcohol, parties, or even a "coarse word" was not exactly accurate—family and friends indicated that Tucker could never refuse a card game—but it was important to distance Tucker from her red hot mama personality when censorship was always a possibility and Tucker's career hinged on her success in film.[21]

Honky Tonk tells the story of Sophie Leonard, a nightclub singer who, after spending her whole life working to further her daughter's education at an expensive European boarding school, is finally ready to retire. Her daughter, Beth (Lila Lee), has been unaware of her mother's true occupation and returns home to discover that her mother has spent decades singing as a hot mama. Beth angrily calls her mother out for dishonesty and moves out of her house. With some intervention from other characters, mother and daughter are reunited, and Beth marries a man, Freddie Gilmore (Tom Keene), whom her mother had at one time objected to. As a compromise is reached and the two reach a better understanding, the film ends happily with Leonard becoming a grandmother. The film allowed Tucker to sing her signature tunes "Some of These Days" and "I'm the Last of the Red-Hot Mamas," while also introducing new Ager and Yellen songs, such as "I'm Doing What I'm Doing for Love," describing the sacrifice she made for her child.

The film is autobiographical in some ways, but Tucker did not personally embrace it as an accurate presentation of her life or her talents. Some in the press remarked that Tucker's screen daughter possessed an outrage about her mother's profession that Tucker's son did not express in real life. This reporter laid out how Bert had found a job as a vaudevillian and had applauded his mother rather than being appalled about her profession. The film seemed ridiculous when paralleled with Tucker's own story: "Of course that was life and not drammer!"[22]

Tucker described sinking down into her seat during the *Honky Tonk* premiere, completely disgusted by the prospect of a horrific film. She was relieved that she looked better than she thought she would on screen—"very nice for a big woman" as she recalled—but she did not find her performance acceptable. To her, the film was a complete disappointment, a "stinkeroo," as she told Morris.[23] A critic writing for the *New York Times* was not impressed, indicating that Tucker would maintain her current fan base but that the film was not likely to provide her with "new admirers." Some claimed that the tired plot and bad acting prevented audiences from seeing Tucker in her full glory and that singing through tears did not serve her well. However, not all reception was negative. Although many criticized the film, others claimed, "Soph is herself here."[24] One writer for a trade journal contended that the film was saved by Tucker's "big, voluptuous figure, the big, voluptuous voice, and a heart that matches both curves and contralto."[25] The film fared better than Tucker imagined, at least in the short term. According to the *Motion Picture News*, in its first week *Honky Tonk* was grossing well and *Variety* predicted that Tucker would have more success in the future. *Honky Tonk* ran through October in major cities, but Tucker's option to make a second picture was canceled.[26]

Tucker's disappointment with her work in *Honky Tonk* may have also resulted from internal comparisons with peers who had made the transition to film with incredible success. The singer's career was much more similar to those of men like her close friends Jolson and Eddie Cantor than to those of females in the industry. By the 1930s, Cantor and Jolson had both acted in short films, and Jolson's *The Jazz Singer* had ushered in the era of talkies. Combining their work as vaudeville singers with comedic acting, both men had a staying power in Hollywood that Tucker did not. Their flexibility in taking on different roles stood in great contrast with the "Last of the Red Hot Mamas," who could only be cast as versions of herself. Similarly, the Marx Brothers were making some of the most innovative films of the Depression era. Current historical memory casts these performers as film artists, but they also had beginnings in vaudeville that mirrored Tucker's early years as an entertainer. None of these artists depended on live performance to the extent that Tucker did, and perhaps none of them were as personally engaged with their audiences. Because footage has not survived, it is hard to determine whether Tucker was so critical of *Honky Tonk* because the film was indeed awful or because it didn't meet the expectations she placed on herself.

All speculation about the film's success ended with the start of the Great Depression, which affected every corner of the economy. After the stock market plummeted in October 1929, gross national product also fell drastically, and one in four people was unemployed by 1933. The years between 1929 and 1933 were particularly treacherous, as many families lost their homes and some of the worse droughts in history left agricultural families itinerant. World War I veterans descended on the Capitol in the summer of 1932 as the Bonus Army, demanding promised compensation from the government for their service. The realities of poverty could not have been more evident. Tents pitched on grounds near the Capitol represented the desperation of citizens and their anger with a seemingly uncaring President Hebert Hoover. When the federal government violently removed the Bonus Army, it was a powerful symbol of political indifference to the needs of ordinary citizens. Franklin Roosevelt's landslide victory in 1932 marked a hope for a new kind of leader, although at the time it was unclear whether the charismatic governor of New York would create the kind of change he promised in his rhetoric.

Culture industries took a major hit, and vaudeville, already crippled by the growth of the motion picture industry, was at its lowest point. There was now an imperative for managers to seek out the least expensive options for putting on productions, if they could put them on at all. Salaries for many top vaudevillians, including Tucker's, had become extremely high before the stock market crashed. These individuals worked at a reduced salary during the Depression years, and demand was at a low point for live shows. Many motion picture theaters closed, and the price of admission dropped from thirty-six to twenty-four cents. Still, people continued to go to the movies, with admissions rising rather than falling. After 1933 and the repeal of Prohibition, the film industry took off. New theaters were constructed annually, but they were smaller and more rustic than the ornate palaces that had popularized the medium in the 1920s. More Americans who had never attended a picture were able to buy tickets after 1933, and theaters were located not only in wealthier urban areas, but also in working-class neighborhoods. The opening of new national markets, technological mastery of talking pictures, and plot-lines echoing Depression-era fears all contributed to the mass appeal of film. This had been the role of vaudeville for decades, but it could no longer be the case.[27]

As motion pictures—in films such as *The Grapes of Wrath* and *Mr. Smith Goes to Washington*—photography, radio, and other forms of mass media captured the plight of everyday people, vaudeville was a reminder of an older, more materialistic time rather than a vital source of cultural currency. Its lavish theaters and long bills seemed extravagant and time consuming. The large variety of performers and the continuous entertainment, once the selling point, now felt out of touch with the need for simplicity. Vaudeville performers encouraged the public not to give up on them, claiming that vaude-ville was far from dead. Touting the comeback of the genre, vaude-ville producers and performers such as Herb Williams, George Choos, and Isabella Patricola (Miss Patricola) wrote off film as a "novel invention," believing that Americans truly longed to see "living people who speak, sing and dance."[28]

Tucker participated in this dialogue, emphasizing individual needs to applaud and respond to live artists rather than a "flat image." Tucker contended that vaudeville was in "hiding" but would natu-rally return, even though the Palace was the only remaining straight vaudeville theater by 1932. Part of the reason for the slump, she explained, was a lack of good material for singers. She admitted that she was having a tougher time finding songs that matched her per-sonality. As songwriters moved from Broadway to Hollywood, she believed, there was a scarcity of new melodies for live singers. For the many who did sing in picture houses before or after films, projecting their voices over a live orchestra to the numerous rows of people who were coming to see another attraction was particularly challenging. Tucker admitted that new, young audiences were growing up with motion pictures and didn't recognize vaudeville stars until they appeared in a film or had the opportunity to perform before a fea-ture. All of this, she insisted, would change once the temporary thrill of a new kind of entertainment wore off.[29]

Still, the effect of the Depression was felt deeply in the show business community. *Variety* estimated that fifteen thousand theatrical workers were unemployed in 1930; with the lingering vaudeville shows using shortened bills and fewer acts, the total of employed variety performers was two thousand. As Times Square employment agencies were "flooded with actors and actresses," the situation was grim for all but established stars.[30] Fortunately for Tucker, she was still a name brand and was able to secure gigs over the course of a year before a scheduled trip to London in June 1930. Although she did not perform with the frequency she was accustomed to in the early Depression era, she fared better than most of her vaudeville peers. She was still receiving a hefty (albeit reduced) salary, with three weeks of performances in Chicago and Detroit totaling $11,000.[31] Not all critics sang the usual praises, however. One report noted that Tucker was less funny than in previous shows and fell flat at Chicago's Oriental. Although she was still able to deliver songs such as "Ain't No Sin" and "St. Louis Blues" with her usual stamina, she was not able to enhance the talents of her fellow performers.[32]

In a hurried attempt to rescue itself amid declining interest in the genre, the Loews circuit hired the biggest names in vaudeville at exuberant salaries to attract audiences. *Variety* doubted that this technique would save the company, but months of performing allowed Tucker and others to avoid the economic woes so many others in the industry faced.[33] Loews promoted Tucker as "the highest salaried and most successful singing star before the public."[34] She also performed in Miami Beach, representing a growing trend among Broadway performers as southern Florida became a winter retreat for the wealthy. Even in the depth of the Depression, the Palm Beach–Miami area was still described as a place for luxury and entertainment, where the rich could "satisfy any longing for action."[35] Tucker would become a staple in Florida hotels and nightclubs over the years; this early visit was more important to her career than she realized at the time.

Tucker recalled that the early years of the Depression and the popularity of motion pictures were "full of headaches for everybody in show business," but she faced another kind of pain when Mollie

Elkins died in May 1930.[36] Although Elkins had not traveled with Tucker for some time due to her failing health, the bond between the two women had remained strong. Several newspapers commented on the passing of Tucker's most trusted friend, who was "just another colored maid to most people," but not to the star, who had cherished her companion and assistant for twenty-two years.[37] The singer was present for the burial of her friend and claimed that Bert attended as well. "It was almost as if his own mother died," she said of the relationship between Elkins and Bert. There is little evidence that Tucker's son and Elkins were very close, and it seems unusual that Tucker would give credit to Elkins, rather than her sister Annie, for raising Bert. Yet Tucker was always inconsistent in publicly describing Bert's upbringing, and pretending to leave him with Elkins while she performed would have meant that she was still close by.[38] However fictional this part of the story, there is no doubt that Elkins was like family to Tucker. She recalled that when Elkins died, "She took a piece out of my life when she went." Tucker would never have another female friend that she considered as influential in her life.[39]

In November 1931, the singer made her national radio debut, appearing on WEAF for a Thursday evening show.[40] Tucker never fully embraced radio because, like recorded sound, it involves singing without a visible audience, but she understood that she would have to become part of it as the popularity of radio grew exponentially during its golden age of the 1930s and 1940s. *Variety* suggested that as with all sites where she performed, Tucker was determined to study the "routine" of broadcasting, even taking courses on the media.[41] By 1933, 62 percent of households owned a radio, and the major networks of CBS and NBC offered widely popular programming such as *Amos 'n' Andy* and the *Jack Benny Show* on 599 different stations.[42] Although Tucker hoped to get a show of her own, for many years she appeared as a guest star on other programs, such as CBS's *Blue Ribbon Town* show and NBC's *Your All-Time Hit Parade*, as well as *The Frank Sinatra Show* and many other programs hosted by friends. One experiment that Tucker participated in was the *Sophie Tucker Music Hall*, which aired in May 1935 and appears to have run through July on the New York independent station WHN. The thirty-minute variety show featured vaudeville talent, and the listeners would cast ballots for those who would obtain "sustaining spots on the station," which was Tucker's idea. This *American Idol* predecessor received positive reviews, but it did not seem to have had staying power.[43]

In 1938, her wish came to fruition when she finally secured her own radio program to be broadcast on CBS three times a week. Featuring her "bluesy" voice and a twelve-piece orchestra, the show gave Tucker an opportunity to sing for fifteen minutes, with an introduction from producers as an international sensation and a "veteran of night-clubs, stage and screen."[44] She considered her radio work utterly unsuccessful, like her dalliances with film, because she could not connect to her audience and resented being scheduled around other acts. Still, Tucker pressed on, with radio appearances extending through the 1950s. Radio spots were never as frequent as her live work, but she could not afford to turn down opportunities to reach the next generation of listeners.[45] This may have been a more common experience among women than men in the industry; one survey conducted in the 1930s indicated that listeners showed a bias toward male voices.[46]

In June Tucker returned to London, accompanied by songwriters Ager and Yellen, as well as Ted Shapiro. This time Tucker would perform in a musical comedy, *Follow a Star*, costarring with English actor Jack Hulbert. With new songs by Ager and Yellen and the kind of intense rehearsals that Tucker wished for in *Honky Tonk*, her spirits were lifted. The show featured two parts: Tucker performing alone with Shapiro and then entering into a comedy as the wife of a conjurer who discovers that he is English royalty. Tucker's character's mishaps among the lords and ladies provided comic relief and opportunities for other actors to showcase their talents. *Follow a Star* premiered in August, first in Manchester before moving to London's Winter Garden Theater. In Manchester, Jewish community leaders welcomed Tucker with open arms, and one newspaper identified the singer as "a prominent member of the Jewish community in America."[47] The opening in Manchester was meaningful to Tucker as well; she always felt most comfortable around Jewish patrons before presenting a new show. Even after countless performances on the stage, she was still quite nervous.

Follow a Star proved to be a worthy career move. The show outsold all other London productions in the first two weeks and was booked for weeks more. Back in the United States, the *New York Times* marveled at Tucker's engagement with British audiences, and journalists in the London press declared the show to be an amazing vehicle for the star to display her "first class personality."[48] Yet there were some who charged that the new songs did not compare to Tucker's classics and that she could never fit into the scheme of a musical comedy. Others agreed that she was at her best "when all such pretense is thrown aside and she sings alone with her pianist."[49] Some reporters commented that Tucker showed some "odd mannerisms," including delivering lines with her head pointed down and laughing at her own jokes.[50]

Even though the show was successful, the Depression led to salary reductions for the cast so the show could continue, which Tucker agreed to. Still, as someone who preserved all her reviews and cared deeply about press reception, it is possible that Tucker chose to work at the Kit-Cat Club a few months after *Follow a Star* due to her need for consistent acclaim. As she performed simultaneously at the Winter Garden and the Kit-Cat, Tucker hoped to enjoy the kind of audience reception she thrived on, while also socializing with British friends and entertainers. When Tucker's role in *Follow a Star* ended in December, she continued at the Kit-Cat Club, as well as at vaudeville houses in London. Economic conditions during the worldwide Depression affected the entertainment industry everywhere, and Tucker did not have the kind of reliable salary she once did, and much smaller audiences. She knew that the climate was precarious. When given the chance to perform in Paris for $7,000, she accepted, though with a great deal of trepidation.[51]

The singer's fear of performing for French audiences was understandable because she did not speak the language, and she lacked knowledge of French sensibilities when it came to entertainment. Tucker learned the chorus of "Some of These Days" in French, and when she performed her theme song on opening night, she received rousing applause. Still, she was booked for two weeks and felt far from becoming an instant hit, especially because she knew only one of her songs in the native language. After various requests for "My Yiddishe Momme," which she customarily received everywhere she went, she decided to perform it for her new crowd. With some French Jews in the audience, Tucker felt it would be especially meaningful, and her English version of the mournful ballad went over well. But when she chose to sing the song in Yiddish, she received boos from the audience and abruptly stopped the song. Several articles in the press later reported that Tucker was confronted with angry responses because she would not perform any encores; others claimed French opposition to "blues singing." *Variety* attributed French hostility to "local prejudice against English lyrics."[52]

In a 1930 article, Tucker confirmed that she could not provide additional songs in encores due to exhaustion; she never mentioned the Yiddish lyrics and the likely presence of anti-Semitism.[53] There is good reason for Tucker's description of the incident at the time to have differed from later recollections in her autobiography. Although many people knew that Tucker was Jewish, she did not brand herself as a Jewish singer. Even though some press reports described Tucker's religious affiliation, there were others in which her faith was unmentioned. In a British article describing Tucker's wish not to perform in *Follow a Star* on Yom Kippur, the author indicated that many people were surprised to learn that Tucker was Jewish, although Tucker's explanation for canceling the show was accepted.[54]

Although it was public knowledge that many entertainers were Jewish, rising anti-Semitism and dire economic conditions led most people in show business to keep their religious identity private. Tucker's intentions in singing "My Yiddishe Momme" in Yiddish for French audiences seemed to be the same as they were in America: to unite people under the universal theme of motherhood. The fact that some Jews had asked her personally to deliver the song gave her the impression that the environment was more tolerant, and unfortunately this was not the case. Yet it is also possible that Tucker's autobiographical account was an invention, perhaps drawing attention to anti-Semitism at the time it was published in 1945. By that point the world had become aware of the atrocities committed against Jews during the war, as well as the plight of Jewish refugees. Even if she was booed off the stage due to a refusal to sing additional encores, Tucker used the event to politicize Jewish struggles in her memoir.

Tucker continued her British engagements through the spring of 1931, but by the summer, she had made plans to return to the States. Before heading to New York, she received the surprise news that Bert had married a "fine Jewish girl." It was not atypical of her relationship with Bert that she had missed his wedding or that he did not wait for her to return from England. We cannot know for sure how much contact the two had, although Tucker did become aware that Bert was working at a New York boot shop rather than on stage. Having been in England for a year, Tucker was disengaged from her son's affairs, and although she recalled being sad about missing his wedding, it was not a subject of lengthy discussion in her memoir. Of more concern to Tucker was the decrepit state of vaudeville when she returned to New York to play movie theaters, which, she remembered, had made the public "very blasé about entertainment."[55]

Tucker managed to stay busy for the next two years working in movie houses and nightclubs, with some shining moments at the Oriental in Chicago, playing with George Jessel at the Paramount Theater, and returning to the Palace in 1932.[56] In one of her most frightening experiences at the Palace, in February the theater's backstage caught fire, and 1,700 patrons fled in panic. Tucker tried to calm the audience by singing, but the episode was terrifying for the singer, who described "horror and dread of the catastrophe which might ensue."[57] Fortunately the theater did not sustain irrevocable damage, and the Palace was running again within a few weeks, but it could not stand as a vaudeville house for much longer. The Palace converted to a film house in November 1932.

Despite this harrowing episode, Tucker continued to stay on course. New York Evening Graphic Broadway columnist Ed Sullivan delighted in seeing the "grand veteran of vaudeville" when she performed live on the stages she knew best. A teary-eyed Sullivan lamented the end of performances by seasoned artists like Tucker, who had graced the vaudeville stage for decades.[58] Sometimes Tucker had to relinquish her headliner status, and full orchestras, lavish sets, and ornate costumes were gone. Regardless, she was still faring well, earning up to $3,000 per week. Her ego was definitely bruised, however. She recalled: "It hurt like hell to have to step down for the 'no talent' stars of the movies" after she had spent sixteen years on her quest to become a headliner.[59]

Tucker was completely devastated when her "boss" and beloved friend Morris died of a heart attack at the age of fifty-nine while playing cards at the Friar's Club in November 1932. The New York Times called him "one of the most respected and honored citizens" in show business, describing his early finds in entertainment, such as Charlie Chaplin and Harry Lauder, as well as his reputation as a friend of the "poor actor." Morris's philanthropy was extensive; he hosted regular benefit performances for children's organizations and religious institutions.[60] Most notably he had been active in various institutions aiding people suffering with tuberculosis, raising funds for a number of clinics and nurseries in the Adirondacks, where he had spent so much time battling his own health problems.[61] Variety explained how Morris saw talent in Johnson and Dean, an African-American duo, but knew they were not dressed for auditions and took them to a clothing shop to help them get started. Rabbi Stephen Wise led Morris's funeral at Temple Rodeph Shalom, and memorial speeches were delivered by leaders of both the Catholic Guild and the Jewish Theatrical Guild.[62]

This time was incredibly difficult for Tucker, who felt more attached to Morris than perhaps anyone except Elkins. Morris's death marked the end of an era because so many of his clients were longtime vaudevillians who adored their faithful agent. As Tucker remembered, "To me, there never was anyone to equal him, or even stand beside him."[63] Tucker had absorbed much more than entertainment advice from her mentor. Although she loved and admired her parents, and particularly appreciated her mother's empathy for those in need, she took life lessons from Morris quite seriously. He taught her how to engage with audiences, emphasized the priority of kindness and reciprocity, and shared his passion for equal rights among all performers. The causes she took up after Morris's death—particularly union work and medically related philanthropy—spoke to her desire to carry out his legacy. Tucker was also quite concerned about how her professional career would fare without the boss. Facing difficulty accepting Morris's death and questioning the longevity of her relevance without his guidance, the singer felt lost. Fortunately Morris's son, William Morris Jr., and Abe Lastfogel, the founder's right-hand man, were able to keep the agency afloat. Morris and Lastfogel had been working to master the business for years, and they were able to sustain the agency's position as one of the top talent agencies over the course of the twentieth century.

In spite of this stability, Tucker knew that she had to move into a space where she would still be the feature act, not an opening for another show. Nightclubs and cafés were the last option for patrons who wanted to enjoy live entertainment, and in major cities such as Chicago and New York, they grew in number, buttressed by the repeal of Prohibition in 1933. With celebrity vocalists as the main draw and no cover charge, these sites fashioned themselves as classy and respectable—far from the speakeasies of previous decades. Institutions like the Chez Paree and the Latin Quarter in New York would become central in providing Tucker continued access to live audiences and would remain on her docket for the next two decades. Tucker still faced steady competition from other performers; crooners and name bands were in high demand at some of the hottest sites. The singer was able to maintain her fan base as she traveled to New York, Chicago, and Florida for nightclub appearances, but she was always concerned about the viability of her career, and she wondered whether she could remain in the headlines as she aged. Describing the state of show business, she clamed, "Never have I seen it so bad or the future so uncertain."[64]

Tucker's personal life was tumultuous. Reports of her divorce from Al Lackey surfaced by February 1933. She seems to have used the divorce to boost publicity; she incorporated material about the failed marriage into her act, and she later recalled, "It didn't hurt me in the café business."[65] Her press agent issued a statement indicating that Lackey and Tucker did not get along due to differing "temperaments," although it was never quite clear what drove the two apart permanently. In April 1934 the *New York Times* reported that Tucker had filed for divorce from "Abe Lackerman" in a secret decree under charges of cruelty. Her autobiography oddly still refers to Lackey as her husband after 1934, and it seems that the two remained companions from time to time after the divorce. Yet when Tucker was scheduled to leave for Britain at the end of April, she could not have been more relieved. Not only was she escaping a "stale" market and gossip about her third failed marriage, she was to be giving a command performance for King George V and Queen Mary.[66]

Appearing at the Palladium Theater as part of an event benefiting variety artists in Britain was a thrill for Tucker, who had performed for the king and queen once before during her stint in *Round in Fifty*.[67] As Tucker took the stage, she almost lost her composure when she saw the incredible reception she received. After a few years of unpredictable audiences in America, this kind of welcome was more than comforting, as Tucker reminisced: "These people loved me and wanted me and weren't too high hat to let me know it."[68] By December she was organizing a benefit for a national memorial honoring George V, with American performers such as Marlene Dietrich and Douglas Fairbanks participating. Tucker explained that she was organizing the event because she appreciated all the kindness the British had shown her and other American performers, who as a "queer wandering tribe" basked in royal recognition.[69] She remained in England until October, playing at many of the theaters she had frequented in the past—the Empire, Finsbury Park, and the Winter Garden. Upon her return, the Morris Agency's Abe Lastfogel took out a page in *Variety* to display the glowing press from her British engagements, about everything from the cheering crowds at the command performance to her amazing shows in Yorkshire and Manchester. Tucker's team was determined to keep her actively employed in the United States.[70]

For the next several months, Tucker began to make her mark in the nightclubs that would become steady venues for the rest of her career. Chicago's Chez Parce, Miami's Hollywood Country Club, and New York's Hollywood Restaurant provided the singer with commitments spanning several months.[71] Although it seems her voice was becoming more and more strained—she often spoke the lyrics and shifted to witty exchanges with Shapiro—audiences did not seem to care or notice: the press declared after an Orpheum Theater performance, "Reception was tremendous, and the applause that greeted her after every number showed real appreciation."[72]

Tucker also expressed an interest in purchasing the Boston Braves baseball team, sending the press into a flurry of speculation over whether this was a "press agent stunt" or she was actually serious. With the team in a slump, the singer had apparently approached Braves president Emil Fuchs with an offer to "put the team back on its feet" by recruiting her friend Babe Ruth, who had briefly played for the Braves before retiring. In Tucker's opinion, Ruth was being "kicked around," and she felt that she could bring a new element of showmanship to the American pastime. While the press joked that Tucker would make the game significantly more entertaining, her offer did not sustain much momentum because Fuchs refused to supply Tucker with any financial information about the team. Telling her that the Braves were not for sale, Fuchs ended the discussion. This was one of many examples in which Tucker would seek out a leadership role that women rarely aspired to.[73]

Tucker had more success among her peers than she did with sports; in 1935 she was nominated to succeed Cantor as president of the American Federation of Actors (AFA). Formed under the umbrella union of the Associated Actors and Artists of America, the AFA had fifteen thousand members and included a range of industry performers, from circus actors to vaudevillians to nightclub workers, of multiple races and ethnicities.[74] The nominating committee was composed of all men, and this would be the first time a woman was elected president. Tucker took a quite active role in the position, firmly believing in union membership for all entertainers. She had never forgotten her early years, when she wondered whether she could pay the rent or afford the clothes she needed to properly address her audiences. As she took office, she hoped to make a real difference for her fellow actors. Although Ralph Whitehead had been performing most of the day-to-day operations as executive secretary, Tucker worked to promote real equity. As she recalled, "It seemed to me that the actor who paid his due to his union was entitled to relief from that union when he needed it."[75]

Tucker was no mere figurehead. She had launched a hospitalization fund for actors and ensured that women in chorus jobs were paid during rehearsals. She also worked to prohibit the frequent practice of nightclubs promising free talent to wealthy patrons. She advocated that nightclubs sign closed-shop contracts with their entertainers, and by 1937 sixteen clubs, including the Cotton Club and the Rainbow Room, had agreed to this arrangement.[76] AFA executive secretary Whitehead publicly underscored Tucker's effectiveness in negotiating fair employment for actors in clubs and theaters, saying that she exceeded all expectations. "It's the kind of a job that you would think a woman would be least fitted for," Whitehead initially explained, but he went on to describe his amazement at Tucker's level of competency and effectiveness.[77]

People appreciated the tenacity of a woman who showed no inclination to slow down; however, most of the country had moved on to motion pictures, radio shows, and new kinds of music offered by a younger generation. Tucker knew that she had to try to work on the silver screen again and had been hoping that her performances on stage in Los Angeles would translate into a movie opportunity. In 1936 she received an offer from MGM to play a role in the film titled *Broadway Melody of 1938*, with production to begin in January. Unlike the filming of *Honky Tonk*, this was a much more comforting, inviting atmosphere for Tucker. She rented a house in Hollywood, attended parties, and was surrounded by people she had worked with over the years on vaudeville circuits. The cast of the film, which included Buddy Ebsen, George Murphy, Eleanor Powell, and a young Judy

Garland, all shared similar backgrounds, and Tucker recalled that "It was like getting home to the old crowd of the days before vaudeville ended."[78] She was extremely hopeful and felt that this film could secure her future in motion pictures. Sullivan expressed assurance that with the film's release, "The country will be hailing Sophie Tucker as a great cinema star."[79] Yet some *Variety* artists who bemoaned the exodus of live performers to Hollywood could not forgive Tucker, considering it "treason" that she would abandon her stage roots. Still, she felt she had to give Hollywood another chance after one failed film.[80]

The plot of *Broadway Melody* centers on the production of a show backed by a millionaire (Raymond Walburn) and the hijinks that ensue as romance blossoms between the producer and the star, as well as the jealousy of Walburn's wife. Tucker and Garland had minor roles in the film, but they stand out. Tucker played the owner of a boarding house for actors, as well as Garland's mother, who is trying to get her daughter a chance in show business. For Garland, it was her first major singing role, and the shooting of the film fostered a strong relationship between Tucker and her young mentee. The press described the relationship between the two women, and Tucker commented, "I had always hoped to have a girl of my own to carry on the Tucker tradition," and Garland "fits the bill."[81] The two remained close for decades after the film, and Garland would never underplay the influence Tucker had in her career. As she expressed in one interview, the rising star couldn't have been luckier to work with the veteran singer at the beginning of her motion picture work: "She taught me every little trick she had learned from her years as a stage star. If I do put a song over, it's because of Sophie Tucker."[82]

Tucker's relationship with Garland on screen and off may have been the highlight of the film, as Tucker came to realize that most of the scenes she had filmed were cut and her role had been dramatically reduced. Once released in August 1937, the film received lukewarm reviews but praise for the dancing scenes featuring Powell and Robert Taylor and the singing efforts of both Tucker and Garland.

Most agreed that the plot was tired, and some felt that the show was not up to the standards of current musicals, but still, it showcased some incredible talent.[83] Tucker felt that the picture was awful, mainly because she could not shake the knowledge that so many of her scenes had been relegated to the cutting room floor. She lamented that her second foray into film wasn't the success she had hoped for: "It didn't seem to me that my career in pictures was breaking just right."[84] Still, she signed on to make another picture with Garland, *Thoroughbreds Don't Cry*.

With a very small, nonsinging role in the film as the manager of a boardinghouse for jockeys and as Garland's aunt, Tucker was again disappointed. But she was happy for Garland, who was for the first time starring alongside Mickey Rooney. Critics seemed to agree with the singer's dissatisfaction, bemoaning the fact that she was under-utilized. "They're not doing right by our Soph," one reporter claimed, but Hollywood remained unresponsive.[85] With no further interest from studios after the film's release in December 1937, Tucker left Hollywood frustrated and fearful that she might easily become washed up. Still, she relished in the silver lining: the fifteen scrap-books she complied during production that were filled with amazing publicity.

As much as Tucker was stewing in her own disappointment, she was devoting time to helping the causes she would contribute to for decades to come. By the mid-1930s, the persecution of Jews in Europe had heightened, and some in the entertainment industry were making a concerted effort to aid Jewish refugees. By the spring of 1937, the United Jewish Welfare Fund of Los Angeles had pledged to raise $300,000 for "those left homeless and jobless due to the Anti-Semitics purge." Along with Jack Warner, Oscar Hammerstein, and others, Tucker was one of the first contributors to the fund, giving $5,000.[86] Not only was this amount more than most donations, but she was one of only two women who donated.

As she had in the past, Tucker also helped with Jewish refugees, supporting Cantor as he rallied friends and fellow performers to res-cue five hundred Jewish children in Europe and send them to

Palestine. With Jolson and George Burns, Tucker was dedicated to helping Cantor's campaign, which had already been successful in aiding over two hundred children. AP News reported on Cantor's efforts across the country, even in Southern newspapers such as the *Chattanooga Times* and the *Birmingham News*.[87] Tucker and others were professionally affected by Nazi policies because a widespread ban was imposed under Hitler's rule on swing or hot music, particularly that created by Jewish artists. Tucker's records were no longer available in areas under his control.[88] When she learned that copies of "My Yiddishe Momme" were to be smashed, Tucker recalled writing a letter to Hitler that she felt was a "masterpiece." She was never one to sit on her hands.[89]

The singer also continued to support African Americans in the industry. She attended a benefit for the Negro Actors Guild (NAG) in December 1938. Along with others representing the "top rungs of the white and colored theatrical circles," such as Cantor, Milton Berle, Duke Ellington, and Marian Anderson, the group came together to help black performers in need at an event honoring NAG president Bill Robinson. As was frequently the case, Tucker was the only white woman listed as a performer. Some in the black press documented this event as a particularly significant moment of racial cooperation, also mentioning that any performer who followed Tucker on the program faced a "gargantuan feat."[90] Even into the mid-1930s the black press was comparing newcomers with a bluesy style to the white Red Hot Mama, calling singers Mae Alix and Billie Young the "Sun-Tinted Sophie Tucker," and "Sepia Sophie Tucker," respectively. In 1939, when singer Ethel Waters had established herself as one of the most famous African-American performers on stage and screen, she was still described by one reporter as having been a "sepia Sophie Tucker" in her earlier years of singing.[91] It is difficult to know whether Tucker's signature sound, style of performance, or physical appearance led to this kind of labeling, but perhaps reporters felt that she transcended race, at least in terms of marketing new talent.[92]

Tucker never gave up on hoping for a bigger stage, continued stardom, and prestige that would prevent her from becoming a has been.

An opportunity came in the fall of 1938, when New York producer Vinton Freedley called Tucker to talk about performing in a new musical, *Leave It to Me*, with all music written by Cole Porter. Tucker recalled that Porter, who had skyrocketed into the Broadway stratosphere after the smash hit *Anything Goes*, saw her perform at the Riviera and was seemingly taken by her show. Singing Porter's compositions, such as "I'm Taking the Steps to Russia" and "Most Gentleman Don't Like Love," was a thrill for the singer. In thirty years, she had never appeared in a leading role in a high-profile Broadway musical. Starring with William Gaxton, Victor Moore, and Mary Martin, Tucker became part of the Broadway establishment. One Alabama newspaper congratulated Tucker on this coup, stating that it took her thirty years to persuade "skeptics" that she could act "with the best of them."[93]

The show, a satire about the Soviet Union, allowed Tucker to shine as the wife of a US ambassador in the USSR whose unconventional diplomatic actions result only in praise rather than a hoped-for return to the States. Porter's score suited Tucker's signature delivery, and the show, which opened in November 1938, was a huge success. The *New York Post* claimed that *Leave It to Me* gave audiences the kind of "gleeful exhibition" they needed, commending Tucker on her unique, "full blown personality."[94] Others applauded the amusing nature of the show, although some pointed out the perils of spoofing the Soviet Union during a period of international crisis.[95] Although many in the entertainment industry were joining Communist-front organizations at the time and promoting anti-Fascist causes, Tucker did not enter into these kinds of formal political alliances, instead turning to charitable organizations and refugee work. The show ran for close to three hundred performances in New York. Tucker remembered her time in *Leave It to Me* as "show business as I had known it long ago."[96]

By then, the fifty-year-old performer was perhaps one of the busiest women in the industry, between her Broadway gig, radio show, and presidency of the AFA. Tucker's concerns about fading into obscurity abated as she settled into her role as a veteran performer who could be counted on for wisdom, reliability, and leadership. Yet soon Tucker would become embroiled in turmoil as head of the AFA that she could not have imagined when she accepted the post. With the United States on the brink of war, Tucker endured her own hurricane in a political arena that proved much less predictable than her stage shows. In this new landscape she would find out if she was stoppable after all.

7

◇————◇————◇

THE VALUE
OF DEVOTION

*S*ophie Tucker had always delivered progressive messages to audiences and commanded a position at the
highest rungs of the industry. Yet she had never
served in a formal political capacity, instead shying away from the
suffrage movement, organized civil rights events, and other major
activities promoting social change. But because performers' rights
mattered deeply to the singer, she ventured into unknown territory
as president of the American Federation of Actors (AFA) and soon
realized that she would become the center of one of the largest labor
struggles performers had ever engaged in. While Tucker may have
accepted the role with the best of intentions and the sincerest motivation to promote equity for fellow stage workers, she came to realize that the battle among labor unions was often in the spirit of managerial self-interest. The singer's political activity in the AFA went
against the grain of all of her public actions to date, and she would
pay a price for the generosity and fidelity that she was so famous for.

It was not possible for anyone to know that beginning in June 1939, the union would become embroiled in a major scandal that would be covered daily by the *New York Times* and other major newspapers across the country. The saga began with the American Actors and Artists of America (otherwise known as 4A) charging that its subsidiary union, the AFA, was mishandling funds collected at benefits for relief purposes. The controversy centered on Executive Secretary Ralph Whitehead, who had been managing the daily operations of the union and was cited by 4A as the "only executive of importance" in the 4A report of violations. The 4A provided evidence that along with improperly recording finances, Whitehead had purchased an automobile with the funds. Tucker became incensed at these accusations, defending Whitehead with a steely resolve and claiming that the benefit money was placed in a general fund used to help needy members in times of emergency. New to union politics and thinking only about the consequences for union members, Tucker was not open to any possibility of corruption; she truly believed that Whitehead was honest. It is likely that Tucker's stance had more to do with defending a union that she was entrusted with rather than personal feelings for Whitehead. Tucker recalled that the AFA had emerged as the union making the "first concerted move . . . to lift the status of the vaudeville performer." She had strong feelings about the industry where she began her career and believed that everyone in the profession should support the union.[1]

A hearing was set for July 10 to further investigate the charges, with the possibility that the AFA charter could be revoked by 4A. Yet Tucker's reputation was not tarnished. At the same time the *New York Times* was issuing commentary on these labor woes, Tucker was given a lavish luncheon at the Imperial Theater for her thirtieth year on Broadway. The cast of *Leave It to Me* and other friends attended, and the entertainment community was showing Tucker love and appreciation. This would soon change dramatically.[2]

Tucker called for a mass meeting of union members on June 20, hoping to clear things up and to promote a vote of confidence for all AFA leadership, particularly Whitehead. Yet before the meeting,

Tucker received what must have been shocking news that her dear friend Eddie Cantor was resigning from the AFA council. He had served as a past president and an ardent supporter, so Cantor's actions were dramatic. He explained that his reasons for departure would be "sufficiently obvious" when the July hearing took place. Tensions rose even further when Cantor, along with fellow former president Rudy Vallee, encouraged union members to refrain from giving Tucker or Whitehead a vote of confidence. For a woman new to politics and steadfastly loyal to her peers, this was incredibly surprising and hurtful. Cantor adopted a hard line against Whitehead and hoped the executive secretary would "vindicate himself" in the face of mounting suspicion toward the AFA. Tucker was livid, claiming that Cantor had never cared about her union; according to her, he never attended meetings when he was AFA president.[3]

With the best of maternal intentions, Tucker called for her "children" to disbelieve the charges in the June meeting of 1,200 performers at the Hotel Edison ballroom. Whitehead, Vallee AFA vice president Harry Richman, Bill Robinson, and Milton Berle were also in attendance, with Robinson and Berle likely present to support Tucker in an extremely precarious situation. Tucker spoke for an hour, proclaiming that she had never received any compensation for the work she did as AFA president. As she expressed her conviction that opponents were jealous of the union's success, she was constantly interrupted and heckled. Tucker remembered standing with sweat pouring down her face due to the heat while people in the audience raised their middle fingers toward her. The atmosphere could not remain polite. Passions ran high between supporters and opponents of the union, and mayhem erupted despite the protestations of Bill Robinson, who urged everyone to keep the meeting peaceful.[4]

Given a chance to voice their opinions, various performers rushed to the speakers platform. Chorus performer Helen Johnson became entangled with union opponents when she tried to speak. Johnson apparently bit mimic Ernie Mack as he attempted to restrain her, and the rest of the evening was described as complete "pandemonium." Chairs were overturned, food was thrown on the floor, and eight patrol cars finally came to end the chaos. Tucker and Whitehead had dashed out as the melee erupted, but it was clear that there would be no levelheaded discussion among union members. Afterward Tucker claimed that the uproar was a "carefully rehearsed" exercise in violence to force her to resign and that most who attended were not even legitimate actors.[5]

Order was not restored as Tucker hoped it would be. New York City district attorney Thomas Dewey began investigating the financial transactions of the AFA and discovered that close to $13,000 had not been used for relief purposes. Cantor begged Tucker to resign from the AFA, arguing that she had been "misled" by Whitehead; he worried she would continue to "innocently" defend him from serious accusations. Tucker would take none of Cantor's advice, proclaiming that "even a murderer is entitled to a trial" and suggesting that no evidence had yet been formally presented faulting the AFA. She even urged Cantor to go through the AFA's accounting books himself. The singer was not willing to accept that what Cantor called her "bigness of heart" had made her blind to "gross mismanagement."[6] As a woman who had handled all aspects of her own career for years, she did not need to be patronized or accused of simplemindedness.

Tucker saw the mission and purpose of the AFA as crucial to the values she had promoted throughout her life. By the time things became incredibly contentious, she was in too deep to change course. The singer emphasized again and again that any funds that were said to be missing were used for "legitimate and necessary" causes and that Whitehead's car was used for union member business. As she explained, "What is more important to those needy members and to the members who have made substantive economic gains for themselves through our organization, the continuance of our organization or the distribution of the small sum of approximately $12,000 to needy members?"[7] Tucker had invested a significant amount of her time over the years in union matters and was also quite proud of her role as the first female president. She would not be easily pushed aside by others, especially men like Cantor who moved with ease from heading one agency to the next.

When the AFA stood trial on July 10, 1939, Tucker led a walkout. Even as the details of the case were unfolding inside the courtroom, the singer and other union delegates refused to participate on the grounds that the charges were not prepared "in good faith." AFA leaders who were opposed to the trial protested that delegates were not unbiased, that they were acting on behalf of the 4A for personal gain, and that they were beholden to other unions.[8] All of these claims were denied, and the court stripped the AFA of its charter, declaring the union guilty of "misusing relief funds and mismanaging its affairs." Incensing Tucker further, the American Guild of Variety Artists (AGVA) was to take over the membership of the AFA, with Cantor as temporary president. Once she understood why Cantor was so desperate to have her resign, she sarcastically called the ordeal "all very amusing."[9] Refusing to allow the AGVA to interfere in the affairs of the AFA or to "solicit federation members," Tucker and others petitioned New York Supreme Court justice Edward McGoldrick to issue an injunction against the AGVA. Many felt that the AFA charter had been illegally removed and that the AFA's contract with its membership was inviolable.[10] With the list of acronyms growing, the situation become increasingly complicated—"confusing and annoying" as Tucker described it.[11]

While the decision on the injunction was pending, the AFA applied for affiliation with the International Alliance of Theatrical Stage Employees and Motion Pictures Machine Operators (IATSE), a union representing backstage workers both in Hollywood and on Broadway under the auspices of the American Federation of Labor (AFL). At the time AFL president William Green would not indicate whether he recognized the legitimacy of the AFA. The world of labor was witnessing what the *New York Times* called a "virtually unprecedented" case in which two parent unions were claiming to be chartered for the same branch members.[12]

Green eventually granted the AFA charter status under IATSE. George Brown, president of IATSE, explained that because both the 4A and IATSE were AFL affiliates, his union had the right to recognize the AFA even if the 4A did not. Tucker was quite pleased with this compromise, but the 4A was not, calling the actions of IATSE "treasonable." Issuing an action against anyone who participated in "betrayal," the 4A had the power to prevent Tucker from continuing her work in *Leave It to Me*, which fell under its jurisdiction. IATSE members stated that if Tucker did not go on, neither would the stage-hands necessary for production. The show was scheduled to reopen on August 21, but it seems to have been at a standstill until labor relations improved.[13]

The 4A leadership kept its word. Tucker was suspended from the Screen Actors Guild and shortly thereafter received the same treatment from the American Federation of Radio Artists. When Tucker was also suspended from the Actors' Equity Association, pending a trial for her "treasonable" act, the entire production of *Leave It to Me* was affected because all other Broadway actors were forbidden to appear on the stage with her. The cast opposed the suspension and attested to Tucker's "backstage popularity," which they thought would result in a walkout by all of the stagehands.[14] Tucker was confident that her suspension would not stick and assured the public that the leadership of IATSE were not "schoolchildren, but on the contrary, are past masters in the sort of strategy that it takes to win." Yet as petitions circulated among members of the 4A, thousands of actors expressed a willingness to go on strike to uphold the principle that the AFA was no longer a part of the AFL.[15]

Hollywood was called to action as performers such as Katharine Hepburn, Joan Crawford, and Helen Hayes backed the 4A and begged Tucker to "come back home where you belong." In a letter to Tucker, Hayes expressed regret for the "spanking" Tucker had received in her suspensions, but saw them as a necessary measure to protect the integrity of the 4A and the employment of its membership. Tucker seemed not to care very much about her own plight. She remarked, "I am not looking for an easy way out for Sophie, but I am looking for justice for my associates, my organization, and my children, and I am sure I will get it." A meeting of AFL executives to decide the status of the AFA within the competing umbrella organizations was imminent, and a strike was a very real possibility.[16]

Mid-August was a period of intense negotiations. By August 16 it seemed that the AFL executive council had put plans in motion for a peace settlement. The 4A could bring in AFA union members, as well as revoke the AFA charter after findings of misconduct. Under this agreement, the AFL also stated that IATSE was required to withdraw its charter to the AFA. While this seemed like a victory for the 4A, it was found to be problematic by 4A leadership when the agreement also called for the possible reelection of Whitehead. The 4A leaders were more than willing to reinstate Tucker, but Whitehead was viewed as the root of corruption and the initial problem. Under these circumstances, a compromise could not be reached.[17]

Pressure continued to mount for Tucker's resignation from the AFA. A plea in the Actors' Equity Association's magazine stated: "With the welfare of the entire acting profession at stake . . . [one] must rise above the issues of personalities and align themselves with their brothers and sisters of the stage. And that does not mean the stagehands."[18] Meanwhile, stagehands professed a compelling loyalty in refusing to work on *Leave It to Me* should Tucker remain suspended. As a result of this uncertain atmosphere, the show was first postponed until October 9, when Tucker either would be permitted to perform or could be replaced; it was then rescheduled to open on September 4. Producer Freedley reached an agreement with Equity that if the stagehands were to walk out on behalf of Tucker, he would be freed of contractual obligations to the others in the cast. Yet, stagehands abandoning one performance could have led to a widespread walkout, and therefore Tucker's persistence in supporting the AFA led to a logistical nightmare for many on Broadway. By the end of August, eleven Broadway shows were threatened with closing because actors were ready to strike; if stagehands would not accept 4A directives, actors had no choice but to protest.[19] With this stalemate not only facing those on the stage, but also spreading to film workers in Hollywood, the industry reached a moment that the *New York Times* deemed "the most disastrous union warfare the amusement industry has ever known."[20]

Freedley begged his star to reconcile with the Actors' Equity Association for the good of the cast, but she would not budge. Tucker received many other pleas to resign, one of which read, "Don't provide the spark which will explode the theatrical profession."[21] She was undoubtedly conflicted, knowing that a strike would cause many actors serious financial hardship, particularly those who were not big names. While she expressed her lifetime motivation to help all performers, she blamed Equity for the current climate and was seemingly intransigent. Loyal to the AFA and committed to the stagehands who had offered her union sanctuary in a storm, Tucker could not have broken with the principles she had committed to for months. At her core, she simply felt that she had not been given a fair hearing back in July, and she refused to cooperate with any further actions on behalf of the 4A, on the basis that they would not be impartial.

As much as she enjoyed being a headliner, she always identified much more with people in the audience and with the workers in the makeup room and creating her costumes than she did with other big stars. And perhaps because stagehands knew this about her, they felt ready to walk off the job in a unified front if she was not allowed to appear in *Leave It to Me*. In the press Tucker never stopped talking about her humble beginnings, and both her philanthropic work and her union devotion testified to her genuine regard for people on the bottom. As the media couched the conflict as one of stagehands versus actors, there was a real class dynamic at play, particularly with a bevy of big Hollywood stars coming out to support the 4A. Tucker was clearly not comfortable on that side, as much as she expressed concern for the chorus girls and the less established actors who were enveloped in the fight.

At the very moment when a strike seemed most imminent—with the 4A even reaching out to New York mayor Fiorello La Guardia to intervene as a mediator—a settlement was reached. Thousands of actors came to the September 4 meeting ready to vote for a nationwide strike, but instead they were calmed. Under the agreement, the AFA would be part of the 4A, and the charter granted by IATSE would have to be revoked. Members of the now defunct AFA would be represented by the AGVA, which Whitehead now supported and encouraged members to join while remaining "alert and vigilant." Whitehead's role in union affairs was over. There was no mention of his reelection, and it was understood that his only role was to cooperate. With this consent, Tucker was reinstated by Equity and permitted to appear in *Leave It to Me*, which was opening that same night. Crisis was averted. Some said that the peace agreement was influenced by the "outbreak of war in Europe," but the timing of the settlement, the day of the *Leave It to Me* opening, suggests the true reason it was reached.[22]

The debacle left a dark stain on industry relations. Prominent theater critic Brooks Atkinson bemoaned the lack of integrity among labor leaders in the period of conflict: they had passed union members back and forth without discussion and a seemingly disaffected AFL was content to see a violation of its constitution. Atkinson called the whole affair a "disgraceful exhibition of labor union politics," but he had hoped that memories of the conflict would fade. Emphasizing Tucker's critical role in prompting what would have been a national strike, he lamented in his review of *Leave It to Me*, "Out of loyalty to her beaming talents let us hope that the anger aroused by internal strife may quickly pass away."[23]

With the dissolution of the AFA, Tucker joined the AGVA and distanced herself from Whitehead, explaining that she had no connection with his "future plans" and was hoping to "mind her own business." It seemed that Whitehead might still have been hoping to keep the AFA alive by representing workers in carnivals and circuses, but Tucker claimed that she had little use for membership in a union entirely comprised of "nonperformers." Most likely, Tucker decided to accept the demise of the AFA for the good of the industry and because she realized that the achieved settlement was the best possible outcome. She was pleased to get back to work after defending Whitehead so adamantly for months, and it seems he was willing to move into the shadows. Whitehead soon suffered a heart attack, which prevented him from attending to union business. He was ultimately found guilty only of moving funds in an "unauthorized manner." The events that precipitated one of the largest union battles ever within the entertainment industry were brushed under the rug as the actors unions were granted the autonomy they sought.[24]

All that had transpired during the AFA conflict affected Tucker's further participation in politics. She felt foolish and humiliated by the affair, and she had learned that trusted friends would turn on her and that the unyielding acceptance she had among audiences over the years did not extend to her activities in an overt leadership role. Yet she didn't give up on unions. She reminisced, "You think after these experiences that I would have lost faith in the value of a union," but she insisted that performers needed to be active in union activities and to insist on fair treatment from the industry.[25] She would remain under the radar in union politics from then on but would continue to support actors unions financially.

Tucker's support for those who struggled was not lost on the public. Her reputation as a champion of underdogs everywhere would deepen. She turned her major focus to charity work, becoming a leader in a much more controllable atmosphere and receiving uncomplicated recognition for her dedication. Her efforts as a woman in a leadership position were criticized in ways that she had never been subject to before, and although she supported her fellow theatrical workers, particularly those outside of the limelight, the internal politics were not tolerable for the singer. As much as she admired women such as Eleanor Roosevelt who pushed for change in the face of criticism, this was not her calling, and after the AFA debacle, she understood the limits of her own political engagement much more clearly.[26]

Leave It to Me remained in New York before traveling beginning on September 16. The show ran a successful tour through 1940, playing in major northeastern cities as well as smaller southern ones such as Shreveport, Louisiana, and Birmingham, Alabama. Bad weather in the South and Midwest hampered audience attendance by the end of January, and the show ended after sixteen weeks on the road.[27] Thereafter, Tucker, continued her nightclub work in Miami Beach, at Chicago's Chez Paree, and at Jack Dempsey's spot in New York, where she was promoted as the "Sarah Bernhardt of nightclubs"—a label once given to her for her ragtime greatness. She also performed with Harry Richman and Joe Lewis at Loew's State Theater in New York, hearkening back to the old days of vaudeville. With nostalgia running high through the show, *Variety* mentioned that these three old timers were very much at the top of their game, while also calling attention to guest stage appearances by both Cantor and Ed Sullivan. From this collaboration it seemed "very evident" that Tucker and Cantor had put their dispute over the AFA behind them and reconciled as friends.[28] There is little evidence that the labor dispute led to Tucker's alienation from others in the industry. In one instance, Tucker's friend playwright Noel Coward told the singer she was his "favorite entertainer" and that he regretted the fact that she could not participate in a cabaret show he was headlining with several other major stars.[29]

The political struggles Tucker had endured in 1939 did not slow her down; if anything they piqued public interest and provided her with more theatrical opportunities. Beginning in 1940, the press began to document Tucker's efforts to write her autobiography, with the singer eager to provide a foreshadowing of what would appear in print. Describing her process of writing—going back to her hotel after a night performance and writing until four or five o'clock in the morning—Tucker indicated that the book was a labor of love, allowing her to relive moments that gave her "joy to no end."[30]

In the spring of 1941, Tucker's old friend George Jessel asked her to perform in his new musical *High Kickers*, depicting the lives of two burlesque performers. She could not have been more delighted to work with Jessel, especially in a vehicle that would capture what one reporter called her "inward ache for the past." Playing herself, Tucker was a burlesque veteran taking care of producer Jessel as he put on a show. Involving a show within a show, *High Kickers* required Tucker to perform a striptease as well as some of her racier numbers. When the show opened at the Forrest Theater in Philadelphia on October 14, it was said to be "dirty as all get out," with Tucker as good as ever.[31] While some critics questioned the effectiveness of combining both "senti-ment and humor," the show performed above expectations, earning $26,300 in its second week in Philadelphia before moving on to New York's Broadhurst Theater, where it ran for 171 performances.[32]

The attention performers and critics were devoting to *High Kickers* was quickly diverted when the United States was attacked by the Jap-anese on December 7, 1941. Two-thirds of the economy was directed towards the war effort, and 15 million men and women enlisted in the armed forces. Civilian society was quickly converted to a military arsenal, and theaters witnessed spottier attendance as both the draft and conservation efforts affected leisure pursuits. Popular entertain-ers like Tucker were called upon to inspire patriotism as they had during World War I, but this time on a larger scale. Two hundred famed musicians volunteered for USO tours, while others, such as bandleader Glenn Miller, enlisted in the army.[33] Morale-building films in Hollywood abounded, and military benefits offered celebri-ties a new sense of national purpose. Tucker did not hesitate to do her part. *High Kickers* soon incorporated patriotic elements to enhance the show's relevance, and it entertained hundreds of servicemen who took in the performance for free, as was customary in theatres. One reporter touted Tucker as a "familiar face" among the military, with men in the audience of *High Kickers* whose fathers had been enter-tained by her during the Great War. The show went on the road to Washington, DC, Pittsburgh, and Chicago in the spring of 1942 until it closed in May. By November, *High Kickers* was on the production schedule for screen adaptation by MGM, due to its success as one of several long-running stage comedies.[34] The film was never made, but the stage show had a good run.

As part of her longtime support for African Americans, Tucker performed in a "Salute to Negro Troops," a pageant at New York's Cos-mopolitan Opera House celebrating black contributions to the mili-tary, with profits benefiting recreation facilities for black soldiers in New York. Tucker and other white entertainers worked alongside Bill Robinson, Paul Robeson, Count Basie, Marian Anderson, and other

African-American luminaries for an audience of thousands, many of them black soldiers. During the war the government and the members of the entertainment industry conducted a variety of programs aimed at African Americans, often with the help of white stars. Countering Nazi racial policy was critical to democratic propaganda, and with segregation still very much alive, films, posters, and benefit shows could promote the guise of unity. The benefit at the Cosmopolitan was a wide-scale display of interracial creativity and cooperation. As the *Daily Worker* reported, "Shoulder to shoulder the white and Negro actors of America stood together in a great demonstration against the oppression of minorities."[35] The event was chaired by Eleanor Roosevelt, and audiences heard pleas for racial equality in the military as New York City Council member Adam Clayton Powell Jr. urged the first lady to recommend that black soldiers be removed from "glory holes" in battleships and given positions as pilots and ship commanders.[36] The pageant was anything but apolitical.

Tucker's participation in benefits extended over the course of the war as she contributed to various fundraisers and war bond drives, and visited training camps across the country. Tucker sang her patriotic ditty "If He's Good Enough to Fight," urging women, "If he's good enough to fight for his country, then he shouldn't have to fight for his love." She heralded her own wartime service during both World Wars, boasting, "What I did for the fathers, I can still do for the sons."[37] She was called the "sweetheart of the Navy" in one flyer advertising her appearance at a Naval recreation facility. Tucker's age did not prevent her from becoming a popular figure among servicemen; Lt. Henry Fritner's "date" with the singer was publicized as a great opportunity for the young man.[38]

Armond Fields suggests that there were almost ten thousand requests for Tucker's picture from people in the armed forces; a particular group of officers in Newport, Rhode Island, expressed their disappointment that they could not look at the singer in person "constantly" but noted that a pinup would be the "next best thing."[39] Pinups of stars like Betty Grable and Rita Hayworth abounded in military camps and ships, not only as outlets for men's sexual desires, but also as reminders of the women they were fighting for at home. Tucker was far from a young, sexy starlet. Her popularity as an untraditional pinup was a result of her motherly affect. Tucker embodied values of generosity and nurture, albeit with a flirtatious twist, and her picture reassured some servicemembers that they were fighting on behalf of their mothers and sisters—that their obligation as citizens to die for their country was well worth it.[40]

Yet not all of her efforts were appreciated. She was reprimanded for her "spicy" material during one navy relief show in Buffalo that apparently had the audience "gasping." Fifty thousand people attended—a record audience for a war benefit—and Tucker's risqué performance apparently exceeded the bounds of "propriety" set by organizers. They promised more "wholesome and inspiring entertainment" in the future.[41] One local radio station gave Tucker what *Variety* called one of the "worst verbal castigations" any performer had received for a very long time, pointing to the "obscene songs and speeches" that were carried over the stadium loudspeakers, with "smut predominating." Initial reports focused more on Tucker's "peppery dialogue" than her songs, which one critic described as "routine," but this audience was clearly different from those at other military engagements. The singer was appalled by the verbal smackdown, claiming that Buffalo authorities had no right to criticize someone who offered her services for charity, but also that they knew she was billed as the "Red Hot Mama." Explaining that she performed the identical show at two other venues for servicemembers in Ohio with "no adverse criticism," Tucker dismissed the Buffalo organizers as prudish, hypocritical, and unappreciative.[42]

Some of Tucker's songs had always been ahead of the times in terms of sexual suggestiveness, and by the 1940s she had fully embraced the "Last of the Red Hot Mamas" as a literal self-description. Tucker was at a point in her career when she had more autonomy, and with the war reviving her celebrity status and pumping up the economy, she felt very secure. Tucker's hallmark work in nightclubs provided the best format for longer diatribes on life and love, with sexual innuendo abounding, as well as stories about her own romantic mishaps. One of her newer hits, "Life Begins at Forty," empowered older women as the singer urged others to be like her, who had "just begun to live all over again."[43]

Returning to Chicago's Chez Paree in November 1942, Tucker offered a repertoire the media described as "primarily the concern of adults," filled with her signature double entendre and playful exchanges with Ted Shapiro. As she told her fans, for her coupledom was an option, not a necessity. Tucker's classic, "I'm Living Alone and I Like It," validated the singer's joy in taking care of herself: she proudly proclaimed, "There's nobody growling at me, where the hell have you been?" The raunchy "Soph and Ernie" jokes that inspired Bette Midler's early career were built on Tucker's earlier observations on the silliness of human nature. Women always had the upper hand. Tucker's revelations about her fictional boyfriend Ernie poked fun at male incompetence: "I will never forget, you know, my boyfriend said to me, 'Soph, if you could learn to cook we could fire the chef.' I said to him 'Ernie, if you could learn to fuck we could fire the chauffeur!'"[44]

Critics noticed that she was doing more speaking that singing due to strains on her vocal cords over the years, but this had little impact on her success. Her recorded version of "Aren't Women Wonderful" was almost entirely spoken, yet just as effective in relating Tucker's ironic descriptions of women's abilities to multitask more than any man. This was also the case for Tucker's defensive "I Don't Want to Get Thin," in which she insisted conversationally that even though many urged her to diet and reduce her "stout" figure, she was fine as she was, attracting more men than her petite rivals. Unlike her self-pitying "Nobody Loves a Fat Girl," her later songs were all about the untouchable nature of being a red hot mama. When Shapiro chided her to lose just a few pounds, she retorted, "All the married men who run after me have skinny wives at home." The singer dug in her heels—"I'm fat and I know it and I intend to stay fat"—unafraid to admit that her scale read 163 pounds. With songs like these, it's not surprising that for those attending her shows, "La Tucker" was as good as ever. One reporter testified, "You double up in red-faced laughter and feel quite happy when you look up and find you're not alone in your enjoyment."[45]

One significant personal development for Tucker during the war years was the intense friendship she developed with Margaret Chung, the first Asian-American woman to become a physician in the United States. San Francisco–based Chung had become a legend when she hosted hundreds of Bay Area aviators in the 1930s, adopting the "fair hair bastards" as her "sons." Each "son" received a number in the order that Chung "adopted" him as part of her network, and by the end of World War II, there were fifteen hundred men in her group. Hosting parties and hunting and camping outings, and serving as a surrogate mother to her clan, Chung also performed traditional maternal roles, cooking and tending to the men when they were ill. The once engaged but never married physician was quite unconventional. Although her sexual orientation was never publicly revealed, many assumed she was a lesbian. She had had a close relationship with lesbian poet Elsa Gidlow before her recognition as "Mom Chung" to hundreds of servicemen.[46] With female independence encouraged during wartime, women were freer to move outside traditional gender norms—even wearing pants. Homosexuality was not condoned by society, but women's close relationships were accepted and sometimes casually overlooked. In the absence of "flagrant homosexual" behavior, women were even permitted to serve in the military. Cities such as San Francisco became major military bases during the war, allowing for the gradual development of a lesbian subculture as the population became more cosmopolitan and diverse.[47]

Chung adopted many celebrities in the 1940s who frequented Sunday dinners at her home, such as Ronald Reagan and Henry Fonda; however, Tucker was her favorite "daughter." It seems that Tucker and Chung had previously met when Chung was in medical school at the University of Southern California and Tucker was touring in vaudeville in the early 1910s, but the two became fast friends when Tucker began spending more time in San Francisco nightclubs in the 1940s. When Chung conducted a ceremony inducting new members into the family, Tucker became Kiwi number 107, taking on a group name given to celebrities and politicians who did not fly but were important to Chung's cause. By 1945 Tucker often visited Chung's house, and Chung even had a special room reserved for the singer. Chung's philanthropic gestures and unbounded generosity matched Tucker's, and the two worked together to support war morale, in one case organizing a combined effort that resulted in the sale of close to $8,000 in war bonds.[48]

It is not difficult to understand why the singer became so close to the physician; their backgrounds were very similar, as were their ambitions. Chung's family came to America around the same time as Tucker's, and the two were born only a few years apart. The Chinese Exclusion Act had passed in 1882, a few years before Chung was born, and hostility toward the Chinese was at its apogee. Although Chung was a citizen due to her American birth, her parents were considered aliens. Like Tucker, Chung always felt like an outsider, and she was determined to defy expectations for Chinese women. While the poverty Chung experienced was far more severe than Tucker's, she had also worked in a restaurant, and she possessed a similar motivation to do something exceptional. Chung attended the University of Southern California College of Physicians and Surgeons from 1911 to 1916, assimilating into a male profession. She also scoffed at gender norms for women by wearing men's suits and sometimes identifying herself as "Mike" to her friends.

Chung adored Tucker. She traveled to her shows and wrote her loving letters expressing the value of their friendship. While some of Chung's sentiments were of an intimate nature—she asked Tucker to wear a blue nightgown she had mailed so she could virtually experience physical closeness to the singer from afar—it is difficult to know whether these kinds of feelings were reciprocal. Tucker never wrote in this manner to or about Chung. Chung is absent from Tucker's autobiography, even though the singer claimed to have written the book at Chung's home. In the autobiography Tucker focused mostly on individuals who were part of her professional career, so this omission may be more related to the nature of the memoir as a show business tell-all than a conscious effort to exclude the physician.

Although her scrapbooks include clippings about Chung, as well as correspondence from "sons" that conveyed the deep friendship between the two women, there is nothing to suggest that Tucker had sexual feelings for Chung. It is much more likely the physician fully understood Tucker on a professional and personal level, and also successfully navigated a world dominated by powerful men. Tucker's "boys"— Cantor, Jessel, Shapiro, and others—were not unlike Chung's sons, and both women engaged in motherly actions while maintaining their own powerful status. Tucker also delighted in being part of the celebrity scene that revolved around Chung's home in the 1940s, and the site provided her stability during incessant movement. The two women continued their friendship over the course of the next two decades until Chung's death in 1959.[49]

Tucker may have felt close to Chung also because she saw less of her siblings, particularly Moe and Annie, than she would have wished. Annie was living her own married life, and Tucker's itinerant lifestyle kept her from staying with family for a great length of time. She attended the Dayton, Ohio, wedding of her nephew Zachary, son of her brother Philip, in July of 1942.[50] The press reported that Bert had returned to show business after ten years away doing stints in the shoe and drug businesses; he now was managing a band for the William Morris office. By 1943 Bert had moved on to the position of café booker after another agent was drafted. Tucker offered no comment on these developments. Bert was still married to his wife, Lillian, though without children. His presence in his mother's life was only tangible through yearly birthday and Mother's Day cards.[51]

Tucker's popularity during the war years led Hollywood, which had seemingly given up on the singer, to invite her back to perform a cameo role in Universal Pictures' *Follow the Boys* (1944), a musical review packed with the biggest stars of the day, including Orson Welles and the Andrews Sisters. The film was regarded as a "Hollywood tribute to show business in the war effort." The *Motion Picture Herald* admitted that the film didn't have much of a plot, but that was compensated for by the vast amount of talent offerings.[52] Although Tucker only sang her signature, "Some of These Days," the film was profitable domestically and popular among troops stationed at home and abroad. Soon afterward, she shot a similar musical revue, United Artists' *Sensations of 1945*, this time performing two songs written for the film. With another all-star cast, the film scored well with audiences—so much so that the director Andrew Stone planned for a sequel.[53] Although Tucker did not experience the disappointment making these films that she had in the past, they would be her last motion pictures. Nearing sixty and committed to her nightclub work, she knew that movie options were limited and that she belonged on the stage.

After years of reports about Tucker's autobiography, Doubleday Doran finally published it in 1945. It sold for $2.50, and according to Fields, a thousand special-edition autographed copies sold for twenty-five dollars each.[54] It was written in collaboration with *Saturday Evening Post* reporter Dorothy Giles, and all proceeds went to charities that Tucker had supported over her lifetime, from several actors guilds to her mother's treasured Hebrew Home for the Aged in Hartford. Tucker sold the book at her various engagements and marketed it as a way for audiences to learn more about the stories she delivered in her acts. "There are no breaks, just plain hard work," she told one Chicago radio interviewer as the main lesson to take from the memoir.[55] The autobiography was part reflective and part prescriptive, and Tucker hoped that it would "answer some of the questions beginners in show business ask me about how to get started, and how to make a success as entertainers." It contained little about her family, particularly Bert, and the book did not reveal anything about the singer that wasn't already part of public record in interviews and press reports. Several friends and colleagues received copies and some requested them; William Green, still president of the AFL, asked for a "de luxe edition" presuming that there would be "some things left out of the book." Recent events that had transpired between his labor organization and Tucker's when she was president of the AFA were not exactly flattering.[56]

Critical reception was laudatory. *Variety*'s Abel Green commended Tucker for her bravery in telling her story of success and failure, bad marriages, and rifts within her family. "Her ardent Jewishness is honest and inspirational," Green attested, writing that her immigrant background clearly propelled the choices she had made and the affection she had for Jewish communities across the globe.[57] One BBC radio host called the autobiography a "brilliant record of early life," while John Cavanagh, managing director of the *Catholic Register*, was impressed with the singer's message that "bitterness and vindictiveness are men's worst enemies."[58] For Tucker, most satisfying was the money being donated to charity. One 1947 report indicated that in seven weeks of Tucker's nightclub appearances, fifty-five charities had received at least a thousand dollars each in donations resulting from the sale of the book.[59] By 1948, tens of thousands of dollars had gone to philanthropies.[60]

Letters from friends and admirers indicated a profound attachment to the singer and her life. The autobiography was a way for fans to take home a reminder of Tucker after her shows, as her voice permeates the narrative in the same way that she performed. Much of the fan mail attested to the inspiration of Tucker's rags-to-riches story and the values of kindness and empathy that resonated throughout. The book also captured a period in American vaudeville culture that had dissipated while highlighting the central themes of the postwar era: liberal inclusion of all races and creeds, individualism, and the celebration of a burgeoning celebrity culture. A public that flocked to the movies and would soon fully embrace television lapped up Tucker's encounters with the brightest stars in Broadway and Hollywood. By offering a window into an unknown world, with all its pitfalls and mishaps exposed, Tucker fed her fans' insatiable appetite for the lives of the rich and famous.

Shortly after the publication of her autobiography, Tucker's brother Phil died at the age of sixty-one. The singer took only three days off from her engagement at Chez Paree to return to Hartford for the funeral.[61] Philip's death caused a rift in the family after Tucker sued her sister-in-law Leah for $500,000 in securities and stocks, which Tucker claimed were hers and had been illegally taken from a New York Bank. As the press reported, Philip had been her business manager, and Tucker felt that the money was hers, even though Leah disputed this claim. After two years of legal battles, Leah was left with nothing, and according to Tucker's nephew Henry Abuza, the conflict resulted in a stark division between Philip's side of the family and the other three siblings, Sophie, Moe, and Annie. According to Henry, Tucker was adamant about holding onto the money, although she offered to take care of Leah financially. Leah refused the offer. After this incident, Henry Abuza claimed, Tucker only recognized Moe's son, Charles, as her nephew even though Philip had two sons, Henry and Zachary, and a daughter, Sadie. Henry was left with extreme bitterness after all that transpired. He considered Sophie, Moe, and Annie a major disappointment.[62]

Henry Abuza's depiction of his aunt as "single minded and devoted to her career," may have had some truth, but major inconsistencies in his account point to a closer relationship between Tucker and her brother's family. She took Philip's daughter, Sadie, on tour with her and left Henry $5,000 when she died. When it came to family, Tucker was uneven, but never negligent or disinterested. Even the scorned Henry admitted Tucker's generosity toward Bert, whom she supported during his adult life even though he always "took her money and ran." Henry claimed that she also supported her grown siblings. As all of Henry Abuza's published comments are based on a 1994 interview with his cousin, Lois Young-Tulin, that was conducted when he was quite elderly, his memory was most likely fuzzy and events distorted. Clearly, Henry felt detached from Tucker, expecting a relationship that he never had, and he was perhaps jealous of his cousin Charles, whom Tucker adored. After getting the intricacies of the family drama off his chest, he admitted that his aunt was something special. As a child he had access to her Palace Theater engagements and would peek behind curtains backstage. "There were certain exotic things about having an aunt like Sophie Tucker and going back stage and seeing her in the theater . . . and seeing 3500 people, and she could turn them on and she could turn them off."[63]

Back in the world of nightclubs, Tucker's appearances became even more demanding, especially after the Japanese surrender in

August 1945. The end of the war inspired joy among audiences, who returned to theaters in great numbers to celebrate. Tucker felt certain that her comedic material was playing well because patrons were not drawn to depressing content. As people did after the Great War, "They just want to forget," the singer explained; the world had witnessed so much loss and devastation over the past decade.[64] Tucker had made a home at the Chez Paree and was also becoming a regular at New York's Copacabana and La Martinique, earning $5,000 a week for two performances a night, at the top of performer salaries.[65] She would soon expand her circuit of nightclubs. By 1947, she had a draw that was competitive with her peak years in the 1920s; as the "hottest attraction" at Hollywood's Florentine Gardens, the singer's act grossed approximately $80,000 over the course of two weeks, with $10 charges per plate for dinner and audiences clamoring to see the show.[66]

Tucker focused even more on Jewish causes in the postwar era. Like most Jews in America, she was moved into action after the horror of the European Holocaust became fully exposed to the world. If Jewish entertainers were hoping to assimilate in previous decades when they first entered show business, the period after World War II witnessed a newfound imperative to extend help to Jews in need, even if it only remained part of their personal lives. Hollywood films such as The House I Live In (1945) and Gentleman's Agreement (1947) condemned religious intolerance, and with Judaism conceived as a "third faith" acceptable to Protestants and Catholics, more American Jews affiliated formally by joining synagogues and becoming more observant in their homes. A rise in synagogue construction coupled with more children attending religious school indicated that Jews felt it was important to practice religion in some fashion. With Jewish life obliterated in Europe, it was now the responsibility of American Jews to defy anti-Semitism and to speak for the importance of Jewish culture and values. The creation of the Jewish state of Israel in 1948 only fueled the commitment of American Jews to protect their own security, and Zionism became a central part of mainstream Jewish philosophy.[67]

Tucker became established as an ambassador of the faith. All who sought to organize against anti-Semitism and for Jewish education, refugees, and memorials understood her deep dedication and relied on her for assistance. In 1946, Albert Einstein, hoping to expand the Institute for Jewish Religion, wrote to Tucker asking for her support in organizing a luncheon and conference. To Einstein, the genocide of European Jewry made it critically important to disseminate "centers of learning." As he told Tucker, "We need teaching. We need leaders. Without them our present status and dignity will be seriously impaired."[68] The singer was also becoming more involved in American congregations, in particular providing financial support for the Actors' Temple in New York, which included several Broadway and film stars as congregants, and Los Angeles's Temple Emanuel, another sanctuary for Hollywood celebrities. As Rabbi Ernest Trattner told his friend Tucker in thanks for her contribution to a new building, "You are one of our dearest and most beloved member [sic] of the Temple."[69] In 1947 the Jewish Theatrical Guild recognized Tucker—its first female honoree—for her fortieth anniversary in show business. Jessel, Cantor, Irving Berlin, and a crowd of 1,500 in "overflowing attendance" celebrated at New York's Hotel Astor. Berlin wrote a special song for Tucker testifying to her tremendous success and her motivation to keep going.[70] Tucker's activities were continually appreciated; in 1951, Jewish War Veterans named her Woman of the Year, an honor previously bestowed only on Eleanor Roosevelt.[71]

Tucker was also assisting Zionist organizations, participating in benefits to support the establishment of a Jewish homeland and then to sustain it after Israeli statehood in May 1948.[72] When she planned a trip to London at the time of Israel's founding—her first to Europe since 1937—Jewish organizations were thrilled that she would be coming back across the Atlantic. They expressed interest in having the singer attend events supporting refugees, education, and settlement areas in Palestine that were under attack.[73]

One Holocaust survivor living in Britain felt a need to reach out to the singer when she learned of Tucker's visit because she associated "My Yiddishe Momme" with her own mother, who was killed by the

Nazis along with all of her other relatives.[74] Twenty-seven-year-old
Ryvka Slodjinska, a Polish-Jewish refugee whose family members
had also perished in concentration camps, begged Tucker to take
her on as an employee so she could travel to America and live with
family there. This young woman felt that "as one of our people,"
Tucker might consider her plea.[75] Receiving letters from strangers
was not uncommon, and although it is difficult to know how Tucker
responded, she internalized the words of individuals when she made
her larger contributions to Jewish charities and funding for Israel.
During one radio interview, Tucker expressed that "Some of These
Days" was not just a song, but a hope in Israel, where "her people"
could live without fear or threats. She urged listeners to aid, visit, and
otherwise support the nascent state, to "get your family to be a Zionist family." This kind of advocacy became even more significant to
Tucker in the 1950s and 1960s.[76]

The singer appeared at the London Casino for six weeks beginning on May 31, with advance sales for shows exceeding anything that
the site had previously experienced. During her stay, Tucker took part
in benefit concerts sponsored as part of the United Nations Save the
Children Appeal as well as the Jewish National Federation's support
for Israel; she also invited 150 children from a Jewish orphanage to be
her guests during a matinee. While not all of her shows were philanthropic, the singer was widely appreciated for her humanitarian
efforts, and the "air [was] heavy with nostalgia."[77]

Along with introducing twenty new songs, Tucker employed African-
American comic and impressionist George Kirby as part of her act.
Kirby had not worked with a white performer up until that time, but
Tucker did not shy away from his talent. His mother and aunt were
both vaudevillians whom Tucker knew from her days in vaudeville,
and the singer was pleased to give Kirby, who had already appeared
with Duke Ellington, his English debut.[78] There was no doubt that
she was beloved as ever; the British press still talked about the "tingly
delightful feeling" audiences internalized during a Tucker performance, and even King George and Queen Elizabeth sent notice that
they enjoyed Tucker's autobiography.[79]

Between her cabaret circuit, charity benefits, and the friendships she had cultivated for decades, Tucker's life was finally in a more consistent routine. She bought an apartment on Park Avenue, though she was always on the move. Championed as "easily the largest consistent money-maker," she packed in audiences at San Francisco's Bal Tabarin nightclub, as well as at the Latin Quarter in New York, owned by impresario Lou Walters. Not only did some in the press claim that Tucker possessed more clout than any "Hollywood luminary," but her fans continually adored her.[80] One fan wrote a poem that included the line, "No man has lived if he doesn't know how the 'red hot mama queen' can glow."[81] Apparently Hollywood agreed; in January 1948 MGM purchased the film rights to Tucker's autobiography for an estimated $200,000, and many in the press reported that Judy Garland and John Garfield would be cast in leading roles.[82] The autobiography continued to bring in a tremendous amount of money; one 1949 estimate revealed that $10,000 had been donated to charity during the singer's Las Vegas shows over four weeks.[83]

In January 1949, Tucker made a bold gesture, donating her personal scrapbooks, compiled since the beginning of her career in 1906, to the New York Public Library. The scrapbooks reportedly weighed "ten times her 180 pounds." They were a rare collection of every clipping, program, greeting card, and other piece of ephemera that Tucker had acquired over forty-three years in the business. This massive undertaking began with the first "little ledger" Tucker bought at a five-and-dime store, into which she pasted documentation of her first performance. While other public libraries had expressed interest in the collection, Tucker made New York curators quite pleased to have the "most comprehensive collection on 20th Century vaudeville." The singer hoped her archives would be of immense value to historians, fellow performers, and anyone with an interest in "vanishing variety theater." The donation of hundreds of scrapbooks for archival preservation while a person was still alive was very rare, especially among figures outside of formal politics. Tucker knew her legacy was becoming cemented, and true to her generosity, she chose to share her greatest treasures with the public rather than to keep them locked in a private estate. She also recognized that the era of vaudeville was a precarious memory; longtime drama critic, friend, and Tucker chronicler Amy Leslie had died in 1939, and Eva Tanguay had passed away in 1947. Few others who had built their lives in the genre were living to tell its history. Tucker expressed sadness in parting with her memories, commenting that a large portion of her life was between the pages of those albums, something she could never quite get back.[84]

Although contact with her family was sporadic, she never stopped caring about Bert's welfare. A California newspaper published a photograph of Tucker, Bert, and Lillian in 1946, taken before the singer boarded a plane in Miami, with the comment that this was a rare image.[85] In 1948 she bought him a hotel—the Robert E. Lee located in Miami Beach. Intending it as a wedding anniversary present for Bert and Lillian, Tucker spent $55,000 on the property that would perhaps keep her "former agent" son gainfully employed for a long period.[86] One press report indicated that this might be Tucker's permanent home, although this did not prove to be the case. It is difficult to know the singer's intentions behind this grand gesture, except that she always wished for Bert's stability and hoped that he could find something to permanently invest himself in and provide for his wife. In accepting responsibility for the hotel, Bert could settle in for a while after bouncing between occupations. His time as a hotel manager did not last long, however.

By the end of the decade, Tucker was receiving a kind of acceptance among her fans and friends she could never have dreamed of. Tucker's longtime friendship with Fannie Brice had weathered all the changes in show business. Brice told the singer that she hoped they could visit together soon and that she cherished Tucker's "love" and "friendship."[87] Her male confidantes were still by her side. Cantor told Tucker he hoped to be as old "as I think you are." He called himself Tucker's "grandson," and Jessel and Al Jolson were also part of the Tucker "family."[88] These feelings of endearment extended to the larger industry; in November 1949, Tucker made history as the first woman to be honored by the male-only Friars Club, a Hollywood institution that for a night turned its focus to the Red Hot Mama. For two hours Tucker's male peers and colleagues "lampooned the lingerie off their guest of honor," and the singer could not have been more delighted. "They stood up and prayed that God would never take me away from my job of entertaining people," she boasted. "I was tingling in every one of these old bones."[89] Just a year later, Jolson died from a heart attack; after she lost her dear friend, she must have cherished his presence at the Friars Club event even more.

Tucker continued to work on behalf of African Americans in the industry. She lost another good friend when Bill Robinson died in 1949. The black community honored the legendary performer in several ways, and Tucker was there to commemorate him as well. Robinson had been president of the Negro Actors Guild (NAG) for many years; a 1950 NAG benefit concert in his honor included Tucker, Ed Sullivan, and Ethel Waters. Tucker returned the following year to perform at the second Robinson Memorial NAG benefit as well.[90] By 1952 Tucker was working with an interracial committee comprising several key industry figures to establish the Bill Robinson Memorial Clinic at Harlem's Mount Morris Park Hospital to "aid underprivileged people in the Harlem community."[91]

In addition, Tucker contributed to the racial integration of nightlife when she made special efforts to introduce "the toast of Paris," Josephine Baker, at Miami's Copa City nightclub. American-born Baker, who had lived most of her life in Paris, was married to a white Frenchman and feared "inter-racial embarrassment." She initially refused to perform at the club, concerned about potentially hostile conditions, and she had told reporters she did not intend on performing in the United States. Yet the managers of Copa City reassured Baker that she and her husband would be welcomed in Miami; indeed, she was the first black guest at the Arlington Hotel. Baker stipulated that African Americans would face no restrictions attending her performance; this would be her first integrated audience in America and an affront to Miami's strict segregation policies. A fixture herself at the Copa City, Tucker played a role in "familiarizing" the nightclub's owners with Baker's repertoire and appeal, and her presence and influence may have made the atmosphere safer for the African-American singer. Apparently, Tucker told the audience, "Well if they come to blow up the place they'll blow me up." The two women graced the cover of *Ebony* magazine together in 1951, publicizing their friendship and Baker's return to the United States for a longer tour.[92] Tucker never involved herself formally in the politics of the civil rights movement the way that other performers, such as Harry Belafonte and Bob Dylan, did. However, even as she was nearing her late sixties, she worked to create an atmosphere of equality for African-American entertainers, with book proceeds going to the NAG and other charities.

Tucker never stopped working to promote better conditions for others. She was as busy as ever performing and spent the last decades of her life even more devoted to charity. It is hard to imagine that in her fifth decade as a performer Tucker would still have new experiences, but she continued to move outside her comfort zone and connect with new audiences, particularly on an international level. With a new generation of artists building careers in the new genre of rock and roll and the new medium of television gripping audiences, it might seem that Tucker would become obsolete. Yet the singer pressed on to defend the value of live entertainment, and she began to inspire new female artists who mimicked her self-effacing humor. She was celebrated as the grande dame of entertainment on her golden jubilee anniversary in the mid-1950s, but in some ways, this still seemed like just the beginning. Although the world had become a completely different place from when Tucker first started as a young performer in New York rathskellers, it was hard for anyone to imagine that she could ever move away from the spotlight.

8

<hr>

SOPHIE TUCKER
FOR PRESIDENT

I n 1955 the Yiddish *Forward* explored the private world of Sophie Tucker. Tucker gave reporter S. Regensberg a tour of her New York apartment, showing pictures of herself from her early days in show business, as well as images of her famous friends Frank Sinatra, Bing Crosby, and Bob Hope. Regensberg was impressed with Tucker's vast collection of Judaica and with the cherished mementos displayed on her walls—a map of Israel, certificates of philanthropic recognition, and military emblems from soldiers. Everything in the apartment told the story of Tucker's life, from the British landscape painted on a wall in her dining room to the multiple photographs and an oil portrait of her mother. Even though it appeared as if the singer had accomplished all that she hoped to achieve, Regensberg indicated that Tucker would never retire: "She loves people and people love her." She planned to keep performing as long as she was able, remaining in the spotlight while exploring new adventures for the rest of her life.[1]

At the time of this interview it would have been hard for the child of immigrants to believe that she was still living in the same America of her youth. What had once seemed like a wonder of urban growth— with towering skyscrapers, fully stocked department stores, and subway cars crisscrossing the metropolis—was now rolling out into suburban life. Americans hunkered down as families in front of the television, living among familiar neighbors and a burgeoning consumer culture. Tucker profited tremendously amid this postwar economic growth; she was listed among ten of the biggest nightclub "moneymakers" at the beginning of 1952, an elite group that also included Sinatra, Lena Horne, Dean Martin, and Jerry Lewis, with salaries reaching $15,000 a week in some cases.[2]

Tucker worked with new technologies, and her recording career evolved. In 1950 she made a twelve-inch record with the Mercury Records label, embracing a new technique that could play longer sections of music. The record featured greatest hits like "Some of These Days" on one side and newer songs such as "Please Mr. Siegel Make it Legal," on the other. Armond Fields posits that she was one of the first to work in this format. During the 1940s, Tucker had recorded a variety of songs with Decca Records, but in the 1950s and 1960s, she would create longer albums, primarily with Mercury, that captured thematic moments. *Billboard* commented that Tucker's marketing plan was unconventional for the time: she sold records during her nightclub performances as well as in stores. This sales method proved to be quite effective, and perhaps the personal touch of autographing records allowed Tucker to reconcile with the fact that she "canned" her voice frequently. Now it is harder to find a Sophie Tucker record without her signature than with it.[3]

Tucker also made her television debut on the Jimmy Durante show in April 1951. The new medium became a fixture in most households by the end of the 1950s, with 90 percent of households owning at least one television set. Marketed as perhaps the most significant consumer item of the 1950s, television reinforced Cold War ideologies by keeping families glued to network-controlled shows.[4] The singer entered into television performance with mixed feelings. As with audio recordings, Tucker did not enjoy the scripted format or the guest spot status. Still, her first appearance was hailed by one critic as the "greatest debut" since Durante himself had performed, with the sixty-three-year-old Tucker looking smashing in her gown, furs, and jewels. Combining sassy numbers such as "It's Never Too Late to Have a Little Fun" with oldies like "Darktown Strutters' Ball," the singer gave viewers the same thrill as when they saw her on stage.[5] One viewer was extremely happy to see an "old timer" like Tucker on television, especially compared to young performers who seemed "amateurish." Watching Tucker appear "so steeped in tradition, so sprinkled with stardust" made the medium more legitimate for older viewers who were skeptical of technological changes.[6]

Tucker continued to perform on television, most famously for her friend Ed Sullivan, whose program *Toast of the Town* first aired in 1948. Sullivan professed that the Red Hot Mama was one of the "greatest femme 'pop' singers" *Toast* had ever presented, and Tucker would visit the Sullivan show several times in the following decades.[7] Still, she shied away from longer television commitments. As she told one London newspaper, when she appeared on TV, her songs became "public property," and her ability to change up routines and offer fresh material for live audiences was a signature part of her brand. Television required her to scrap familiar songs heard in living rooms across the country.[8]

The world seemed to be changing around the aging singer, and younger audiences and the newest Hollywood celebrities grasped her attention. Tucker expressed distaste for the sexual shenanigans of Hollywood starlets, and she expressed the need for a sanctimonious home. She criticized the frequency of Hollywood divorces, claiming that celebrities provided a despicable role model as "spoiled" young women cavorted outside of marriage. The singer was also concerned that current celebrities were only concerned with a "fast buck" and took little time to get to know each other and their audiences. Tucker warned that this would not lead to longtime success in show business. "Make everyone seem important," she advised, and "they'll never let you down."[9]

Claiming that her poker habit had given way to gin rummy, which was very unlikely, and that she had no taste for alcohol, Tucker insisted in one interview that she sang "off color" songs only because it was good for business. "I am basically just a plain old time gal with a big voice," she remarked. Although she said she was able to make sex "good clean fun" for her audiences, she expressed that such talk did not come naturally. She was actually quite a prude, living a "Jekyll and Hyde" existence as a hot mama onstage and a reserved woman in private. Tucker also spoke of the need for American women to recognize their husband's place in the home and not to try to "wear the pants."[10] This was an odd statement for a woman who was fiercely independent and whose songs championed women's power over men. She was always adjusting her act for her audiences; these statements were most likely geared toward one interview intended for rural New Hampshire readers who were steeped in more traditional values.

Yet Tucker was fairly consistent in her disappointment with new generations in show business. It is difficult to understand whether this was a genuine response to changing morals in the entertainment industry—the current scandal involved Elizabeth Taylor divorcing hotel heir Conrad Hilton after only nine months of marriage—or whether Tucker was trying to downplay her own unconventional lifestyle in the hostile climate of the Cold War. In her sixties by this time, she may have become more personally conventional and out of touch with the younger generation, who promoted a different set of values from those her vaudeville-era peers held dear.

Tucker was recognized by several organizations for her philanthropic work. The Beverly Hills chapter of B'Nai B'rith honored the singer as woman of the year, a title that had previously been conferred on Eddie Cantor and Harry Warner.[11] By the beginning of 1953 a scholarship had been set up in Tucker's name at Brandeis University, supporting the tuition of a young woman raised by a single mother in Roxbury, Massachusetts. A. L. Sachar of Brandeis let the singer know that the scholarship recipient shared her interest in the arts. He also underscored the importance of "people of vision," believing that the world could only progress through the efforts of college-educated citizens. Tucker felt strongly about college for women, especially because she had received so little formal education herself. Tucker remained close with Brandeis, donating scrapbooks from the last two decades of her life to the esteemed Jewish university.[12] In 1955 Brandeis University approved a Sophie Tucker chair for a faculty member in the theater arts department, supported by the Sophie Tucker Foundation, which was amassing funds into the millions. She was thrilled to be on the university campus, explaining that it was her first time on any college grounds. Tucker expressed that Brandeis was the "embodiment of true Americanism" because it allowed all to study when so many universities had instituted quotas limiting the number of Jewish students.[13]

As the industry was reflecting on Tucker's impossibly long career, African-American performers were part of the narrative. The singer publicly bragged about Josephine Baker as "one of the world's greatest," and still, after forty years had passed, she showed her appreciation for the gift composer Shelton Brooks had given her in "Some of These Days." During one *Toast of the Town* appearance, Tucker showed Ed Sullivan's audience the original copy of the theme song that Brooks had written, expressing tremendous pride. Brooks had gone on to write several hit songs including "Walking the Dog," "Jean" and "All Night Long," which earned him annual royalties of $35,000; he had also enjoyed a career as a comedian and stage performer in his own right.[14] Negro Actors Guild president Noble Sissle expressed deep appreciation for Tucker's support over the years. He wrote to her as "My Dear Girl-friend" and relayed thanks from Fannie Robinson, Bill Robinson's widow, as well as "the rest of the bunch." The guild clearly valued Tucker as a friend of and staunch advocate for African-American entertainers. Its board of directors included all of the most noted black performers, and political figures such as Mary McLeod Bethune served on the advisory board.[15]

Tucker expressed her gratitude to many African-American performers in a lengthy article in *Ebony*, declaring that she had borrowed a great deal from her black contemporaries. "Negroes and their music mean much to me, always have," she wrote, stating that she was "indebted" to African Americans for her musical style, rhythm, and songs. The singer talked a great deal about her relationship with Mollie Elkins, explaining that it was Elkins who "taught her how to live, to take the bitter with the sweet in life, and to understand people." Her friend also made her truly aware of racial discrimination, as well as the great significance of black culture. Pictures of Tucker with Cab Calloway, Sammy Davis Jr., Duke Ellington, and Elkins's widower, Bill, adorned the article, and while Tucker was upfront about her early work in blackface, she dismissed it as a product of the time. Tucker expressed great pride in the progress that African Americans had made in show business over her fifty-year career, exclaiming that race or religion should never determine an entertainer's ability to share his or her talent. It was the most candid statement about race Tucker had given up to this point, especially considering her admission that ragtime originated among black musicians and that all "popular music" had a "Negro tinge."[16]

Preparations were a flurry in the months before Tucker's golden jubilee celebration, held on October 4, 1953, at the Waldorf Astoria in New York City and sponsored by the Jewish Theatrical Guild. The guild had previously honored Tucker in 1947 for all of her contributions to show business, as well as for serving as a major donor to that Jewish organization. Cantor and George Jessel had previously received galas in their honor, and Tucker's jubilee would be no different. The press chronicled all of the major celebrities and political figures who would be in attendance, and at Tucker's insistence all proceeds would go to seven charities, including the Episcopal Actors Guild and the Negro Actors Guild. When she was honored at the Friars Club a month before the Waldorf Astoria event—the only woman to become a lifetime member—it was revealed that $97,000 had already been raised for the gala, between tickets and advertising in the program. Tucker's Jewish Theatrical Guild fete had already drawn more revenue than tributes honoring Cantor and Jessel; it was estimated that the event would meet the 1,500-person capacity that the hotel could accommodate. Tucker was beaming with pride,

especially among the Friars—former vaudevillians who had worked
in the "dumps and dives" decades before.[17]

It is hard to imagine an event of this magnitude honoring only one
celebrity, but as many in the press proclaimed, few people reached
a fiftieth anniversary in show business. Tucker's friends and family
came from all over the country to honor her, and the program read
as a who's who of show business. Guests seated on the dais included
old friends such as Jack Yellen, Abe Lastfogel, William Morris Jr., and
Shelton Brooks, but also stars such as Deborah Kerr, Tallulah Bankhead, Edward G. Robinson, and Milton Berle. Tucker's family was not
on the dais. Still, many from the Abuza clan had come to see their
famous relative, and her brother Moe, sister Annie, and son Bert
were together at the same table, seated with her dear accompanist
Ted Shapiro. Margaret Chung would not have missed the night, and
corporations such as the Motion Pictures for Television and Twentieth Century Fox had purchased tables. The 1,500 people in attendance included some of the largest power players in entertainment.
The event was a concrete testament to how much influence Tucker
wielded and how many people she had touched over the previous
fifty years.

A long tribute to Tucker included a reenactment of key elements
of her life. Jessel served as master of ceremonies. Berle remarked,
"Sophie Tucker is to show business what Eleanor Roosevelt is to politics." Film pioneer Adolph Zukor, also celebrating fifty years in the
business, talked about Tucker's early years in dingy vaudeville houses
where one-reel films were dismissed by audiences clamoring for live
material. Kerr and Bankhead testified to Tucker's enormous popularity in Britain, unmatched by virtually any other American star.
Former commanding general of American forces in Korea, General
James A. Van Fleet thanked the guest of honor for her years of dedication to the military and her status as one of the celebrities most
committed to troop morale. In addition, civil rights leader Ralph
Bunche, who proclaimed that he was one of Tucker's "most enthusi-
astic fans" recalled his boyhood days in Los Angeles, where he pushed
to be the first in line at the Orpheum theater when Tucker played.

Remarking on the strong bond between Tucker and Mollie Elkins, Bunche said he believed that Tucker's gratitude for Elkins's friendship lasted with a "loyalty and a love" that extended beyond her dear friend's lifetime. He was inspired to see "theatrical groups of every race and creed" at the golden jubilee, a testament to the values that Tucker prioritized.

Peppered with jokes, heartfelt and sincere, this presentation demonstrated how well Tucker's friends knew her, her struggles, and her never-ending quest to achieve fame and recognition. They continued to emphasize how much Tucker had given back through philanthropy, mentorship, and individual acts of kindness. The Yiddish *Day-Jewish Journal* heralded her altruism: "Her nature flourishes and her heart dances, and her song is struck up only when it yields immediate emotion for someone."[18] It was just what she would have wanted for her jubilee—something that would have been a surreal dream when she was a little girl. Her family was watching, her famous friends were surrounding her, and legions of fans would be reading about the event in newspapers across the country. She could not have been more successful.

Tucker's speech at the occasion began by honoring a generation that had passed, the immigrants living in clustered ghettos whose hope for a better life materialized in show business. She reminisced about Cantor, Irving Berlin, Belle Baker, Fanny Brice, and several others whose "life stories are pretty much the same," who initially moved among the lowest rungs of entertainment venues and stayed in "flea-bag hotels." These were her comrades, who "shared the same tears, the same laughter." She mourned the recent passing of Jolson, Brice, Willie Howard, and others, and spoke of the tremendous talent of a new generation of artists such as Berle, Eddie Fisher, Dinah Shore, and Sid Caesar. "Show business will go on and on," Tucker promised, but it was a new era. Few entertainers conceptualized their historical context as much as she did; certainly few preserved it in an archival record of scrapbooks. Though she knew the night was a celebration of her individual career, she emphasized that it remembered the larger world of vaudeville.

Tucker also spoke of her childhood as Sonya Abuza, the girl from Hartford who followed the "irresistible beckoning of a dream." She recalled that as a child she hoped to find the "yearnings of the heart" in a man, and she could not imagine that a woman could be satisfied without a solid marriage. Yet Tucker had found her love, the one that she was ashamed of wanting for so many years. She was finally ready to admit it. She proclaimed that everyone at the gala had given the young Sonya Abuza "the comfort of your affection, your tender esteem, your love." Tucker "found compensation for the other love" that never manifested in a romantic relationship, and it was more than enough that the family she had built was among millions of fans. This love may have come from an untraditional place, but she relished it anyway.

Riding the jubilee wave, Mercury Records worked with Tucker to issue a special album of her greatest hits, dating back to songs she had recorded on Edison cylinders. *Variety*'s Jim Walsh commented that it was unique for a performer to be represented on "cylinders and disks, mechanical and electrical" and still be in demand for the "platter purveyors."[19] It seemed that Tucker was everywhere, with her face appearing on advertisements for products such as Fannie Mae candy. She had performed on Sullivan's *Toast of the Town* twice in six months, the first time in December 1953, appearing with Joe E. Lewis, and the second time commemorating the show's fifth anniversary with Eartha Kitt in April 1954.[20] The singer kept on going, playing for several months over the winter season of 1953 at the South Florida Beachcomber Club, a hot spot seating six hundred people. Paid $7,500 per week, with the ability to take off for TV gigs or personal vacation, Tucker had full control over her engagement at the club. Her spot was called "Sophie Tucker's Beachcomber."[21]

The Beachcomber provided audiences with an elaborate program listing Tucker's accomplishments. The venue was thrilled to feature a "living, vibrant legend."[22] She shared a bill with Nat King Cole, Harry Richman, and the Amin Brothers, performing with Cole and Richman in a vaudeville-inspired act. When she was photographed with Cole, Richman, and Shapiro, the image was captioned "four-way partnership."[23] Miami's tolerance toward integrated acts had become more prevalent since Josephine Baker's appearance years before. As the Florida spot became a draw for the rich and famous in cold winter months, clubs had to feature the hottest acts. To attract patrons, club owners were making a concerted effort to advertise entertainment "regardless of color or creed," spending over a million dollars on a public relations campaign. By 1955, Billie Holiday had performed in Miami for interracial audiences, as had Ivory Joe Hunter; many more African-American celebrities would soon follow.[24]

Tucker continued on her nightclub circuit with shows at her regular spots, such as New York's Latin Quarter. "Sophie Tucker can still out sing nine tenths of those so-called chanteuses, song stylists," one critic admitted after watching her perform at the top of her game, when Tucker was decked out in a poodle hairdo, matching poodle dress, and diamond collar and leash.[25] Although one woman wrote in to a Detroit newspaper complaining that Tucker was "too emotional to give a good show any more" due to the singer's advanced age, continuous bookings indicate that this was not a majority opinion.[26] Appearing in clubs such as Winnipeg's Rancho Don Carlos and on television shows such as the *Milton Berle Show* in 1955, she was hailed as "America's Sweetheart Number One," as well as "Her Royal Highness of Show Business"—titles that did not extend to many other women in the industry.[27] As long as she could continue to "pack 'em in," the singer would continue to dominate the nightclub scene.[28]

Always aware of the need to change with the times, Tucker tried her best to embrace the new genre of rock and roll. Although it is dubious whether she actually connected with young people hungry for the sounds of Chuck Berry, Little Richard, and Elvis Presley, she claimed that the new generation of "bopsters" loved her, and she invited them to see her show. "They hand me down from one generation to the next," she laughed. As much as she tried to position herself among this new musical genre, she also blamed it for the declining state of nightclubs. "Killing the business" that the singer had shaped for so long, teenagers and college students were boosting the position of television, large outdoor concerts, and concept albums like those recorded by the Beatles.[29]

She was also deeply critical of young performers, who seemed, in her mind, to be "gimmick singers." Tucker thought that these entertainers all sounded alike and, even worse, sang the same songs. Elvis was not top on her list (she jokingly called him Alvin) because she thought he did not put in the time and work required for quality material. Tucker also claimed that Elvis was nothing new, stating, "For years, I've been doing the same thing he does. The same rhythm and even the same wiggle."[30] Side by side, it is hard to imagine Presley and Tucker as similar, yet she did point to the continuing thread of risqué behavior in American popular culture. Instead, she seemed to prefer more polished crooners. In speaking of Frank Sinatra, she remarked, "Now you're talking of the top."[31] She also was impressed with Tony Bennett, who started out rather awkwardly in her opinion, even though she admitted he could sing well. After a few years of practice Bennett become a much more seasoned performer, meeting Tucker's high expectations and even winning her recommendation to entertain overseas.[32]

Tucker was engaging in new friendships with other women in the industry, particularly Bankhead, Marlene Dietrich, and Carol Channing, who had perfected imitations of Tucker. Channing and Tucker were corresponding by the beginning of the 1950s, and by 1958 Tucker, delighted by Channing's on-spot mimicry, considered her a friend. The press commented that Channing used a "Sophie Tuckeresque" method of delivering her "brand of fun," with witty, biting commentary on all subjects, including Hollywood episodes. The new star also seemed to mirror many of Tucker's signature moves.[33] Even in the late 1950s female comediennes were still a rarity, and by taking a page from Tucker's playbook, Channing put herself on the map. Writing to Tucker after seeing her on the Jerry Lewis show, Channing expressed astonishment at Tucker's enduring talent, admitting, "I cried all by myself because I was so completely entertained." Tucker's ability to "do the impossible"—perform at the age of seventy with the same vigor as when she began—gave many in their prime a sense of hope for their futures.[34] Tucker was close to Carol Channing for decades and attended her performance in the smash hit *Hello Dolly* in May 1964.

Channing was only one of several industry admirers. As Durante explained, "When I listen to her I know I'm hearing an awful lot of show business." It seemed, almost unthinkably, that Tucker was still one of the hottest celebrities. Dietrich invited her to the premiere of her film *Witness for the Prosecution*, she was an attendant at the wedding of Paul Newman and Joanne Woodward, and she was asked to participate in a Tony Awards dinner. She delivered a rock-and-roll version of "Some of These Days" with Maurice Chevalier that "brought down the house." Even former first lady Eleanor Roosevelt couldn't miss a Tucker performance at Los Angeles's Ambassador Hotel, and Roosevelt was duly impressed with the singer's talent and philanthropic efforts—Tucker had given away over $3 million to this point! Though Tucker and Roosevelt had intersected through Tucker's charity work over the years, they had never formally met until this time. Roosevelt commented, "I could not help but thinking what an extraordinarily vivid personality she has." The singer naturally ended up providing the former first lady with an autographed copy of her memoir.

When Barbra Streisand came on the scene, it was the dawning of a new force in entertainment. Streisand appeared in the Broadway production of *Funny Girl* in 1964, and Tucker was delighted to see the memory of her dear friend Fanny Brice embraced by the public. Tucker asserted, "I saw her in the clothes of dear Fanny Brice's era, and spent an evening enjoying her tremendous talents." However, she was quite disappointed when she encountered Streisand a few days later in Sardi's restaurant "dressed like a beatnik." In the press Tucker offered unsolicited advice to the young star to always look her best in public. It is dubious whether Streisand cared what "Aunt Sophie" said about her outfit, but she probably appreciated the confidence in her voice. Tucker followed moments in Streisand's career in her scrapbooks, knowing that a star who could rival her was rising in the industry.[35]

Tucker declared that she had a "special eminence" among the press that had made her "immune" from negative reviews. Considering that the singer was still maintaining personal relationships with fans and friends by sending 5,500 Christmas cards, scribbling down seventy-five to a hundred letters a day, this is not surprising. Tucker's support for Jewish causes did not prevent her from reaching out to friends across faiths who had supported her for decades, and even though she did not observe the holidays of Christmas and Easter, she received hundreds of cards wishing her happy holidays, which she pasted into the scrapbooks.

Singing new favorites like "I'm Hotter Than I've Ever Been" and "There's a Fountain of Youth You Can Find," Tucker capitalized on her age to offer inspiration that life could still be spicy after the age of seventy. Tucker's circuit of the plushest clubs continued to delight audiences, and people over forty found her irresistible. She continued to thrill at the Tropicana and El Rancho in Las Vegas, and she was the headliner at Chez Paree in 1957, celebrating the spot's twenty-fifth anniversary. When she performed at the Latin Quarter, "a table [was] harder to get than a ticket for a World Series game" and club owner Lou Walters said that he would hire Tucker if she lived to be in her nineties. Yet reporters indicated that she did not captivate the younger generation in the ways she believed. Young people who by 1962 were screaming for the newest sensation, the Beatles, may have found Tucker "too schmaltzy, too plush in her emotions, gestures, and wardrobe." This perception speaks volumes and explains a great deal about the perception of Tucker as cartoonish in the longer cultural memory.[36]

Although she performed on television, Tucker was constantly critical of the medium, explaining that the "blue pencil" used to censor her lines prevented her from delivering her best material. Tucker also believed that some thought of television as a "short cut to fame and riches," whereas she had put in blood, sweat, and tears learning and perfecting her craft.[37] She loved being close to audiences, and although fans begged her to host her own television program, she had no interest. "The only time Tucker can be Tucker is on the night club floor where she can let her hair down," the performer insisted. Television and radio producers were afraid to air her most entertaining, most risqué material.[38] By this point, she had the great luxury of choosing every appearance carefully and taking the time to give her best to fans. "I'm going to go on and on and on" she exclaimed, "Because the people love me."[39]

Tucker never backed down on her production value or continuing to promote herself even in the campiest of ways. In 1959 the singer indicated she had already spent $35,000 on gowns for a year of bookings in cities such as Las Vegas, Chicago, and Miami.[40] She also donned a sequined Western outfit, complete with guns, that she wore at many of her shows, lampooning the style of contemporary television heroes. Tucker's "presidential" campaign, originated by her popular 1952 "Sophie Tucker for President" anthem, became a running joke, and it seemed many were quite enthusiastic about the concept. Insisting, "I think it's a crime, and just about time that we women have our way," she lambasted male domination of the Oval Office. Promising that women would have "better days and much more enjoyable nights" and "better loving conditions," she joked about men who neglected their wives in bed. Tucker's insistence that she would "put controls on all your guys" sat well with her fans and even the press, as she promised to circulate the Kinsey Report to any man who could not satisfy his partner. Although it was all in good fun, the idea of Tucker becoming president sounded "pretty logical," one reporter exclaimed, but concluded that taking her out of show business circulation would "never do."[41] The singer ran with the mantra and incorporated it into more of her shows, telling one London newspaper, "This Red Hot Momma's gonna melt that Iron Curtain Down." She threw campaign buttons out to her audiences, and fans wrote to her requesting more campaign materials; she happily obliged.[42]

Her stage work was in demand more than ever, but Tucker's film biopic was less promising. Her life story had seemed lucrative for Hollywood executives eleven years before, when MGM optioned the film rights to her autobiography. With the success of *The Jolson Story* in 1946 and public interest in Tucker at a high point, it was a fitting time for Hollywood to make the picture, with Betty Hutton in the lead role.[43] Tucker pushed for the film, hiring established screenwriter Norman Lessing to work on the script. Nevertheless, momentum died down for reasons that are difficult to determine. Betty Hutton had reportedly retired from film, and although Tucker would have loved for Judy Garland to play the lead role, Garland's trouble with drugs and alcohol, leading to "misbehavior" on sets, was now well known. In fact, Garland's sister Jimmie Thompson wrote to Tucker at one point, hoping Tucker could "straighten her out" because Garland had little communication with her own family. Thompson believed that the singer could get through to Garland, as Tucker was one of the few "real" people Thompson thought her sister had met in her life.[44]

The film was also doomed because Tucker was now much older than she was when her autobiography was released, and less appealing to the younger public. Ironically film biographies had been made of male figures like Cantor and Glenn Miller in the early 1950s. Cantor's career had slowed down significantly by the mid 1940s, and Miller had died in 1944, so it is possible that biographical treatment seemed less necessary for a figure like Tucker who was still very active in the profession. Or perhaps Tucker's story fit less evenly with the gender norms of the time. Although she was a beloved figure, calling attention to her self-sufficiency, and particularly her abandonment of Bert, was likely not appealing to filmmakers.[45]

The singer's disappointment over the failure to launch a motion picture was alleviated by the announcement that a Broadway musical based on Tucker's life was in development in the spring of 1962, with a release date for the following year. Producers Len Bedsow and Hal Grossman excitedly reported that they had persuaded the singer to agree to the production, with ex-TV comedian Steve Allen writing the music and lyrics. All of the songs for the show were Allen's compositions rather than Tucker's original material. Tucker was happy with the prospect. She approved of unknown singer Libi Staiger, who was to play the lead, exclaiming of Staiger's bellowing voice, "She'll knock you down." The show was to chronicle Tucker's early years in the business, from 1906 to her first London debut, and Tucker seemed to feel confident that the production was in good hands.[46]

When the musical *Sophie* opened in the spring of 1963, it had less fuel than the singer herself, drawing criticism for a mediocre score and stiff writing. Although many enjoyed Staiger's performance, the show's run was shortened in Philadelphia and cancelled in Boston before its Broadway premiere. It played only eight times in New York. "Draggy and episodic," words used to describe the show, were not usually associated with Tucker, and some critics charged that the musical portrayed Tucker as "ruthless, ambitious, and unappealing." Perhaps it was difficult for the show to achieve success when its subject was still performing to such acclaim. Expectations for Broadway patrons were not fulfilled the way they were for the singer's nightclub audiences. Sadly, no major production based on Tucker's life has ever been made again.[47]

As she aged, Tucker spoke more candidly about her family than she had in the past, indicating that they were spending more time together and calling them a "clannish little bunch." Moe was acting as her business manager, and it seems she saw Annie as much as she could, in addition to other relatives whom she visited when she performed near their hometowns. Her son was more difficult to follow, due to his unsteady career. Bert lost the Robert E. Lee Hotel in Florida due to a "bad deal," and after staying in the hotel business by working as a cashier at the Weylin Hotel in New York City, he moved to the furniture business. He and Lillian visited with his mother from time to time, and it seems Tucker was the one who helped him enter the furniture business, introducing him to her friend Bill Holabird. The singer was always trying to keep Bert in line, and this gesture, which led to him becoming the eastern representative for the Holabird Furniture Company, was no different. Yet it is hard to say how present Bert was in her life.

By the mid-1950s, Tucker had also connected with her cousins Milton and Marion Young, and especially their young daughter Lois, who penned a memoir about her time with her famous relative. Tucker spent many dinners reminiscing with her cousins about the old days and the way her parents' generation had run a household according to strict orthodox principles. Lois Young-Tulin recalled playing gin rummy with her much older cousin, helping her address her many Christmas cards, and most of all the advice that Tucker offered. The singer felt strongly about her young cousin focusing on her studies rather than her social life in college, but Young-Tulin got engaged a year before graduating from Pennsylvania State University. Upon hearing the news, Tucker discouraged her cousin from going through with the wedding, concerned that she would give up her own writing career. Tucker did not attend the wedding, explaining that she would be in Europe at the time, but her cousin worried that Tucker "wouldn't want my acquaintance anymore." These fears proved unfounded as the two saw one another soon after the marriage, and all seemed like water under the bridge. Still, Young-Tulin recalled it as a formative moment in her relationship with Tucker.[48]

Ted Shapiro began to discuss his relationship with the singer, something Tucker rarely mentioned at length in her interviews. The two had worked together for thirty-one years, and Shapiro had spent more time with her than anyone else. Shapiro remarked that although Tucker was "Soph" to everyone else, she was always "Ms. Tucker" or "Boss" to him. This formality pleased the singer, as it was the "highest mark of respect anyone's shown her yet." In spite of this manner of address, the two were like family, and Shapiro felt like a son. The pianist joked that Tucker would run to find half the doctors in the city if he even sneezed. There was a great deal of reciprocity between the two; Shapiro felt like he was really the boss when they were on stage, keeping Tucker in tune and letting her know how the audience was responding. "She obeys implicitly," he explained. As they perfected their act together, he took equal credit for Tucker's rise to the top.[49]

Tucker's friendship with Margaret Chung continued over the years—Chung had visited Tucker several times when she was performing in Las Vegas. Young-Tulin and her parents had dined at Chung's house when they visited San Francisco and had toured the city with the physician. Chung wrote to Tucker in January 1958, calling her "My Precious 107" and inquiring whether her friend had received the Christmas gift she had sent, as well as expressing regret that she could not see the singer that year for her birthday because she was "too broke" to travel. Chung had not stopped caring for her "sons"; she sent 2,500 Christmas cards in 1958 alone![50] Yet by November 1958, Chung had become quite ill, and it is unclear whether Tucker had the opportunity to visit her; however, Chung did receive a letter from President Eisenhower, wishing her a speedy recovery and expressing gratitude for the "tremendous contribution you have made to the people of our armed forces." The physician died in January 1959. There is no record of Tucker's response to Chung's death, but it was most certainly a huge loss for the singer.[51]

Tucker's travels abroad intensified as she overcame her fear of flying. She visited Britain between April and June 1952, most likely accompanied by her sister Annie, returning to the London Palladium for the thirtieth anniversary of her first opening in the city. Reflecting on what had been the start of Tucker's relationship with the British, newspapers reported the singer's return with enthusiasm, and audiences demanded five encores during her first night. She never seemed to let her audiences see her in anything but full command; routines continued to astound the crowds, who were stunned by her energy and tales of a half-century of life experience. Although the six-week schedule of performances in London tired her, Tucker was happy to be back among her beloved British fans.[52]

By the spring of 1957, Tucker was headed back to Britain on what she called her "farewell tour," joined by Annie, Shapiro, three musical writers, and nine trunks of dresses and gowns.[53] During her five weeks in London, she performed at the Café de Paris, appeared on two television shows, and finished in Manchester. At her opening, Tucker looked "like an empress about to address a midnight gathering of loyal subjects." She was drowned in so many flowers that she sent many of them to local hospitals.[54] London newspapers waxed nostalgic about the influence of the entertainer since her first appearances at the Kit-Cat Club in the 1920s, in particular her delivery of "My Yiddishe Momme." Tucker had caused quite a sensation when she performed the song, and *Jewish Chronicle* writer Robert Weltsch felt that "My Yiddishe Momme" was of the utmost importance as a "true landmark of Jewish intellectual history." Because most Jews had assimilated, Weltsch wrote, all that remained of Judaism was the "vague sentiment primarily rooted in family reminiscences."[55]

Tucker was always concerned about Britain's Jewish community. During visits, she spent some time visiting a Jewish home for the aged in Birmingham, where she astounded the elderly residents with her "wisecracking" in fluent Yiddish.[56] During her 1957 trip, Tucker spent her second Passover Seder there since 1922, visiting kosher restaurants and other Jewish establishments in the city. Annie told the *Jewish Telegraph*, a Manchester newspaper, that they were both "orthodox Jewesses" with strict observance of Shabbat and other religious customs. While it is difficult to know how observant the singer was, it is unlikely that she identified as Orthodox, as her Friday night bookings would have conflicted with the Sabbath, and there is no indication that Tucker kept kosher. Perhaps for the sake of the elderly people she visited, the *Telegraph* wanted to provide reassurance that the singer had not broken with tradition; however, this was a very different characterization from any she would have offered in the American press.

She expressed great enthusiasm about the efforts British Jews were making for Israel and hoped to visit Israel for her seventieth birthday in January.[57] Her passion for ensuring safe, productive sites for Jewish activities only grew stronger; by mid-decade, Tucker was relentless in galvanizing support for Israel. She became the first Israel Bond trustee in the entertainment field, having already committed $50,000, with a pledge to donate $10,000 for every remaining year of her life.[58] She always asked famous friends to join her in this mission. When she invited Berlin to a luncheon, she stressed, "Everything that Israel has achieved as a democracy now hangs in the balance," unless the country could build an "unbreakable economic structure."[59] As the population of Israel had surged due to the influx of refugees, many were living in dilapidated housing with few possessions, and help for the Israeli people came primarily from private sources within the United States.

In April 1959 Tucker fulfilled her dream of traveling to Israel, with her sister and her brother Moe accompanying her as well as Shapiro and several friends. Her two week trip was jam packed with events, as she visited the cities of Jerusalem, Tel Aviv, and Haifa and toured a kibbutz and the campus of Hebrew University. Israeli reporter Tikvah Weinstock described her as a "fat woman with hardly any neck with white hair," but nevertheless demonstrated amazement at all she had accomplished over her lifetime, which revealed what is in the "American Jewish Heart." Stunned by the singer's busy schedule and the fact her engagements were still booked a year in advance, Weinstock declared, "Sophie Tucker is running against the clock and is winning the race." During her trip Tucker talked to ordinary citizens in the Yiddish slang she still remembered, met for an hour with Prime Minister Golda Meir, and was the guest of the Israeli air force for the first Passover Seder. Tucker was elated to engage with Israeli leadership, having spent so much time fundraising for the country in the United States. She also participated in a Youth Aliya benefit concert with prominent Israeli artists, entertaining 2,500 people at Tel Aviv's Mann Auditorium. The visit was a mix of personal moments, such as taking in the beauty of the mountaintops at the Lebanese border, and political engagements with various organizations she had contributed to for years.[60]

The most significant event of her trip was the dedication of the Sophie Tucker Youth Center at Beit Shemesh in the Jerusalem Corridor. This was a place for young people to learn trades and for working youth to take academic classes. Tucker had contributed $40,000 for the center and handed over a $2,500 check for beautification purposes during her visit. The ceremony was an amazing, moving experience for the singer, and she declared that visiting Israel was the greatest experience of her life. There, she felt connected her with her roots in a way that she could have never fully imagined. Although she told a crowd of thousands that she was just "a singer of silly songs," clearly she had become much more in the eyes of Israeli leaders, who declared that Tucker's contributions had done much to "keep us in the heart of U.S. and World Jewry." With tears in her eyes in front of the children of Beit Shemesh, Tucker promised to provide as much as she could for the community: "If you ever want anything, write to Aunt Sophie and you will get it fast," she assured.[61] A month after her trip, she told the American press that she had become a "new Momma . . . all over again" to the Israeli children, witnessing the result of her tremendous charity. In Israel she could be the kind of mother that she never was to Bert.[62]

In September 1960, Tucker lost her sister. Although there are no records expressing Tucker's feelings at the time, it was undoubtedly one of the most difficult moments of her life. Annie had raised Bert, had accompanied her in the United States and abroad for so many of her performances, and had been a source of stability and a reminder of family throughout the singer's life. Annie never had children of her own, although her marriage to Jules Aronson seemed to be a happy one. After Annie's death, Tucker set up a memorial fund, the Annie Abuza Aronson Temple Fund benefiting Congregation B'Nai Israel. Located near Annie's home in Auburn, New York, the synagogue was a source of happiness for Tucker's sister, who was an active congregant, bringing food, good wishes, and other kinds of help to those who were needy. The memorial fund was to support synagogue activities, and it also purchased an adjoining building for expansion. It seems that Tucker also intended to dedicate sites in Israel and Hartford to the memory of her sister, who was described as an incredibly selfless, "angelic" woman.[63]

Travel remained on the singer's mind, and she planned an ambitious itinerary. In 1961 Tucker made another journey to London in May and June and a visit to Israel in July. By the time she arrived in Israel, the township of Beit Shemesh had planted a "Freedom Forest" honoring Tucker's birthday, and the performer had donated $50,000 for the establishment of another youth center, this time at Beeri, a kibbutz in the Negev Desert. She had become an important figure in Zionist philanthropy, and Tucker's contributions were reported across the American press. For the generation of Jewish vaudevillians who had found such success in America, Israel was now an important point of focus. Berlin donated to Tucker's youth center, and Jessel was also active in raising money for Israel Bonds. Cantor was also recognized by the Israel Bonds organization, which hosted a large birthday gathering when Cantor turned seventy.[64]

Tucker's trips to Israel encouraged her to explore the world more fully. In June 1962 she traveled to Australia, a visit that was reported in the Aussie press from the first minute her plane hit the ground in Sydney. Tucker was the highest-paid female performer to work in the country to date, raking in a reported $2,240 weekly. Jews in Australia were particularly proud of the singer's arrival. A group of students from Moriah College, a Jewish institution, greeted her with a song in Yiddish. In addition, one of the Jewish newspapers urged its readers, "I beg of you, go, admire, and be able to say to your children, 'Yes, I remember Sophie Tucker—what a marvel she was!'" She delighted Australian audiences, performing for sixteen days at Melbourne's Tivoli Theatre, which was deemed a "milestone" in the theater's history. She also appeared on a radio program on the Melbourne station 2CH. *Variety* reported that she received more coverage from TV, radio, and press than any other American entertainer who had traveled to the continent. Sol Schwartz of Columbia Pictures wrote to the singer, amazed and thrilled that she was able to show Australians her "tremendous personality." Few entertainers, especially in their seventies, had aspirations to become a global sensation.[65]

This impulse continued as Tucker traveled to South Africa in August with Shapiro and her brother Moe, touring under the auspices of the African Consolidated Theatres. Many American entertainers and political leaders expressed outrage at the oppressive policy of Apartheid, so it is unclear why Tucker, who felt very strongly about social justice, agreed to this visit. She was the guest of Mrs. Buddy Daitsh, the sister of her daughter-in-law Lillian. Perhaps loyalty to Bert and an appearance on behalf of his sister-in-law were deeply important to her. She was already on a whirlwind travel experience, and perhaps she felt it was difficult to decline the invitation. Formal boycotts of South Africa, initiated by the British Anti-Apartheid Movement, did not begin until months after Tucker's visit, and it is likely that she did not feel as compelled to protest as other entertainers would in the following years.

Her visit included a performance at the Alhambra in Cape Town, as well as trips to Johannesburg, Durban, Port Elizabeth, and Pretoria; she was scheduled for twice-nightly performances and was battling laryngitis. The Cape Town press commented on Tucker's warm personality, fabulous wardrobe, and tireless correspondence with her fans, while the *South African Jewish Times* expressed amazement that Tucker was relatable and "unassuming" during their talk about clothes, charity, and Jewish food. All was going well until the singer broke down twice during a performance in Durban, experiencing labored breathing and problems with her throat. She recovered from the episode, but was frustrated to have disappointed audiences. She would not think of canceling the rest of her South African tour. The incident was a sign, though, that as much as Tucker thought the dirtiest word was *retire*, she would have to face the limits of her own stamina. It was also an indication that perhaps she should take better care of herself. She was a heavy smoker, worked late-night hours, and had an erratic sleep schedule; Tucker's itinerant lifestyle was catching up with her.[66] Still, she traveled to Israel for a third time after leaving South Africa, dedicating a forest of ten thousand trees in the Judean Hills and attending a lavish gala reception at the King David Hotel in her honor.[67]

Tucker did not have time to slow down. To her delight, she was invited to appear before the queen of England in the Royal Variety Performance on October 29—her third command performance in her lifetime. She would be appearing with other American acts such as Bob Hope, Eartha Kitt, and Rosemary Clooney; the show was a tremendous honor, even after so many engagements in Britain. Wearing a mink stole and a glittering blue gown, Tucker was brought to tears when audiences roared after her twelve-minute act, and she blew a kiss to the royal box. As she greeted Queen Elizabeth and Prince Philip afterward, Tucker was on top of the world, especially knowing she had entertained the queen's grandparents in 1934. She apparently received the "loudest and longest ovations in the history of the annual vaudeville event."[68]

In 1964, even though the press declared her "ancient," she returned to the city she loved so much. Two years after her command performance, feeling ready to "compete with the Beatles," the singer appeared for three weeks at the London cabaret Talk of the Town and on a television program, *Blackpool Night Out*. After her second song on the show, she almost collapsed and was assisted off stage by other performers. She recovered by the next day but was clearly wearing thin. This seemed to matter little to Tucker. Her motivation baffled all who talked to her. As reporter Harold Stern commented, "When you're 76, you knit. You don't play 30 weeks a year."[69]

Back in the United States, Tucker's charity work continued apace. She supported the Actors' Temple in New York, a literal sanctuary for Jewish dramatists and entertainers; sent money to the United Negro College Fund; and still provided charity for Jewish inmates at Clinton prison.[70] Among the larger contributions she made was a $10,000 donation to her mother's beloved Hartford Hebrew Home for the Aged, which required building renovations, and she was working on a committee to develop the Eleanor Roosevelt Institute for Cancer Research, corresponding with Congressman James Roosevelt on the particulars. Tucker respected the former first lady enormously and hoped to work with her on the cause that she felt most passionate about—the only institution Roosevelt had allowed the use of her name.[71] In addition, Tucker funded the Sophie Tucker Free Maternity Clinic at the General Rose Memorial Hospital in Denver, where the singer was proud that babies of "every race, creed, and color" were born each day.[72] Famous friends like Jerry Lewis visited the clinic to publicize its existence, and the hospital board of trustees called it "one of the most valuable humanitarian services."[73] Tucker had supported women's ability to act independently since the time she befriended prostitutes in the German Village in the beginning years of her career; this center allowed women with financial constraints to obtain health care and to deliver their babies safely.

In May 1964 Tucker passionately spoke to an audience of show business peers at a charity event at New York's Latin Quarter, declaring her dreams for the future. It was her first return to the club after an absence of more than five years. She looked out over the crowd and declared that although show business folks are often "temperamental" and egotistical," they are also the most "warm hearted" people one could ever encounter. She spoke with great candor of her onetime hope to have her own children, resulting in only one "firecracker"—Bert. Yet, she now felt this happiness in her relationships with children all over the world. They were, she said, "as dear to me as if I had given birth to them." Reflecting on her time in Israel, Tucker could not offer enough superlatives. She stated that her dream would be to establish a Sophie Tucker Youth Center for Arab children, in hope of bringing about peace and goodwill for all who resided in the nation. As much as she had embraced Judaism, she was always more determined to witness interfaith cooperation. Through sales of her autobiography, golden jubilee tickets, and honoring of individual requests, she had contributed hundreds of thousands of dollars to Episcopal and Catholic charities over the years. She was more than proud of the $3.5 million she had raised for charity as the "Queen of Schnorrers," displaying a talent for begging equal to her stage work.[74]

She also talked openly about the "shameful spectacle" in Congress during the filibuster of the Civil Rights Act of 1964, a law intended to provide black Americans with federal protection from discriminatory practices. The civil rights movement was being waged in full force by this time, with groups such as Martin Luther King Jr.'s Southern Christian Leadership Conference and the Student Nonviolent Coordinating Committee organizing protests across the South to secure integration and voting rights. This public statement on civil rights was very rare for the singer. She was bemoaning racial inequality in a way that was not just confined to the plight of actors, as in previous years. But these kinds of appeals from celebrities were becoming more common. Jessel had also denounced the actions of segregationists such as Alabama governor George Wallace, and more people in Hollywood were aligning themselves with black political organizations. Tucker spoke of the stain of segregation and the injustice toward children "whose only crime is that they were not born with white skin." By the end of the speech, she laughed at the prospect of her own immortality, then ended with the motto, "Old Red Hot Mamas never die; they just go up in smoke." This was perhaps the most honest self-assessment Tucker had made in recent years; less nostalgic about her humble beginnings or her past successes in the industry, and focused on what she had come to embody in the present. Here, she was not the wittiest of women on stage, but a living legend discussing political realities more candidly than she ever had before.[75]

Tucker's work of calling attention to the plight of refugees never waned. In 1964 she served as master of ceremonies at a Carnegie Hall event celebrating exceptional women, sponsored by the Women's Division of the United Jewish Appeal of Greater New York. Esteemed pianist Halina Neuman, opera singer Halina Nadi, and dancer Hadassah Badoch had all survived unthinkable horrors; Neuman and Nadi had endured life in the Warsaw ghetto before escaping, and Badoch had fled anti-Semitic Yemen, moving through the desert for days to pursue a life in Israel. This was the first time Tucker was on stage in a nonperforming capacity, but she was very grateful to be there as an emcee. Tucker recalled the terror of the Holocaust and the miracle these women represented on stage. She thanked the United Jewish Appeal for its decades of aid, stating, "We need to be reminded of what life saving really means."[76] Tucker continued this mission, urging the White House to act to protect the 3 million Jews in the Soviet Union. Although correspondence indicated that the State Department was discussing the issue, no detailed information was available. The White House counsel applauded Tucker's continuing appeals for "all who suffer."[77]

The singer celebrated her seventy-fifth birthday on the Ed Sullivan show in Miami Beach, singing "The Saga of Sophie Tucker" and "Don't Stop the World for Me." She offered advice for youth, telling them, "Be sure you start in the right direction." Listeners embraced Tucker's call to young people. "I'm sure you reached our teenage son with your stirring ovation," one listener wrote in to the show. The press reported this as a rare guest spot as she was booked in clubs for the next four years. The "Tucker hurricane" was in "high gear," and she saw no reason to spend more time in studios.[78] Yet this hope of longevity may have reflected wishful thinking. Tucker's voice was wearing thin, and others around her were facing health problems that made her more aware of her own mortality.

She felt this reality most deeply with the death of Cantor in October 1964. He was seventy-two. With the deaths of Gracie Allen and Harpo Marx having occurred weeks before Cantor passed, it was a time for reflection.[79] Cantor left behind an enormous legacy in show business, as well as efforts in philanthropy that paralleled Tucker's. President Lyndon Johnson recognized Cantor for his charitable activities, and Israeli organizations honored him for his support of the state in its formative years. Although Cantor's failing health had prevented him from performing for the last decade of his life, he never lost touch with the show business community. Former vaudevillian turned columnist Louis Sobol compared the end of the genre to the "passing of a dear cherished friend," although Seattle writer Maureen Englin was more optimistic, declaring a resurgence of vaudeville acts. Believing that this kind of entertainment was "making a comeback" in New York City and Hollywood schools, Englin expressed hope that future generations would see the value in performing live—the "best proving ground for beginners in show business." Tucker's beliefs, expressed in hundreds of interviews, were resonating among those who cherished America's rich cultural history.[80]

Tucker worried that her principles were perhaps becoming obsolete. In the fall of 1964 Nora Ephron, then a young *New York Post* reporter, engaged in a long interview with Tucker and found that the singer was no longer trying to provide advice for the younger generation, who believed her to be "outdated." Tucker showed Ephron all the ephemera going into the latest batch of scrapbooks and told the reporter that she was still continuing the now uncommon practice of sending a note of thanks and a Christmas card to everyone she interacted with. "And when you leave here, toots," she chided Ephron, "you get a note of thanks and a Christmas Card, too."[81] As she performed into 1965—with an appearance in Johnny Carson's third season—Tucker committed herself to looking as good as ever, calling glam-squads when she came to town and spending approximately $40,000 yearly on her beautification. "No woman alive is too old to pay strict attention to the way she looks," Tucker emphasized in her late seventies.[82] She was very confident in her physical strength, planning to visit Honolulu, Paris, and Rome, as well as to make another trip to Israel. She was, in one reporter's words, "the only living performer who is booked up solidly for the next three years."[83]

Yet as Tucker sang her faithful Jack Yellen melodies at the Latin Quarter in the fall of 1965, her health took a turn for the worse. She missed a few shows due to what was reported as a virus and she appeared noticeably thinner. Although she bounced back to perform for a few weeks in October, she was hospitalized by the end of the month, with reports varying from "lung inflammation" to "intestinal inflammation." It was later revealed that the singer had been diagnosed with lung cancer months before but wished to keep her illness from the press. She desperately wanted her fans to believe she could keep going, was never weak, and would never give up. By December, however, she was confined to her home, with only close friends and family visiting and very few ventures outside her apartment building. She continued to write her thousands of Christmas cards and post materials into her scrapbooks, and one reporter exclaimed that this was the first time in the singer's life that she had spent her birthday on the sofa. She hoped to keep working, was dictating the contents of what might become another book into a recorder, and would be throwing a "Jewish luau" brunch for friends at the beginning of January. Her letterhead apparently read, "Sophie Tucker . . . Working at Home . . . Not Retired."[84]

Tucker continued to express interest in the goings-on in show business, and her voice was still "loud and lordly." She received thousands of get well cards, and birthday cards when she turned seventy-eight on January 13. In this batch was a special card from Bert, in which he had written his mother a lengthy note. This was unusual; most cards from Bert and Lillian bore only signatures, but this one expressed the conviction that Tucker was very strong and could overcome her illness. "We know you can do it, Mother Dear, so for your sake, as well as Lil and I—we really want you to fight hard."[85] They needed her, as did everybody else.

Tucker died on February 9, 1966, from lung cancer and kidney disease. She died knowing that her son loved her. She died knowing that her youth centers in Israel were successful and thriving. Love abounded from friends like Ed Sullivan and Carol Channing, William Morris Jr., and so many of the organizations she had worked with throughout her life. She also knew that she had become an important, serious figure in American culture. Before her death, Yale University School of Drama saluted Tucker for forty years in the theater—the same forty years since the founding of the esteemed drama program at Yale. Tucker had always wondered about her place as a legitimate performer—not just a "singer of silly songs"[86]—and this recognition provided real reassurance, not just from her beloved friends in Hollywood and on Broadway, but now in one of the most respected dramatic training programs in the country.[87] The girl from Hartford ended her life with a note from New Haven, most likely not the message she was expecting, but one that was undoubtedly deeply satisfying. She knew she was wanted, and it was finally enough.

EPILOGUE

*S*ophie Tucker's death was recorded in a final scrapbook. With great care, Bert compiled all the materials his mother would have wished to be preserved: the last cards she sent to Bert and Lillian, the black, torn *shiva* (mourning) ribbon he wore for weeks after her funeral, the prayer he recited during the months of her illness, as well as all of the cards and condolence messages sent from family, friends, and fans all over the world. Declared a "lovable mother" on the front of this scrapbook, Tucker would have treasured this characterization from her son. As Bert gave the New York Public Library this incredible piece of history—proclaiming the end of the "Era of the Last of the Red Hot Mamas"—he passed on the dramatization of his mother's death as part of her larger legacy.[1]

News of Tucker's passing moved quickly through the entertainment industry. *New York Post* critic Earl Wilson described the aftermath of the singer's death, portraying a grief-stricken Ethel Merman watching a young Liza Minnelli perform. After hearing about Tucker,

Merman exclaimed, "Isn't fate strange, the night one star dies another is born?" Reports indicated that those who had seen Tucker in her final months witnessed a woman in serious physical decline, considerably shrunken in size, moving about her apartment in a wheelchair.[2] Ted Shapiro was by her side when she died, and she still asked for her performance clothes and music, pleading that she was ready to practice. Shapiro was thankful that Tucker could not accept her state of illness: "She would have been miserable if she had known she was never going on again," he said.[3]

The New York Times indicated that she was seventy-nine when she died, although some in the press noted Tucker's wavering on her real birthdate and speculated that she could have been anywhere between seventy-eight and eighty-two, "depending on whether you believe her or the reference books."[4] Reports of her passing circulated around the United States and in the nations she had visited all over the world. As a London writer declared, "She was that rare thing in show business, . . . not only the last of the red hot mamas, but the model, and the greatest of the breed."[5] Cape Town's Times indicated that there would never be another star to match Tucker's longevity.[6] Ironically, Tucker died the same day as famed lyricist and Broadway producer Billy Rose, once the husband of Fanny Brice. Another Jew born at the turn of the century who had risen to fame in the industries that Tucker moved through, Rose was also deeply dedicated to Israeli causes. The passing of two giants of the stage created a tangible void. "The lights of Broadway are dimmer today, and that old show-biz fizz is a little flatter," British reporter David Nathan lamented.[7]

Over a thousand people attended Tucker's memorial service at New York's Riverside Chapel, crowding inside to make room for more mourners. Outside, another three thousand lined the streets behind barricades, watching both famous and ordinary people enter to pay their respects to the singer. Tucker's pallbearers included Shapiro, Ed Sullivan, William Morris Jr., and Abe Lastfogel, as well as Abel Green, editor of Variety; Barney Balaban, head of Paramount Pictures; and the heads of the Negro and Catholic Actors Guilds, Charles Coles and Horace McMahon, respectively. With Rabbi Isidore

Aaron presiding, the atmosphere was sullen, yet speakers could not help but remark on the joy the singer had brought to the world. Wherever she went, Aaron stated, "she lit a bright candle in a dark corner." George Jessel's eulogy testified to the strength of their fifty-year friendship. He urged mourners to remember Tucker's full, amazing life rather than "the voice that had been stilled." From New York, Tucker's body was taken to Hartford for another service, after which she was buried in Emanuel Cemetery in Wethersfield, Connecticut.[8] She had wished to be buried with her parents at Zion Hill Cemetery, but it had run out of burial room.[9] In addition, hundreds of London mourners held their own service at a synagogue in the district where Tucker had performed.[10]

Tucker's estate was valued between $500,000 and $1 million, and she had written a twenty-two page will two years before her death, with particular requests for allocation. Her estate was divided equally among Moe, Albert, and her nephew Charles, with the money for Bert and Charles left in trust. Given Bert's financial irresponsibility in the past, his mother most likely thought it best for him to receive his inheritance in increments. According to Armond Fields, Bert would receive 50 percent of the total amount on the fifth anniversary of her death, and the remainder on the tenth anniversary of her death. The singer requested that $30,000 go to the Sophie Tucker Foundation for charitable use, $25,000 to Ted Shapiro, and $10,000 to the Hebrew Home for the Aged in Hartford. Her stage clothes were donated to the Screen Actors Guild. After all the money she had raised for charity in the last decades of her life, the singer knew that after she died she would have taken care of all the people and organizations that mattered most to her.[11]

Moe was heartbroken after the death of his sister. He was already mourning the death of his wife, Blanche, who had died a few weeks before Tucker in January 1966, and Tucker's passing took a tremendous toll on her brother. Although in following years he enjoyed spending time with his grandchildren (Charles married and had two children), traveling, and spending time with the larger Abuza clan, Moe never fully recovered from all of the loss in his life. He died from a stroke in 1978 and was buried alongside his sister and his wife. Bert's whereabouts after his mother's death are more difficult to discern, but he died in 1982 after a lengthy struggle with his health, leaving Lillian to inherit the rest of Tucker's estate. As much as his mother's life was filled with many joys, Bert had lived what was often a troubled existence. He had Lillian as his partner, yet it seems he was completely without direction.[12]

Tucker's legacy within her immediate family was more short-lived than her influence on American entertainment at large. The singer's talent for philanthropy proved one of her greatest gifts, spearheading wide-scale international charity initiatives. While politics in the Middle East were continually precarious, the contributions that Tucker had made were tangible. The youth centers bearing her name were thriving, with capable instructors and students learning a variety of trades that would prepare them well for employment. Young men and women came from fourteen different countries and found stability in these institutions. One Israeli solider, Yitzhak Bar-Shasheet, had learned the trade of plumbing while a student at the Sophie Tucker Youth Center and used his training while serving in the army in the late 1960s.[13] There were undoubtedly many more like Bar-Shasheet who carried on Tucker's wish for a prospering Israeli state. As students came into the youth centers with a large picture of Tucker hanging in the entrance, they knew of her generous spirit. "You can take great pride in this accomplishment," Mrs. Alfred Herz, director of the Women's Division of United Jewish Appeal, had written to the singer.[14]

Tucker was part of creating an industry standard in the $4 million she raised for charity; charitable contributions are now something that celebrities come to understand as a responsibility of tremendous fame. When Steven Spielberg was first inculcated into Hollywood living while becoming one of its most successful directors, Steve Ross of Warner Communications introduced him to the "pleasures of philanthropy."[15] Speilberg's Righteous Persons Foundation and Shoah Foundation uncover the testimony of Holocaust survivors while also supporting educational initiatives to promote tolerance across race, religion, and sexual orientation. Speilberg is one of many celebrities who conduct this now-expected philanthropic work, and the millions of dollars that stars have raised for AIDS research, the environment, humanitarian causes, and many other issues are connected to the inner workings of the fame machine. Today a name in lights requires giving to those who are less fortunate. The amount of money Tucker raised by 1966 may today seem less exceptional because over decades others have hoped to exceed that kind of generosity.

Famously, in 1963 the Beatles declared that their favorite American musical group was "Sophie Tucker." Tucker's size could always draw laughs, but because she had become one of the most beloved American performers in the United Kingdom, it is no wonder that she came to the mind of Paul McCartney. After her death, she was less regarded for her body image than her willingness to speak her mind and break down gender conventions, inspiring other women in the industry. Like Tucker, Carol Channing, Ethel Merman, Joan Rivers, and others shed inhibitions and challenged men to top their brand of humor. Many in Bette Midler's early audiences were most captivated with her routine titled "Those Wonderful Sophie Tucker Jokes," partly because they disbelieved that Tucker used such brazen humor so many years ago. At the mention of Tucker's name, people still refer to the common Tucker/Midler joke: "I was in bed last night with my boyfriend Ernie, and he said to me, 'Soph, you got no tits and a tight box.' I said to him, 'Ernie, get off my back.'" They want to know more about the woman Midler held in such esteem, the woman who dared to talk about sex with such frivolity. Tucker was both an icon of a bygone era and a motivating force for women who hoped to make it on their own terms, to reinvent or even bypass the fads of popular culture.

In the winter of 2013 I attended a performance of *Sophie Tucker: Last of the Red Hot Mamas* at Philadelphia's Walnut Street Theater, featuring actress Kathy Halenda impersonating Tucker. Performers such as Halenda and Sharon McNight star in one-woman shows depicting Tucker's performances and life story in theaters and Jewish community centers around the country. As I took my seat in the crowded theater as one of the youngest patrons, I could feel the excitement around me. Some in the audience actually had seen Tucker perform live, and they acted as if they were going to witness her again. When Halenda came out in sequined gowns, feather boas, and a pianist playing Ted Shapiro, I understood what I could not have comprehended through archival material. This version of Tucker looked into the eyes of the audience members, asked them witty questions, brought them on stage for gags, and reassured them that she would return. She spoke with passion about family, heartbreak, and aging, asking men and women if they understood how she felt, and they nodded their heads sympathetically. There was a lot of laughter and also some very somber moments. Even though it was an imitation of Tucker, I left knowing that fifty years later, audiences still loved Tucker's show; they begged for encores and roared at the end. I knew what had made her truly special.

Sophie Tucker worked to create the largest, most fantastic career, never forgetting the dreams she had as a girl while working in her parents' restaurant. The guilt that she felt for abandoning Albert and the romantic difficulties she had with men were initially made bearable by the forgiveness of her family and the affection of her fans. Those nagging feelings were finally alleviated by the role she played as a maternal ambassador across nations. Her words, lyrics, and writings urged people to learn from each other, to listen carefully, to study hard in the pursuit of any trade. Formally she was an entertainer, but for most Americans, she transcended the arena of performance. Dare to think big, help people in need, never back down no matter who you are—these were the most important messages Tucker conveyed to all who listened. The "First Lady of Show Business" but also everyone's "Yiddishe Momme," she molded the concept of fame at the moment when mass culture came to dominate American life. She lived the American Dream—not the one her mother would have wanted for her daughter when they arrived as immigrants, but the remarkable course she set out for herself.

ACKNOWLEDGMENTS

This book could not have come to fruition without all of the support I have received from so many individuals and institutions. A University of South Carolina Provost Humanities Grant funded years of research, and I thank those at USC, particularly chairs Dean Kinzley and Christine Ames, for working with me to assure that the momentum for this project never stopped. I am so lucky to have Christine as a dear friend, who always reminds me what is important, makes me laugh really hard, and exemplifies the best kind of scholarship. Thanks to Abby Callahan and Lori Vann for all of their hard work keeping the USC History Department running, performing essential tasks that we could not function without. I am so appreciative of my colleague Lacy Ford, now dean of the College of Arts and Sciences, who has believed in me since I was hired at USC over a decade ago.

I am fortunate to have received a National Endowment for the Humanities Public Scholars Fellowship, which allowed me to focus entirely on writing the majority of the book. This is a gift for any academic, and it is even more meaningful that I have been part of an NEH initiative that can bring academics and the broader public closer together. Thank you to my Columbia friends who always express their support for my work—Jennifer Kahn, Eveda Matzner, Kelly Stein-Marcus, Erica Serbin, Rachel Hedley, and Sara Weinberg—and those in the wider community who have come to listen to me talk about Sophie Tucker, particularly at Beth Shalom Synagogue in Columbia, the Katie and Irwin Kahn Jewish Community Center, the Philadelphia Jewish Film Festival, and the Pop Conference in Seattle. It was a pleasure to give my first public talk on the book as part of the USC History Center Faculty Spotlight initiative, and I appreciate the dedication of director Patricia Sullivan, a terrific colleague. I also had the opportunity to interview Tucker's cousin Lois Young-Tulin about her favorite relative, and I appreciate Lois's time and confidence in me. It has been a joy to work on a topic that allows me to move beyond academia and to hear people's own experiences, especially from those who saw Tucker perform live. The hardest part of my public engagements has been my delayed response to the most asked question, "So when is this book coming out?" I am so glad that I can now officially provide the goods.

I agree with *Hamilton*'s Schuyler Sisters that New York is the greatest city in the world, and it was a dream to conduct most of my research at the New York Public Library's Billy Rose Theater Collection. This archive is invaluable for anyone interested in American cultural history, and even though I spent years examining materials, I know they are only a tiny part of the histories of theater, dance, music, comedy, and so many more elements of history that still warrant attention. I benefited from a short-term New York Public Library Fellowship that allowed me to sift through Tucker's hundreds of personal scrapbooks. Archivist Annemarie van Roessel could not have been a more patient or receptive guide to the Tucker materials, and I am indebted to her for helping me through this overwhelming collection, along with many other holdings. Thanks to Jeremy Megraw for assisting me through the process of image reproduction from scrapbook findings, and for others at NYPL who led me through digital recordings, pulled sheet music, and made the process more manageable.

At Brandeis University, I had the wonderful help of Chloe Morse-Harding, who assisted with another hefty portion of scrapbooks and with procuring images. At the University of California–Los Angeles and the University of Southern California, I also encountered the enthusiasm and expertise of archivists during the late stages of the project that allowed me to respond to unanswered questions. I am grateful to the late Armond Fields for his useful biography charting Tucker's professional activities, but even more so for the personal papers he donated to the University of Southern California. His manuscript notes and images were helpful for understanding her early life and the Abuza family's immigration to America. At the Library of Congress the help of David Sager in the Division of Recorded Sound enriched my experience, as he pointed me to important broadcasts and sent me discographies even after I had left Washington, DC. The Museum of the City of New York houses a treasure trove of amazing photographs, and Lauren Robinson made it so easy for me to procure reproductions that would made the book sparkle. Many thanks also to Brad Kay of Superbatone Records, who supplied me with critical recordings and welcome musings on Tucker. I am indebted to Kathy Snediker, a Zotero angel, and to my translators, Maia Evrona and Risa Strauss.

Scholars who I have known throughout my career and others who I have met more recently have been critical in supporting and inspiring this book. There are too many important influences to name each individually, but I extend special thanks to Larry Glickman, Burton Peretti, Lew Erenberg, Steve Waksman, Stephen Whitfield, Mark Smith, Don Doyle, Marjorie Spruill, David Weinstein, Harvey Cohen, Woody Holton, and Dan Carter. Kathy Fuller-Seeley provided amazing feedback on the entire manuscript, and I am so grateful for her expertise and camaraderie. An anonymous reader also offered many valuable and detailed suggestions for improving clarity and providing more texture. In addition, creative, energetic graduate students keep me thinking outside the box, and my scholarship is better because of Megan Bennett, Stephanie Grey, Stephen O'Hara, Sam King, Madeline Steiner, Jillian Hinderliter, and Andrew Walgren. I will probably include this in every book I author: Pete Daniel and Charlie McGovern created the most formative intellectual experience when I was a Smithsonian fellow years ago, and even though that time has long passed, I could not be the kind of scholar or teacher I am without their model.

I can identify with how strongly Tucker felt about William Morris because I have had that kind of stewardship in my agent, Lisa Adams, and my editor, Robert Devens. Lisa agreed to represent me when the book was in a very formative stage. She felt that Tucker's story was worth telling, even when I wavered on my ability to do justice to the biography. I am so thankful for all of her hard work and encouragement, introducing me to the world of trade publishing and writing for a broader audience. Working with my editor, Robert Devens, at the University of Texas Press has been one of the best parts of writing this book. He is in sync with my sense of humor, rapid on email, and admirably candid, and I could not have found a better person to help me turn years of research into a finished product. Thank you to all the folks at Texas—Sarah McGavick, Lynne Chapman, Robert Kimzey, Meg Wallace, Nancy Bryan, and the marketing team—for all of their faith in this project and their effort in making something special. I appreciate Bob Ellis for his work on the index.

My parents, Ellen and Neil Sklaroff, taught me to love music, particularly from Broadway, from a very young age. I was always the first to run up on the stage and belt out "Memory" from *Cats*, and although I didn't move away to become a star, I've dedicated my career to preserving American culture because it was a priority in my house as I was growing up. Along with helping me in the archives and reading the entire manuscript, my mother made the tough tasks of the project a lot of fun. I treasure soaking up New York City with her, walking through neighborhoods that once featured Tucker's favorite haunts, and enjoying the shows, fashion, and food that were always present in the scrapbooks. My mom knew I could do this before I did, and I'm glad I listened to her when she told me that it was about time people knew that Sophie Tucker was not the same person as Fanny Brice. In this spirit, I dedicate this book to Ellen Sklaroff, who never gives up and who loves with her whole heart.

Writing a book while raising three kids is no easy feat, but my sweethearts Jack, Alex, and Hope have kept me going through their infectious energy, curiosity, and delectable smiles. Over the years they have come to understand why I am frequently going out of town and why I always have a computer sutured to my lap. "Mommy is an author" has an amazing ring to it when uttered by a seven-year-old, and as they watched me wrestle with this book, they have hopefully learned about the importance of sticking to your goals, the necessity of revision, and the value of choosing a career that permits you to do what you love. This biography is about following big dreams, and perhaps when they read this they will learn from Tucker that those dreams are possible—hard, but possible.

I could never say enough to thank my love, Jim Lamey, for everything he does. My head stays above water largely because I am married to him. Jim cared for the children when I was away, made sure I had writing time, and helped with images and other details that I am too disorganized to handle. In addition, he read the entire manuscript and found all of the tiny errors that I could never spot, providing amazing feedback. His reassurance led what was once the scariest thought on earth (a second book!) to become a tangible reality. For all of this, I am forever grateful. As Tucker sang, "You've Got to Be Loved to Be Healthy"; because of my family, I am certainly the "healthiest gal in town."

NOTES

INTRODUCTION

1. Bette Midler, *Live At Last* (Atlantic, 1977).

2. Irv Saposnik, "Jolson, *The Jazz Singer*, and the Jewish Mother: Or How My Yiddishe Momme Became My Mammy," *Judaism* 43, no. 4 (Fall 1994): 433.

I. BREAKING WITH TRADITION

1. Charles Abuza, 1900 US Federal Census, Hartford, CT, Roll 136, Page 4A, Enumeration District 0145, FHL microfilm 1240136 (Ancestry.com, February 16, 2016).

2. Johnny Abuza, 1900 US Federal Census, Hartford, CT, Roll 136, Page 4A, Enumeration District 0145, FHL microfilm 1240136 (Ancestry.com, February 16, 2016); Jennie Abuza, 1920 US Federal Census, Hartford Ward 7, Hartford, CT, Roll T625_183, Page 17B, Enumeration District 96, Image 608 (Ancestry.com, February 16, 2016). There is a discrepancy in the date of birth for Jennie Abuza in these two census reports; the 1900 census (calling her "Johnny") reports date of birth as 1853, while the 1920 census lists date of birth as "abt 1848."

3. Irving Howe and Kenneth Libo, *World of Our Fathers* (New York: Harcourt Brace Jovanovich, 1976), 5–7; Jonathan D. Sarna, *American Judaism: A History* (New Haven, CT: Yale University Press, 2004), 152.

4. Philip Abuza, 1900 US Federal Census, Hartford, CT, Roll 136, Page 4A, Enumeration District 0145, FHL microfilm 1240136 (Ancestry.com, March 5, 2016). This census lists Philip as sixteen years old in 1900, which would place his date of birth in 1884. It incorrectly lists his birthdate as 1863. Later census reports place his birthdate in 1885 and 1886, with the family emigrating to the United States in 1887.

5. Howe and Libo, *World of Our Fathers*, 58–59.

6. Sarna, *American Judaism*, 63–64.

7. Howe and Libo, *World of Our Fathers*, 42–49.

8. Sophie Tucker, *Some of These Days: The Autobiography of Sophie Tucker* (privately published, 1945), 2.

9. Sophy Abuza, Philip Abuza, and Johnny Abuza, 1900 US Federal Census, Hartford, CT, Roll 136, Page 4A, Enumeration District 0145, FHL microfilm 1240136 (Ancestry.com, March 5, March 5, and February 16, 2016, respectively); Tucker, *Some of These Days*, 1. All of these 1900 census reports cite 1887 as the year of immigration.

10. Tucker, *Some of These Days*, 2.

11. Leonard Dinnerstein, *Antisemitism in America* (New York: Oxford University Press, 1994), 35, 58–77. For more on racial ideologies concerning immigrants, see Matthew Frye Jacobson, *Whiteness of a Different Color: European Immigrants and the Alchemy of Race* (Harvard University Press, 1999).

12. Armond Fields, *Sophie Tucker: First Lady of Show Business* (Jefferson, NC: McFarland, 2003), 9–11.

13. "Diamonds! David Mayer, Jeweler and Importer," *Hartford Courant*, January 22, 1890; "Before Inventory Bargain at Schall's!," *Hartford Courant*, January 22, 1890; "Mandlebaum's Great Annual Clearance Sale: Surpassing All Other Sales Held in This City," *Hartford Courant*, January 3, 1891.

14. David G. Dalin and Jonathan Rosenbaum, *Making a Life: Building a Community* (New York: Holmes & Meier, 1998), 51–53.

15. Tucker, *Some of These Days*, 5.

16. Dalin and Rosenbaum, *Making a Life*, 53; Tucker, *Some of These Days*, 10.

17. Nicholas E. Tawa, *A Sound of Strangers: Musical Culture, Acculturation, and the Post-Civil War Ethnic American* (Metuchen, NJ: Scarecrow, 1982), 113–114.

18. Tucker, *Some of These Days*, 11.

19. Katharina Vester, "Regime Change: Gender, Class, and the Invention of Dieting in Post-Bellum America," *Journal of Social History* 44, no. 1 (Fall 2010): 54.

20. Tucker, *Some of These Days*, 11.

21. Paula Hyman, "Gender and the Immigrant Jewish Experience in the United States," in *Jewish Women in Historical Perspective*, ed. Judith Raskin (Detroit: Wayne State University Press, 1991), 231.

22. Kathy Lee Peiss, *Cheap Amusements: Working Women and Leisure in Turn-of-the-Century New York* (Philadelphia: Temple University Press, 1986), 6–7.

23. Tucker, *Some of These Days*, 12.

24. Ibid.

25. Ibid., 12–14.

26. Louis Tuck, 1900 US Federal Census, Hartford, CT, Roll 136, Page 5B, Enumeration District 0147, FHL microfilm 1240136 (Ancestry.com, March 3, 2016); Sophia Abuza, (Massachusetts Marriage Records, 1840–1915, Springfield, MA, n.d.), Massachussetts Vital Records, 1840–1911, New England Historical Genealogical Society, Boston, MA (Ancestry.com, March 3, 2016); Tucker, *Some of These Days*, 14.

27. Fields, *Sophie Tucker*, 17.

28. Tucker, *Some of These Days*; Kristin Celello, *Making Marriage Work: A History of Marriage and Divorce in the Twentieth-Century United States* (Chapel Hill: University of North Carolina Press, 2009), 21–23.

29. Tucker, *Some of These Days*, 20.

30. Ibid., 22.

2. FINDING A PLACE IN THE CITY

1. Tony Pastor, "Tony Pastor Recounts the Origins of American 'Vaudeville,'" *Variety*, December 15, 1906.

2. Robert Clyde Allen, *Horrible Prettiness: Burlesque and American Culture* (Chapel Hill: University of North Carolina Press, 1991), 178–180.

3. Ibid., 185–186.

4. Robert W. Snyder, *The Voice of the City: Vaudeville and Popular Culture in New York* (New York: Oxford University Press, 1989), 26–41.

5. Craig H. Roell, *The Piano in America, 1890–1940* (Chapel Hill: University of North Carolina Press, 1989), 32.

6. Isaac Goldberg, *Tin Pan Alley: A Chronicle of American Popular Music* (F. Ungar, 1961), 123.

7. Roell, *Piano in America*, 31–65.

8. David Suisman, *Selling Sounds: The Commercial Revolution in American Music* (Cambridge, MA: Harvard University Press, 2009), 28–35.

9. Jack Gottlieb, *Funny, It Doesn't Sound Jewish: How Yiddish Songs and Synagogue Melodies Influenced Tin Pan Alley, Broadway, and Hollywood* (Albany: State University of New York, 2004).

10. "Fight Shylock in Schools," *New York Times*, March 9, 1907, 2.

11. "The Jew on the Stage," *Variety*, December 10, 1910, 23.

12. M. Alison Kibler, *Censoring Racial Ridicule: Irish, Jewish, and African*

American Struggles over Race and Representation, 1890–1930 (Chapel Hill: The University of North Carolina Press, 2015), 116–130.

13. "Hotel Affronts Senator's Sister: Mrs. Frank of Baltimore, Sister of Isidor Rayner, Told that Jews Are Not Wanted," *The New York Times*, May 18, 1907, 1.

14. Sophie Tucker, *Some of These Days: The Autobiography of Sophie Tucker* (privately published, 1945), 21

15. Ibid., 26.

16. Mary E. Odem, *Delinquent Daughters: Protecting and Policing Adolescent Female Sexuality in the United States, 1885–1920* (Chapel Hill: University of North Carolina Press, 1995), 22, 53.

17. Armond Fields, *Sophie Tucker: First Lady of Show Business* (Jefferson, NC: McFarland, 2003), 18–20.

18. Snyder, *Voice of the City*, 46–52.

19. Tucker, *Some of These Days*, 30.

20. Ibid., 33–34.

21. Pamela Brown Lavitt, "First of the Red Hot Mamas: 'Coon Shouting' and the Jewish Ziegfeld Girl," *American Jewish History* 87, no. 4 (December 1999): 253.

22. Michael Rogin, *Blackface, White Noise: Jewish Immigrants in the Hollywood Melting Pot* (University of California Press, 1998); Eric Lott and Greil Marcus, *Love & Theft: Blackface Minstrelsy and the American Working Class* (New York: Oxford University Press, 2013); David R. Roediger et al., *The Wages of Whiteness: Race and the Making of the American Working Class* (London: Verso, 2007).

23. M. Alison Kibler, *Rank Ladies: Gender and Cultural Hierarchy in American Vaudeville* (Chapel Hill: University of North Carolina Press, 1999), 126–134; Lori Harrison-Kahan, *The White Negress: Literature, Minstrelsy, and the Black-Jewish Imaginary* (New Brunswick, NJ: Rutgers University Press, 2010); Steve Waksman, "A Woman's Place: Staging Femininity in Live Music from Jenny Lind to the Jazz Age," in *The Routledge Research Companion to Popular Music and Gender,* ed. Stan Hawkins (London: Routledge, 2017), 215–228.

24. Tucker, *Some of These Days*, 35.

25. Ibid., 39

26. Ibid., 42.

27. "Pleasure Bay Park Orpheum Theater Program," 1908, MWEZ + n.c.

10,833, Sophie Tucker Scrapbooks ,*T-Mss 1966-004, Billy Rose Theater Division, New York Public Library (hereafter Sophie Tucker Scrapbooks).

28. "Proctor's Bijou Dream," 1908, MWEZ + n.c. 10,833, Sophie Tucker Scrapbooks; "Souvenir Program, Hathaway Theater," August 24, 1908, MWEZ + n.c. 10,833, Sophie Tucker Scrapbooks.

29. "Unidentified Clipping on Sophie Tucker at the Plaza Music Hall," 1909, MWEZ + n.c. 10,833, Sophie Tucker Scrapbooks.

30. "New Orpheum," 1908, MWEZ + n.c. 10,833, Sophie Tucker Scrapbooks.

31. "Unidentified clipping 'Sophie Tucker,'" 1908, MWEZ+ n.c. 10,833, Sophie Tucker Scrapbooks.

32. John J. Niles, "Shout, Coon, Shout!," *The Musical Quarterly* 16, no. 4 (1930): 530.

33. Amy Leslie, "Majestic Is Turning Crowds Away Who Come to See the Trick Monkey, Charles the First," 1909, MWEZ + n.c. 10,833, Sophie Tucker Scrapbooks.

34. "Unidentified Clipping on Sophie Tucker at the Plaza Music Hall," 1909, MWEZ + n.c. 10,833, Sophie Tucker Scrapbooks.

35. "Pleasure Bay Park Orpheum Theater Program," 1909, MWEZ + n.c. 10,833, Sophie Tucker Scrapbooks.

36. Ernest Hogan, "The Negro in Vaudeville," *Variety*, December 15, 1906.

37. Karen Sotiropoulos, *Staging Race: Black Performers in Turn of the Century America* (Harvard University Press, 2008); Lynn Abbott and Doug Seroff, *Ragged but Right: Black Traveling Shows, "Coon Songs," and the Dark Pathway to Blues and Jazz* (Jackson: University Press of Mississippi, 2007).

38. Tucker, *Some of These Days*, 43–45.

39. "Pastor's Theater Program," 1908, MWEZ + n.c. 10,833, Sophie Tucker Scrapbooks.

40. Allen, *Horrible Prettiness*, 221–240.

41. Tucker, *Some of These Days*, 59; Allen, *Horrible Prettiness*; Barbara Wallace Grossman, *Funny Woman: The Life and Times of Fanny Brice* (Bloomington: Indiana University Press, 1991), 20–21.

42. Tucker, *Some of These Days*, 59.

43. Ibid., 57.

44. Grossman, *Funny Woman*.

45. Tucker, *Some of These Days*, 62–63.

46. Sophie Tucker, "How Negroes Influenced My Career," *Ebony*, December 1953, 92.

47. Tucker, *Some of These Days*, 62–63.

3. ACCEPTANCE AS A RISING STAR

1. Linda Mizejewski, *Ziegfeld Girl: Image and Icon in Culture and Cinema* (Durham, NC: Duke University Press, 1999), 41–64.

2. Ibid., 59–61.

3. Anthony Slide, *The Encyclopedia of Vaudeville* (Westport, CT: Greenwood, 1994), 27–30.

4. Rennold Wolf, "Ziegfeld Discovers Sophie Tucker for the Follies of 1909," *Morning Telegraph*, 1909, MWEZ + n.c. 10,834, Sophie Tucker Scrapbooks, *T-Mss 1966-004, Billy Rose Theater Division, New York Public Library (hereafter Sophie Tucker Scrapbooks).

5. Armond Fields, *Sophie Tucker: First Lady of Show Business* (Jefferson, NC: McFarland, 2003), 32–33; Sophie Tucker, *Some of These Days: The Autobiography of Sophie Tucker* (privately published, 1945), 67–68, 72.

6. Tucker, *Some of These Days*, 72.

7. Ibid., 71–74.

8. "Unidentified Follies of 1909 Clipping," n.d., MWEZ + n.c. 10,834, Sophie Tucker Scrapbooks.

9. "'Follies of 1909' Move with Vim: Many Amusing Scenes in Ziegfeld's Latest 'Revue' of the Season. An Aeroplane Introduced Craft Moves Over the Heads of the Audience Atop the New York Theatre," *New York Times*, June 15, 1909, 7.

10. *Sophie Tucker Golden Jubilee* (Mercury Records, 1954), Performing Arts Research Division, New York Public Library.

11. Tucker, *Some of These Days*, 77.

12. Lynn Abbott and Doug Seroff, *Ragged but Right: Black Traveling Shows, "Coon Songs," and the Dark Pathway to Blues and Jazz* (Jackson: University Press of Mississippi, 2007), 56–67.

13. Tucker, *Some of These Days*, 71.

14. Ibid., 83.

15. Ibid., 80, 101.

16. Grace Elizabeth Hale, *Making Whiteness: The Culture of Segregation in the South, 1890–1940* (New York: Vintage, 1999).

17. Tucker, *Some of These Days*, 86.

18. Frank Rose, *The Agency: William Morris and the Hidden History of Show Business* (New York: HarperBusiness, 1995), 17–23.

19. Arthur Frank Wertheim, *Vaudeville Wars: How the Keith-Albee and Orpheum Circuits Controlled the Big-Time and Its Performers* (New York: Palgrave Macmillan, 2006), 118.

20. Rose, *Agency*, 24–31.

21. "Sophie Tucker: The Headliner at the Plaza Music Hall This Week," 1909, MWEZ + n.c. 10,834, Sophie Tucker Scrapbooks.

22. "Sophie Tucker: America's Greatest Coon Shouter," 1909, MWEZ + n.c. 10,834, Sophie Tucker Scrapbooks; "William Morris Plaza Track," November 8, 1909, MWEZ + n.c. 10,834, Sophie Tucker Scrapbooks.

23. "Sophie Tucker Scores Tremendously at the Criterion," 1909, MWEZ + n.c. 10,834, Sophie Tucker Scrapbooks.

24. Tucker, *Some of These Days*, 91, 89–97; Fields, *Sophie Tucker*, 36–41.

25. "Unknown Clipping on American Music Hall in Chicago," 1909, MWEZ + n.c. 10,834, Sophie Tucker Scrapbooks; Karen Sotiropoulos, *Staging Race: Black Performers in Turn of the Century America* (Harvard University Press, 2008), 93–94.

26. "American Music Hall (Chicago)," December 5, 1909, MWEZ + n.c. 10,834, Sophie Tucker Scrapbooks.

27. "Colonial-Vaudeville," February 29, 1910, MWEZ + n.c. 10,834, Sophie Tucker Scrapbooks.

28. Sophie Tucker, "How Negroes Influenced My Career," *Ebony*, December 1953, 88.

29. Sophie Tucker, *Origins of the Red Hot Mama, 1910–1922* (Archeophone Records, 2009).

30. Ibid.

31. Tucker, *Some of These Days*, 94.

32. June Sochen, *From Mae to Madonna: Women Entertainers in Twentieth-Century America* (Lexington: University Press of Kentucky, 1999), 41–59.

33. Tucker, *Some of These Days*, 95.

34. Tucker, *Origins of the Red Hot Mama*.

35. Jody Rosen, "A Century Later, She's Still Red Hot," *New York Times*, August 28, 2009; Tucker, *Origins*.

36. Wertheim, *Vaudeville Wars*, 244–245.

37. "Unnamed Clipping from Pantages Tour," Summer 1910, MWEZ + n.c. 10,836, Sophie Tucker Scrapbooks.

38. "Miss Tucker in Rag Time," 1911, MWEZ + n.c. 10,835, Sophie Tucker Scrapbooks.

39. Tucker, *Some of These Days*, 90.

40. "Coon Shouting and the Stage and What Sophie Tucker Has to Say," November 3, 1910, MWEZ + n.c. 10,836, Sophie Tucker Scrapbooks.

41. Tucker, *Some of These Days*, 104.

42. "One Arrest Not Enough," *Variety*, November 12, 1910; "When Is Coon Act Indecent," November 1910, MWEZ + n.c. 10,840, Sophie Tucker Scrapbooks.

43. *The Edison Phonograph Monthly* 8, no. 7 (July 1910), MWEZ + n.c. 10,836, Sophie Tucker Scrapbooks.

44. Brian Rust and Alan G. Debus, *The Complete Entertainment Discography from 1897 to 1942* (New York: De Capo, 1989), 749.

45. Tucker, *Some of These Days*, 99; David Suisman, *Selling Sounds: The Commercial Revolution in American Music* (Cambridge, MA: Harvard University Press, 2009), 16, 90–124; Emily Thompson, "Machines, Music, and the Quest for Fidelity: Marketing the Edison Phonograph in America, 1877–1925," *The Musical Quarterly* 1, no. Spring (1995): 131–171.

46. Suisman, *Selling Sounds*, 101–124.

47. "Week's Bills at the Theatres," *New York Times*, January 24, 1911.

48. "Sophie Tucker A Big Hit in Ragtime Songs," December 19, 1910, MWEZ + n.c. 10,836, Sophie Tucker Scrapbooks; Fields, *Sophie Tucker*, 41–43.

49. Tucker, *Some of These Days*, 114.

50. Rose, *Agency*, 31–32.

51. Ashton Stevens, "Sophie Tucker Gets Laughs: Chorus Girls Are Lauded," April 1911, MWEZ + n.c. 10,835, Sophie Tucker Scrapbooks.

52. "Merry Mary at the Whitney," 1911, MWEZ + n.c. 10, 835, Sophie Tucker Scrapbooks.

53. Stevens, "Sophie Tucker Gets Laughs."

54. Tucker, *Some of These Days*, 107.

55. Fields, *Sophie Tucker*, 48; Tucker, *Some of These Days*, 109–111.

56. Josephine Hart Phelps, "Untitled Lousiana Lou Review," 1912, MWEZ + n.c. 10, 839, Sophie Tucker Scrapbooks; "Louisiana Lou Is Big and Noisy," 1912, MWEZ + n.c. 10,839, Sophie Tucker Scrapbooks.

57. Tucker, *Some of These Days*, 112.

58. "She's 'Sick' to Get Back into Vaudeville," 1913, MWEZ + n.c. 10,839,

Sophie Tucker Scrapbooks; "Unidentified Louisiana Lou Review," n.d., MWEZ + n.c. 10,839, Sophie Tucker Scrapbooks.

59. "Sophie Tucker Brings Attractive Songs as Well as Sings," n.d., MWEZ + n.c. 10,840A, Sophie Tucker Scrapbooks.

60. Tucker, *Some of These Days*, 106.

61. Jennie Abuza, 1920 US Federal Census, Hartford Ward 7, Hartford, CT, Roll T625_183, Page 17B, Enumeration District 96, Image 608 (Ancestry.com, February 16, 2016).

62. Tucker, *Some of These Days*, 118.

63. "Sophie Tucker at Poli's This Week," *Hartford Courant*, October 19, 1913; "The Pride of Hartford: Sophie Tucker," *Hartford Courant*, October 19, 1913.

64. "Sophie Tucker Meets Old Friends," *Hartford Courant*, October 19, 1913.

65. Tucker, *Some of These Days*, 124–125.

4. THE HAZARDS OF BECOMING A JAZZ QUEEN

1. Sophie Tucker, *Some of These Days: The Autobiography of Sophie Tucker* (privately published, 1945), 126.

2. Ibid., 126–127.

3. "Sophie Tucker Wins Divorce Suit," *Billboard*, June 7, 1913, 7.

4. "Sophie Tucker, Actress, Wins Her Divorce Suit," *The Morning Telegraph*, May 28, 1913, MWEZ + n.c. 10,841, Sophie Tucker Scrapbooks, *T-Mss 1966-004, Billy Rose Theater Division, New York Public Library (hereafter Sophie Tucker Scrapbooks); Tucker, *Some of These Days*, 131.

5. "Topping the Vaudeville Bills," *New York Times*, January 9, 1916, X3; "Brooklyn Amusements," *New York Times*, February 6, 1916, X7.

6. "'Jazzbo's Queen's' Husband, Former Auto Racer, Is Good Entertainer," February 4, 1918, MWEZ + n.c. 10,838A, Tucker Tucker Scrapbooks; Armond Fields, *Sophie Tucker: First Lady of Show Business* (Jefferson, NC: McFarland, 2003), 67.

7. Tucker, *Some of These Days*, 137.

8. Sophia B. Abuza; Cook County, Illinois Marriage Index, 1871–1920; Illinois Department of Public Health records; "Marriage Records, 1871–present"; Division of Vital Records, Springfield, Illinois (Ancestry.com). "Tucker-Westphal Wedding," *Variety*, October 19, 1917, 5.

9. "'Jazzbo's Queen's' Husband."

10. "'Age of Ragtime' Is Sophie Tucker's Gift to Music of All Eras," 1914, MWEZ + n.c. 10,841, Sophie Tucker Scrapbooks.

11. "The Sequel of Sophie's Secession," *The Billboard*, December 19, 1914, 63.

12. Susan A. Glenn, *Female Spectacle: The Theatrical Roots of Modern Feminism* (Cambridge, MA: Harvard University Press, 2000), 13.

13. Tucker, *Some of These Days*, 152.

14. "Sophie Tucker and Belle Baker in Feats of Agility," *Billboard*, July 22, 1916, 9.

15. Glenn, *Female Spectacle*, 126–154; "Sophie Tucker Brings Attractive Songs as Well as Sings," n.d., MWEZ + n.c. 10,840A, Sophie Tucker Scrapbooks.

16. "Sophie Tucker Makes Hit," *The Billboard*, April 25, 1914; "Sophie Tucker's Songs Are Good," 1914, MWEZ + n.c., 10,841 Sophie Tucker Scrapbooks.

17. Tucker, *Some of These Days*, 134.

18. Ibid., 130–131.

19. Ibid., 144–146; Fields, *Sophie Tucker*, 62–63. Charles Abuza; US Find a Grave Index, 1600–Current (Ancestry.com, July 22, 2016).

20. Tucker, *Some of These Days*, 164; Joe Laurie Jr., *Vaudeville: From the Honky-Tonks to the Palace* (New York: Henry Holt and Co., 1953), 59.

21. Jack Yellen and Abe Olman "I'm Waiting for Ships that Never Come In." http://lyricsplayground.com/alpha/songs/i/imwaitingforshipsthat nevercomein.shtml (accessed June 27, 2017).

22. Ferdinand Otto, "Sophie Tucker Reveals the Secret of Her Softening," 1918, MWEZ + n.c. 10,838A, Sophie Tucker Scrapboks.

23. Frank Rose, *The Agency: William Morris and the Hidden History of Show Business* (New York: HarperBusiness, 1995), 24, 37–39; "William Morris Agency," *Variety*, August 26, 1925, 38.

24. Rose, *Agency*, 34–39.

25. Ted Gioia, *The History of Jazz* (New York: Oxford University Press, 2011), 33–37; Gunther Schuller, *Early Jazz: Its Roots and Musical Development* (New York: Oxford University Press, 1986), 71.

26. David Savran, *Highbrow/Lowdown: Theater, Jazz, and the Making of the New Middle Class* (Ann Arbor: University of Michigan Press, 2009), 23; Gordon Seagrove, "Blues Is Jazz and Jazz Is Blues," *Chicago Daily Tribune*, July 11, 1915, E8.

27. Tucker, *Some of These Days*, 141, 138–139; Fields, *Sophie Tucker*, 67.

28. Wynn, "New Acts This Week: Sophie Tucker and Syncopated Band," *Variety*, June 30, 1912, 12.

29. Lewis A. Erenberg, *Steppin' Out: New York Nightlife and the Transformation of American Culture, 1890–1930* (Chicago: University of Chicago Press, 1984), 113–175.

30. "The Real Scoop of the Season," *Variety*, March 28, 1918, 39.

31. Tucker, *Some of These Days*, 152.

32. "Ragtime Queen Explains Real Meaning of Jazz," February 2, 1918, MWEZ + n.c. 10,838A, Sophie Tucker Scrapbooks; "Sheet Music for 'Blue Melody,'" music and lyrics by Maceo Pinkard, 1918, MWEZ + n.c. 10,838A, Sophie Tucker Scrapbooks; "What Is Jazz?," *Kansas City Star*, January 27, 1918, MWEZ + n.c. 10,838A, Sophie Tucker Scrapbooks.

33. Sophie Tucker, *Sophie Tucker: Cabaret Days* (Sepia Records, 2010).

34. "Remarkable Popularity of Vaudeville—More About the Genesis of Jazz," *Dramatic Mirror*, January 25, 1919, MWEZ + n.c. 10,838B, Sophie Tucker Scrapbooks; Louis Raymond Reid, "Evolution of Jazz," *Shadowland*, November 1919, 72.

35. "Colonial," *Variety*, March 9, 1917, 15.

36. Walter J. Kingsley, "Jazz Has Benchmarks," 1919, MWEZ + n.c. 10,846, Sophie Tucker Scrapbooks.

37. Christopher Capozzola, "The Only Badge Needed Is Your Patriotic Fervor: Vigilance, Coercion, and the Law in World War I America," *The Journal of American History* 88, no. 4 (2002), 1360.

38. Philip Furia and Graham Wood, *Irving Berlin: A Life in Song* (New York: Schirmer Books, 1998), 78–83.

39. "Orpheum: The Best of Vaudeville Program," January 8, 1918, MWEZ + n.c. 10,838A, Sophie Tucker Scrapbooks; "What Is Jazz?," *Kansas City Star*, January 27, 1918, MWEZ + n.c. 10,838A, Sophie Tucker Scrapbooks.

40. Sophie Tucker, "An Appreciation," *Variety*, 1918, MWEZ + n.c. 10,838A, Sophie Tucker Scrapbooks; E. F. Albee to Sophie Tucker, April 30, 1918, MWEZ + n.c. 10,838A, Sophie Tucker Scrapbooks.

41. "Temple," *Rochester Times*, November 23, 1918, MWEZ + n.c. 10,838B, Sophie Tucker Scrapbooks.

42. "Charitable Sophie Tucker," *Variety*, September 14, 1918, 6; "United War Work Campaign Benefits," *New York Telegraph*, November 8, 1918, MWEZ + n.c. 10,838B, Sophie Tucker Scrapbooks.

43. Albert Lucas, "American Jewish Relief in the World War," *The Annals of the American Academy of Political and Social Science* 79 (September 1918): 221–228.

44. "Jewish Relief Fund $3,500,000," *New York Telegraph*, December 15, 1918, 00, MWEZ + n.c. 10,838B, Sophie Tucker Scrapbooks; "Century Program for Jewish War Sufferers," December 1918, MWEZ + n.c. 10,838B, Sophie Tucker Scrapbooks.

45. "Actress Raises $45 for Prisoners at Dannemora," *Newark Eagle*, August 31, 1918, MWEZ + n.c. 10,838B, Sophie Tucker Scrapbooks.

46. "Sophie Tucker at Maccabaeans' Dance," *New York Globe*, n.d., MWEZ + n.c. 10,839, Sophie Tucker Scrapbooks; Charles A Cowan to Sophie Tucker, February 10, 1919, MWEZ + n.c. 10,838B, Sophie Tucker Scrapbooks.

47. Sheet music for "It Took the Sunshine of Old Dixieland to Make You a Wonderful Girl," music and lyrics by Al Palmer and Joe McCarthy (Will Rossiter, 1918), MWEZ + n.c. 10,838A, Sophie Tucker Scrapbooks; sheet music for "I Want You Every Day," music by Shelton Brooks, lyrics by W. R. Williams (Will Rossiter, 1918), MWEZ + n.c. 10,838A, Sophie Tucker Scrapbooks; sheet music for "Mammy's Chocolate Soldier," music by Archie Gottler, lyrics by Sidney Mitchell (Waterson, Berlin, and Snyder, n.d.), MWEZ + n.c. 10,838A, Sophie Tucker Scrapbooks.

48. "Sophie is 'Off' Songs of War for Duration," *Newark Eagle*, August 30, 1918, MWEZ + n.c. 10,838B, Sophie Tucker Scrapbooks.

49. Untitled article, *Chicago Vaudeville*, March 21, 1918, MWEZ + n.c. 10,838A, Sophie Tucker Scrapbooks.

50. Sophie Tucker, "A Friendly Suggestion," *Variety*, 1918, MWEZ + n.c. 10,838A, Sophie Tucker Scrapbooks.

51. "Sophie Seeks Divorce, Is Rumor," October 3, 1918, Locke Collection, Billy Rose Theater Division, New York Public Library.

52. Tucker, *Some of These Days*, 168.

53. Sophie Tucker, *Origins of the Red Hot Mama, 1910–1922* (Archeophone Records, 2009).

54. "Sophie Tucker Sues for Divorce," October 1920, MWEZ + n.c. 10,838, Sophie Tucker Scrapbooks; "Sophie Tucker Sues for Divorce from Her Husband, Because He Doesn't Value Her Talent," *New York Forward*, October 7, 1920, MWEZ + n.c. 10,848, Sophie Tucker Scrapbooks.

55. "Sophie Tucker Has Divorce Case Drawn," *Variety*, October 8, 1920, 3; Fields, *Sophie Tucker*, 91–92; Tucker, *Some of These Days*, 168.

56. Tucker, *Some of These Days*, 141.

57. "Sophie Tucker's New 'Kings,'" *Variety*, August 9, 1918, 5.

58. "Sophie Tucker Makes Hit at Reisenweber's," *New York Telegraph*, December 14, 1918, MWEZ + n.c. 10,838B, Sophie Tucker Scrapbooks.

59. Andrew L. Erdman, *Queen of Vaudeville: The Story of Eva Tanguay* (Ithaca, NY: Cornell University Press, 2012), 210.

60. "Bert Leslie Benefit," *Variety*, November 29, 1919, 19; "Sophie Tucker in Jazz Room," *Variety*, December 20, 1918, 5; "Sophie Tucker Extends New Year's Greetings to All," *Variety*, December 27, 1918, 93.

61. "The Spanish Influenza," *New York Times*, October 7, 1918, 12.

62. "5 Theatres Close Tonight: Theatrical Depression Attributed in Large Part to Influenza Scare," *New York Times*, October 12, 1918, 13; "Changes in Opening and Closing Hours Ordered in City's Fight against Influenza," *New York Times*, January 25, 1920; Fields, *Sophie Tucker*, 81.

63. Brian Rust and Allen G. Debus, *The Complete Entertainment Discography: From 1897 to 1942*, 2nd ed. (New York: De Capo, 1989), 748–49.

64. "Puts Ban on Modesty," *New York Telegraph*, April 2, 1919, MWEZ + n.c. 10,846, Sophie Tucker Scrapbooks.

65. "Suggestive Songs Barred," *Clipper*, June 11, 1919, 20.

66. Fields, *Sophie Tucker*, 82.

67. "Winter Garden and Century Advertisement," April 27, 1920, MWEZ + n.c. 10,847, Sophie Tucker Scrapbooks; "B. F. Albee's Palace Theater," March 1, 1920, MWEZ + n.c. 10,847, Sophie Tucker Scrapbooks; "Manhattan Opera House Advertisement," January 25, 1920, MWEZ + n.c. 10,847, Sophie Tucker Scrapbooks; "44th Street Theater Program," December 1919, MWEZ + n.c. 10,847, Sophie Tucker Scrapbooks.

68. "Sophie Tucker and the Critics," *Dramatic Mirror*, October 30, 1919, MWEZ + n.c. 10,845, Sophie Tucker Scrapbooks.

69. "Tucker Resting," *Clipper*, June 11, 1919, 3.

70. Johnny O'Connor, "Who's Who and What's What," *Dramatic Mirror*, February 14, 1920, MWEZ + n.c. 10,847, Sophie Tucker Scrapbooks.

71. "Majestic Chicago," *Variety*, March 4, 1921, 8.

72. "Victory Show Program—Jewish Welfare Board," 1919, MWEZ + n.c. 10,846, Sophie Tucker Scrapbooks.

73. "Start Campaign for New Harlem Temple," *New York Mail*, April 3, 1919, MWEZ + n.c. 10,846, Sophie Tucker Scrapbooks; "Purim Carnival Clipping," *New York Journal*, April 9, 1919, MWEZ + n.c. 10,846, Sophie Tucker Scrapbooks.

74. Philip Solomon to Sophie Tucker, March 21, 1919, MWEZ + n.c. 10,846, Sophie Tucker Scrapbooks; S. Judelson to Sophie Tucker, February 27, 1919, MWEZ + n.c. 10,846, Sophie Tucker Scrapbooks.

75. Sean P. Holmes, "All the World's a Stage! The Actors' Strike of 1919," *Journal of American History* 91, no. 4 (March 1, 2005): 1304; Fields, *Sophie Tucker*, 85–86; "Production of New and Road Shows Has Practically Ceased," *Clipper*, August 27, 1919, 4.

5. EVERYBODY'S MAMA

1. Ann Reinking, *Chicago The Musical (New Broadway Cast Recording)* (Masterworks Broadway, 1997).

2. "With Prohibition Seemingly Established," *Variety*, January 1919, 11; Michael A. Lerner, *Dry Manhattan: Prohibition in New York City* (Cambridge, MA: Harvard University Press, 2007), 51–56.

3. Sophie Tucker, *Some of These Days: The Autobiography of Sophie Tucker* (privately published, 1945), 169; "Federal Dry Raids Put Atlantic City in Bryan's Class," July 1920, MWEZ + n.c. 10,848, Sophie Tucker Scrapbooks, *T-Mss 1966-004, Billy Rose Theater Division, New York Public Library (hereafter Sophie Tucker Scrapbooks).

4. Lerner, *Dry Manhattan*, 61–95.

5. Tucker, *Some of These Days*, 173–174.

6. Sime Silverman, untitled column on the breakup of Tucker and the Five Kings, *Variety*, January 26, 1922.

7. "Sophie Tucker Announcement about Five Kings of Syncopation," *Variety*, August 16, 1918, 23.

8. "Shows and Foreign Halls Drain American Vaudeville," *Dramatic Mirror*, May 20, 1919, MWEZ + n.c. 10,846, Sophie Tucker Scrapbooks.

9. Tucker, *Some of These Days*, 177; "Sailing with Two Pianists," *Variety*, March 17, 1922, 5.

10. Tucker, *Some of These Days*, 184–188.

11. "Sophie Tucker Wins," *Variety*, April 14, 1922, 2.

12. Tucker, *Some of These Days*, 190–192.

13. "London Memoirs, Wednesday, May 17, 1922," MWEZ + n.c. 10,851, Sophie Tucker Scrapbooks.

14. "Tucker Secure," *Variety*, May 19, 1922, 2.

15. "Sophie Tucker at the Rivoli," July 10, 1922, MWEZ + n.c. 10,851, Sophie Tucker Scrapbooks.

16. "Everybody's Pal," *Ideas*, May 27, 1922, MWEZ + n.c. 10,851, Sophie Tucker Scrapbooks.

17. "Royal Censor Cuts Sophie Tucker Song that Names Prince," *New York American*, May 1922, MWEZ + n.c. 10,851, Sophie Tucker Scrapbooks.

18. "Sophie Tucker Says England Is All O.K.," *Vaudeville News*, June 16, 1922, MWEZ + n.c. 10,851, Sophie Tucker Scrapbooks.

19. E and H Gordon-Clifford, "Before the Public," *The Magnet*, May 27, 1922, MWEZ + n.c. 10,851, Sophie Tucker Scrapbooks.

20. Tucker "the singing violinist," "To the Editor of Variety re Sophie Tucker," *Variety*, September 8, 1922, 31.

21. "Sophie Tucker: The American Queen of Jazz," featured clip from *Chicago American*, November 1922, MWEZ + n.c. 10,850, Sophie Tucker Scrapbooks.

22. "Application for Final Closing of Reisenweber's," *Variety*, September 22, 1922, 36; "Appeal from U.S. District Court," *Variety*, February 1, 1923, 26.

23. "Sophie Tucker Now Completing Eight Months in California," *Variety*, October 25, 1923, MWEZ + n.c. 10,853, Sophie Tucker Scrapbooks.

24. Archie Bell, "Few Minutes with Sophie Would Make the World Smile," *Cleveland News*, January 1, 1923, MWEZ + n.c. 10,852, Sophie Tucker Scrapbooks.

25. Rudolph Valintino [*sic*] to Sophie Tucker, 1922, MWEZ + n.c. 10,852, Sophie Tucker Scrapbooks.

26. "Palace," *Variety*, October 13, 1922.

27. "Sense of Proportion Vital in Costuming Stout Woman, Declares Actress," *Women's Wear*, October 5, 1922, MWEZ + n.c. 10,852, Sophie Tucker Scrapbooks; "Organizes Fat Women's Club," *Los Angeles Times*, November 2, 1923, MWEZ + n.c. 10,853, Sophie Tucker Scrapbooks.

28. Eddie Cantor, *Take My Life*, 34, quoted in Lewis A. Erenberg, *Steppin' Out: New York Nightlife and the Transformation of American Culture, 1890–1930* (Chicago: University of Chicago Press, 1984), 196.

29. "Are Women Afraid to Be Funny," *Post*, 1922, MWEZ + n.c. 10,852, Sophie Tucker Scrapbooks; Sarah Blacher Cohen, "The Unkosher Comediennes: From Sophie Tucker to Joan Rivers," in *Jewish Wry: Essays on Jewish Humor* (Detroit: Wayne State University Press, 1990), 105–110.

30. Marshall Winslow Stearns, *Jazz Dance: The Story of American Vernacular Dance*, (New York: Da Capo Press, 1994), 248–257; Jayna Brown, *Babylon*

Girls: Black Women Performers and the Shaping of the Modern (Durham, NC: Duke University Press, 2008), 213–214; "Ida Writes," *Chicago Defender*, October 21, 1922, 6.

31. "'Brown Buddies' Will Have Many Noted Stage Stars in Their Cast: Adelaide Hall and 'Bojangles' Bill Robinson to Head Great Galaxy at Nixon Theater Next Week," *Pittsburgh Courier*, September 27, 1930, 49.

32. George F. Courier Brown, "Play 'Some of These Days' At My Funeral, Says Says Sophie Tucker in TV Tribute to Shelton Brooks," *Pittsburgh Courier*, December 12, 1953, 22.

33. John S. Wilson, "Eubie Blake, Ragtime Composer, Dies 5 Days After 100th Birthday," *New York Times*, February 13, 1983, 36.

34. "A Note or Two," *Chicago Defender*, November 15, 1924, 6; Floyd G. Snelson, "Theatrical Comment," *Pittsburgh Courier*, November 15, 1924, 9.

35. "'Bo' Gets His," *Chicago Defender*, February 16, 1924, 6.

36. Buzzy Jackson, *A Bad Woman Feeling Good: Blues and the Women Who Sing Them* (New York: W. W. Norton, 2005), 38–43; Daphne Duval Harrison, *Black Pearls: Blues Queens of the 1920s* (New Brunswick, NJ: Rutgers University Press, 2000), 200–205; Anthony Slide, *The Encyclopedia of Vaudeville* (Westport, CT: Greenwood, 1994), 535–537.

37. Ethel Waters with Charles Samuels, *His Eye Is on the Sparrow: An Autobiography* (Kingsport, TN: Kingsport Press, 1950), 135.

38. Harrison, *Black Pearls*, 210.

39. "Display Ad 2—No Title," *Pittsburgh Courier*, April 28, 1923, 2.

40. "Bessie Allison, Chosen by Sculptor for Beauty, Has Prize-Winning Essay," *Pittsburgh Courier*, August 9, 1924, 2.

41. Chappy Gardner, "'Imposters Steal Race Material': Colored Actors Loafing while Whites Work 'Blacked Up' for Effect," *Pittsburgh Courier*, May 10, 1930, 2.

42. Karl Hagstrom Miller, *Segregating Sound: Inventing Folk and Pop Music in the Age of Jim Crow*, (Durham, NC: Duke University Press, 2010), 190–192; David Suisman, *Selling Sounds: The Commercial Revolution in American Music* (Cambridge, MA: Harvard University Press, 2009), 210.

43. Miller, *Segregating Sound*, 206–208.

44. *Bessie Smith: The Complete Recordings*, Vol. 1 (Legacy/Columbia 1991).

45. "Display Ad 36," *Pittsburgh Courier*, January 22, 1927, A3.

46. "Defender Forum," *Chicago Defender*, September 7, 1929, A1.

47. Lyrics accessed at www.lyricsvault.net/php/artist.php?s=41507 #axzz4lExiCHkp.

48. "Dame Sophie Tucker," *Variety*, April 15, 1925, MWEZ + n.c. 10,855, Sophie Tucker Scrapbooks.

49. "Prescribe Yiddisha Mama," May 26, 1925, MWEZ + n.c. 10,856, Sophie Tucker Scrapbooks.

50. Irv Saposnik, "Jolson, *The Jazz Singer*, and the Jewish Mother: Or How My Yiddish Momme Became My Mammy," *Judaism* 43, no. 4 (Fall 1994): 437–439.

51. Tucker, *Some of These Days*, 260.

52. "The Stage and The Jew," *Jewish News*, May 10, 1921, MWEZ + n.c. 10,848, Sophie Tucker Scrapbooks.

53. A. B. Cummins to Sophie Tucker, 1925, MWEZ + n.c. 10,856, Sophie Tucker Scrapbooks.

54. Jerry Koslow to Sophie Tucker, June 2, 1925, MWEZ + n.c. 10,856, Sophie Tucker Scrapbooks.

55. Lillian Woods to Sophie Tucker, May 23, 1925, MWEZ + n.c. 10,856, Sophie Tucker Scrapbooks; Troy Goldfarb to Sophie Tucker, May 19, 1925, MWEZ 10,856, Sophie Tucker Scrapbooks; a Hebrew scholar to Sophie Tucker, June 19, 1925, MWEZ + n.c. 10,856, Sophie Tucker Scrapbooks.

56. Evelyn Wells, "Says 'Red Hot Momma Age Is Waning,'" *San Francisco Call and Post*, June 6, 1925, MWEZ + n.c. 10,856, Sophie Tucker Scrapbooks.

57. Ibid.

58. C. Navier to Sophie Tucker, September 22, 1925, MWEZ + n.c. 10,857, Sophie Tucker Scrapbooks.

59. "Best Paid Variety Star in U.S.," *London Star*, September 19, 1925, MWEZ + n.c. 10,857, Sophie Tucker Scrapbooks.

60. Ad for William Morris clients at the Piccadilly Hotel and Kit Cat Club, *Variety*, October 27, 1925, 33.

61. Amy Leslie, "Glad Tidings from Deserting Actors," *Chicago Daily News*, October 3, 1925, MWEZ + n.c. 10,857, Sophie Tucker Scrapbooks.

62. "William Morris," *Zit's Column*, October 17, 1925, MWEZ 10,857, Sophie Tucker Scrapbooks; "Lettres de Londres," *L'Italie*, November 15, 1925, MWEZ + n.c. 10,857, Sophie Tucker Scrapbooks.

63. "Sukes in the Jewish Shelter," *London Jewish Times*, October 7, 1925, MWEZ + n.c. 10,857, Sophie Tucker Scrapbooks.

64. "Berlin Sings to Wife in London Night Club," *New York Evening Post*, January 18, 1926, MWEZ + n.c. 10,857, Sophie Tucker Scrapbooks.

65. "Valentino Returns, Calls Worries Over," *New York Evening Post*, January 27, 1926, MWEZ 10,859, Sophie Tucker Scrapbooks; "Star Loses in Death Flight," *Boston American*, January 25, 1926, MWEZ + n.c. 10,859, Sophie Tucker Scrapbooks; "Sophie Tucker's Mother Dies; Soph on Ocean," *Variety*, January 27, 1926; "Singer's Rush to Sick Mother," *Sunday Chronicle*, January 1926, MWEZ + n.c. 10,857, Sophie Tucker Scrapbooks.

66. Tucker, *Some of These Days*, 224.

67. Eddie Cantor to Sophie Tucker, February 20, 1926, MWEZ + n.c. 10,858, Sophie Tucker Scrapbooks.

68. Ernest Trattner to Sophie Tucker, February 25, 1926, MWEZ + n.c. 10,859, Sophie Tucker Scrapbooks.

69. Jennie Abuza to Sophie Tucker, January 1926, MWEZ + n.c. 10,859, Sophie Tucker Scrapbooks.

70. Tucker, *Some of These Days*, 225–226.

71. Armond Fields, *Sophie Tucker: First Lady of Show Business* (Jefferson, NC: McFarland, 2003), 124; Tucker, *Some of These Days*, 226.

72. "Sophie Tucker's Playground Next," *Morning Telegraph*, March 7, 1926, MWEZ + n.c. 10,859, Sophie Tucker Scrapbooks.

73. "Sophie Tucker Playground," *Variety*, March 17, 1926, 44.

74. "Sophie Tucker Playground to Run All Summer," *Variety*, April 17, 1926, 22.

75. Fields, *Sophie Tucker*, 125; Tucker, *Some of These Days*, 228, 234.

76. "Sophie Tucker, The International Star," June 1927, MWEZ + n.c. 10,863, Sophie Tucker Scrapbooks; "It's Toasted" Lucky Strike ad, 1927, MWEZ + n.c. 10,863, Sophie Tucker Scrapbooks.

77. Nellie Revell, "Right off the Desk," *Variety*, December 1926.

78. "Sophie Tucker's Son, Alfred, Goes on Stage in Publix Piece," *Morning Telegraph*, February 20, 1926, MWEZ + n.c. 10,859, Sophie Tucker Scrapbooks.

79. Tucker, *Some of These Days*, 236.

80. "Sophie Tucker's Son in *Le Maire's Affairs*," *Billboard*, August 7, 1926.

81. "Sophie's Son Signs With Paul Ash," *Chicago News*, August 17, 1926, MWEZ + n.c. 10,860, Sophie Tucker Scrapbooks.

82. "Oriental Advertisement for Paul Ash," *Chicago America*, August 17, 1926, MWEZ + n.c. 10,860, Sophie Tucker Scrapbooks.

83. "Sophie Tucker's Son Impersonating Mother," *Variety*, August 18, 1926, 68.

84. Tucker, *Some of These Days*, 238.

85. "Soph in M.P. Houses," *Variety*, February 9, 1927, 22.

86. "Soph and Son," *Variety*, November 23, 1927, 29.

87. "Sophie Tucker and Bert a Sensation at the Oriental," *Billboard*, December 10, 1927, 19.

88. "Paramount," *Variety*, February 8, 1928, 34.

89. Fields, *Sophie Tucker*, 135–137.

6. GRASPING FOR RECOGNITION

1. Sophie Tucker, *Some of These Days: The Autobiography of Sophie Tucker* (privately published, 1945), 241–242.

2. Ibid., 216; Armond Fields, *Sophie Tucker: First Lady of Show Business* (Jefferson, NC: McFarland, 2003), 108.

3. Tucker, *Some of These Days*, 247.

4. "Sophie Indulges in Another Brand New Husband," *New York Review*, December 22, 1928, MWEZ + n.c. 10,868, Sophie Tucker Scrapbooks, *T-Mss 1966-004, Billy Rose Theater Division, New York Public Library (hereafter, Sophie Tucker Scrapbooks); "Soph Admits Marriage and Pan Alterations," *Variety*, January 9, 1929.

5. "Sophie Tucker Discusses London vs. United States," *Zit's Column*, June 23, 1928, MWEZ + n.c. 10,865, Sophie Tucker Scrapbooks.

6. Tucker, *Some of These Days*, 242; "Soph's Plaintive Response," *Variety*, May 16, 1928, 2; "Ager and Yellen Wrote Soph's Hit," *Variety*, June 6, 1928, 54.

7. Sophie Tucker, *The Complete Early Sophie Tucker (1910–1937)* (Superbatone Records, 2002).

8. Virginia Dale, "Speaking of Plays and Players," November 10, 1928, MWEZ + n.c. 10,867, Sophie Tucker Scrapbooks.

9. Vera Caspary, "An Open Letter to Sophie Tucker," *Gotham Life*, October 1927, MWEZ + n.c. 10,867, Sophie Tucker Scrapbooks.

10. Lary May, *Screening out the Past: The Birth of Mass Culture and the Motion Picture Industry* (Chicago: University of Chicago Press, 1983), 169–177.

11. S. D., Trav, *No Applause, Just Throw Money; or, The Book that Made Vaudeville Famous: A High-Class, Refined Entertainment* (New York: Faber and Faber, 2005), 246–256.

12. "Sophie Tucker on Youth," *Brooklyn Eagle*, January 8, 1928, MWEZ + n.c. 10,864, Sophie Tucker Scrapbooks.

13. Louella O. Parsons, "First National Stars to Stay under Warner Rule," October 21, 1928, MWEZ + n.c. 10,867, Sophie Tucker Scrapbooks; Louella O. Parsons, "Sophie Tucker to Make Film for Warners," *Daily Mirror*, September 11, 1928, MWEZ + n.c. 10,866, Sophie Tucker Scrapbooks.

14. "W.B. Offer Sophie Tucker $85,000 for Vita Picture," *Variety*, September 5, 1928; "Sophie Back Home for a Few Hours," September 19, 1928, MWEZ + n.c. 10,866, Sophie Tucker Scrapbooks; Fields, *Sophie Tucker*, 141.

15. "Soph Admits Marriage and Pan Alterations," 37; "Buxon Sophie Tucker Boasts Third Husband and Postpones Honeymoon to Have Face Lifted," January 3, 1929, MWEZ + n.c. 10,868, Sophie Tucker Scrapbooks.

16. Henry Schireson to Sophie Tucker, October 14, 1925, MWEZ + n.c. 10,859, Sophie Tucker Scrapbooks.

17. "Sophie Goes Talkie," *Motion Picture Classic*, May 1929, MWEZ + n.c. 10,869, Sophie Tucker Scrapbooks.

18. Tucker, *Some of These Days*, 288.

19. Ibid., 290.

20. "Sophie Goes Talkie"; Rob Reel, "Sophie Made Hollywood Let Her Be Herself," *Chicago Evening American*, May 22, 1929, MWEZ + n.c. 10,869, Sophie Tucker Scrapbooks.

21. Amy Leslie, "Closeup of the Real Sophie Tucker: Type of American Woman Admired Her," *Chicago Daily News*, May 25, 1929, MWEZ + n.c. 10,869, Sophie Tucker Scrapbooks; Lois Young-Tulin, *Sophie and Me: Some of These Days* (San Jose: iUniverse.com, 2001), 175–179; William Gazecki, *The Outrageous Sophie Tucker* (Menemsha Films, 2014).

22. "Playwrights Still Dote on Aged Mother-Love Theme," *Cleveland News*, September 12, 1929.

23. Tucker, *Some of These Days*, 291.

24. "Reel Reviews," *Evening Journal*, June 5, 1929, MWEZ + n.c. 10,869, Sophie Tucker Scrapbooks.

25. Mordaunt Hall, "Good Stories Sapped of Drama: Unnecessary Changes Made in Transferring Plays and Books to Screen—Tame Productions of Past Week a Dull Piece. Sins of the Snobs. Father's Vampire. A Buxom Night Club Hostess," *New York Times*, June 9, 1929.

26. "MGM Hollywood Revue Still Leads: Four Feathers and Honky

Tonk Gross Well," *Motion Picture News*, September 1929, 414; "Honky Tonk Advertisement," *Variety*, July 3, 1929, 52; Fields, *Sophie Tucker*, 147.

27. S. D., *No Applause*, 255–256; Lary May, *The Big Tomorrow: Hollywood and the Politics of the American Way* (Chicago: University of Chicago Press, 2000), 16, 122–124.

28. "I Believe in Vaudeville," *New York Star*, May 31, 1930, MWEZ + n.c. 10,872, Sophie Tucker Scrapbooks.

29. "Vaudeville Will Come Back Says Sophie Tucker," *New York Star*, September 6, 1930, MWEZ N.C. 10,872, Sophie Tucker Scrapbooks; "Vaude Coming Back So Says Sophie Tucker," *The Morning Telegraph*, September 3, 1930, MWEZ 10,872, Sophie Tucker Scrapbooks.

30. "25,000 Idle Stage Actors," *Variety*, October 29, 1930, 43.

31. "Soph's $11,000," *Variety*, January 29, 1930, 66.

32. "Chicago Oriental," *Exhibitor's Herald-World*, February 15, 1930, 50.

33. "50 Names and Standard Acts Taken by Loews for 1st Time," *Variety*, March 19, 1930, 40.

34. "Popular Songs Keep Actress in Spotlight," *Loews Flash*, April 1930, MWEZ + n.c. 10,870, Sophie Tucker Scrapbooks.

35. "Broadway Gets Hot in Florida," *New York City World*, February 3, 1930, MWEZ + n.c. 10,870, Sophie Tucker Scrapbooks.

36. Tucker, *Some of these Days*, 247.

37. "Sophie Tucker Loses a Pal," *Zit Column*, May 31, 1930, MWEZ + n.c. 10,872, Sophie Tucker Scrapbooks.

38. Gilbert Swan, "In New York," *New York City World*, May 31, 1930, MWEZ + n.c. 10,872, Sophie Tucker Scrapbooks.

39. Tucker, *Some of These Days*, 248.

40. "Makes Radio Debut," *Motion Picture Herald*, November 21, 1931, 35.

41. "Sophie's Pick Ups," *Variety*, September 22, 1931, 58.

42. Susan J. Douglas, *Listening In: Radio and the American Imagination from Amos 'n' Andy and Edward R. Murrow to Wolfman Jack and Howard Stern* (New York: Times Books, 1999), 128.

43. "Sophie Tucker Music Hall," *Variety*, May 8, 1935, 57; "Welcome Mat out for Vaudevillians as WHN Starts Open Door Policy," *Variety*, April 24, 1935, 44; "Sophie Tucker as Spieler," *Variety*, July 10, 1935, 44.

44. "Columbia News Roundup for Week of November 6–12," October 28, 1938, MWEZ + n.c. 10,909, Sophie Tucker Scrapbooks.

45. "Sophie Tucker Interview" (Chicago: WIND Radio, October 29, 1946), L (Special) 88-67, Sophie Tucker private recordings collection, the Rodgers and Hammerstein Archives of Recorded Sound, New York Public Library for the Performing Arts.

46. Douglas, *Listening In*, 135.

47. "Miss Sophie Tucker: Jewish Community's Welcome for Commedienne," *Manchester Chronicle*, June 8, 1930, MWEZ + n.c. 10,872, Sophie Tucker Scrapbooks.

48. "London Hails Miss Tucker," *New York Times*, September 18, 1930; Herbert Farjeon, "The London Stage," *The Graphic*, September 1930, MWEZ + n.c. 10,872, Sophie Tucker Scrapbooks.

49. "Good Old Soph Back Again," *Daily Herald*, September 9, 1930, MWEZ + n.c. 10,872, Sophie Tucker Scrapbooks.

50. "Untitled," *Daily Express*, September 9, 1930, MWEZ + n.c. 10,872, Sophie Tucker Scrapbooks.

51. "Sophie Tucker Hobnobs in British Society Again," *Billboard*, November 8, 1930; Fields, *Sophie Tucker*, 151–153; Tucker, *Some of These Days*, 252.

52. Tucker, *Some of These Days*, 255–258; "Tucker Explains Paris Incident," *Billboard*, March 2, 1931, MWEZ + n.c. 10,873, Sophie Tucker Scrapbooks; "Sophie Tucker Is Booed Off Stage in Paris," *Pasadena Post*, March 3, 1931, MWEZ + n.c. 10,873, Sophie Tucker Scrapbooks; "Soph's Lyrics Aroused the French," *Variety*, February 25, 1931, 56.

53. "Tucker Explains Paris Incident."

54. "The Question of Yom Kippur," *The Daily Express*, September 14, 1930, MWEZ + n.c. 10,872, Sophie Tucker Scrapbooks.

55. Tucker, *Some of These Days*, 261.

56. "Sophie Tucker Wins Again at the Oriental in Chicago," *Motion Picture Herald*, November 7, 1931; "Paramount, N.Y.," *Variety*, October 31, 1931.

57. "Sophie Tells of Blaze," *New York Evening Journal*, February 18, 1932, MWEZ + n.c. 10,877, Sophie Tucker Scrapbooks.

58. Ed Sullivan, "Ed Sullivan Sees Broadway," *New York Evening Graphic*, February 16, 1932, MWEZ + n.c. 10,875, Sophie Tucker Scrapbooks.

59. Tucker, *Some of These Days*, 266.

60. "William Morris, Showman and Friend," *New York Times*, November 6, 1932, X1.

61. "Saranac Lake Day Nursery Pamphlet," n.d., MWEZ +n.c. 12,927, William Morris Scrapbook Collection, MFL+++12,929, Billy Rose Theater

Collection, New York Public Library; "Third Annual Benefit, Saranac Day Nursery," May 22, 1927, MWEZ + n.c. 12,927, William Morris Scrapbook Collection, MFL+++12,929, Billy Rose Theater Collection, New York Public Library.

62. "Services Held for Wm. Morris and Moe Mark," *Variety*, November 8, 1932, 39; "Bill Morris Incidents," *Variety*, November 8, 1932, 39.

63. Tucker, *Some of These Days*, 265.

64. "No Room for Talent in Show Business: Sophie Tucker Observes During Visit Here," *Asbury Park Evening Press*, July 23, 1935, MWEZ + n.c. 10,892, Sophie Tucker Scrapbooks; Burton W. Peretti, *Nightclub City: Politics and Amusement in Manhattan* (Philadelphia: University of Pennsylvania Press, 2007), 175–179.

65. Tucker, *Some of These Days*, 269.

66. "Sophie Tucker to Seek Divorce From 3rd Husband," *New York American*, February 26, 1933, MWEZ + n.c. 10,879, Sophie Tucker Scrapbooks; "Sophie Tucker Divorced: Singer Got Secret Decree in Chicago Court Sept. 2," *New York Times*, April 13, 1934; "Tucker Sails," *Variety*, March 29, 1934, 48.

67. "Soph Repeats," *Variety*, June 5, 1934, 20.

68. Tucker, *Some of These Days*, 271.

69. "American Stars Help King George Memorial," *Evening News*, December 10, 1936, MWEZ + n.c. 10,899, Sophie Tucker Scrapbooks; "Sophie Would Bring U.S. and Britain Closer," *Rocky Mountain News*, December 21, 1936, MWEZ + n.c. 10,899, Sophie Tucker Scrapbooks.

70. Abe Lastfogel promotional ad, *Variety*, November 13, 1934.

71. "Soph to FL," *Variety*, January 15, 1935, 50.

72. "Orpheum," *Variety*, November 20, 1935, 19.

73. "Sophie Tucker Seeks Braves, Ruth as Pilot," *Washington Post*, July 19, 1935, MWEZ + n.c. 10,892, Sophie Tucker Scrapbooks; Stuart Bell, "Sophie As B.B. Magnate Hotcha Might Help Braves but Keep Her off Bench," *Cleveland Press*, July 19, 1935, MWEZ + n.c. 10,892, Sophie Tucker Scrapbooks.

74. Joyce Antler, *The Journey Home: How Jewish Women Shaped Modern America* (New York: Schocken, 1997), 143.

75. Tucker, *Some of These Days*, 302.

76. "Sophie Tucker Tells Them," *Billboard*, November 20, 1937, MWEZ + n.c. 10,907, Sophie Tucker Scrapbooks.

77. "Sophie Tucker Observes Birthday Today; Friday 13th Holds No

Terror for Her," *Jefferson City Capital News*, January 13, 1939, MWEZ + n.c. 10,917, Sophie Tucker Scrapbooks.

78. Tucker, *Some of These Days*, 294.

79. Ed Sullivan, "Behind the Headlines," *Daily News*, July 6, 1937, MWEZ + n.c. 10,903, Sophie Tucker Scrapbooks.

80. "Old Variety Stars Mourn Sophie, Film Captive," March 1937, MWEZ + n.c. 10,900, Sophie Tucker Scrapbooks.

81. "Sophie Tucker Picks Judy Garland to Be Next 'Red Hot Mama,'" *Harrisburg Patriot*, September 3, 1937, MWEZ + n.c. 10,904, Sophie Tucker Scrapbooks.

82. Judy Garland, "The First Sixteen Years," *Hartford Courant*, March 24, 1940, MWEZ + n.c. 10,930, Sophie Tucker Scrapbooks.

83. "Broadway Melody Reopens the Capital," *Daily News*, September 1937, MWEZ + n.c. 10,904, Sophie Tucker Scrapbooks; "Broadway Melody of 1938," *Motion Picture Herald*, October 2, 1937, 69; John Mosher, "The Current Cinema," *New Yorker*, September 4, 1937.

84. Tucker, *Some of These Days*, 299.

85. "Ronald Sinclair, C. Aubrey Smith, and Sophie Tucker in M.G.M's 'Thoroughbreds Don't Cry,'" *Southern Echo*, December 18, 1937, MWEZ + n.c. 10,905, Sophie Tucker Scrapbooks.

86. "Hollywood Jewish News," April 1937, MWEZ + n.c. 10,902, Sophie Tucker Scrapbooks.

87. "Cantor to Help Send Children to Palestine," *Chattanooga Times*, June 16, 1938, MWEZ + n.c. 10,912, Sophie Tucker Scrapbooks; "Cantor to Aid Jews," *Birmingham News*, June 15, 1938, MWEZ + n.c. 10,912, Sophie Tucker Scrapbooks; "Cantor Will Help Jewish Refugees," *Elizabethtown Star*, June 15, 1938, MWEZ + n.c. 10,911, Sophie Tucker Scrapbooks.

88. "Nazis Bar Benny, J. Dorsey," *Orchestra World*, November 1938, MWEZ + n.c. 10,915, Sophie Tucker Scrapbooks.

89. Tucker, *Some of These Days*, 260; David Weinstein, "Eddie Cantor Fights the Nazis: The Evolution of a Jewish Celebrity," *American Jewish History* 96, no. 4 (December 2010): 235–263.

90. Billy Rowe, "Actors' Guild Stages 'Finest' Benefit: Eddie Cantor Opens All-Star Bill; Marian Anderson Closes It," *Pittsburgh Courier*, December 17, 1938, 21.

91. Dorothy Kilgallen, "Voice of Broadway," *Boston American*, January 10, 1939, MWEZ N.C. 10,917, Sophie Tucker Scrapbooks.

92. "Mae Alix Scoring at Sunset Cafe," *Pittsburgh Courier*, March 14, 1936, A7; "Nite Club Circuit Formed," *Pittsburgh Courier*, November 6, 1937, 21.

93. Mermon Potter, "A 'Red Hot Mama' Thirty Years: Sophie Tucker Gains Heights at Last," *Birmingham Post*, December 6, 1938, MWEZ + n.c. 10,910, Sophie Tucker Scrapbooks.

94. John Mason Brown, "Mr. Throttlebottom Gets a Job as Ambassador," *New York Post*, November 12, 1938, MWEZ + n.c. 10,915, Sophie Tucker Scrapbooks.

95. "Leave It To Me," *New Yorker*, November 1938, MWEZ + n.c. 10,915, Sophie Tucker Scrapbooks; "Attention Dies Committee," *The Nation*, November 26, 1938, MWEZ + n.c. 10,915, Sophie Tucker Scrapbooks.

96. Tucker, *Some of These Days*, 301; Michael Denning, *The Cultural Front: The Laboring of American Culture in the Twentieth Century* (London: Verso, 1998).

7. THE VALUE OF DEVOTION

1. "Actors Union Trial on Funds Ordered," *New York Times*, June 15, 1939, 30; Sophie Tucker, *Some of These Days: The Autobiography of Sophie Tucker* (privately published, 1945), 280.

2. "Sophie Tucker Feted," *New York Times*, June 15, 1939, 31.

3. "News of the Stage," *New York Times*, June 17, 1939, 17; "Cantor Quits A.F.A. Post," *New York Times*, June 18, 1939, 38; "Cantor and Vallee Advise Actors to Withhold Vote on Union Heads," *New York Times*, June 19, 1939, 17; "Variety Artists Bar Sophie Tucker Vote," *New York Times*, June 20, 1939, 29.

4. Tucker, *Some of These Days*, 304; "Actors' Meeting Ends in a Melee," *New York Times*, June 21, 1939; "'Peace' Meet Ends in Riot," *Burlington Times*, June 20, 1939, MWEZ + n.c. 10,922, Sophie Tucker Scrapbooks,*T-Mss 1966-004, Billy Rose Theater Division, New York Public Library (hereafter Sophie Tucker Scrapbooks).

5. "Actor Is Bitten by Chorus Girl as Union Meets," *New York Herald Tribune*, June 21, 1939, MWEZ + n.c. 10,922, Sophie Tucker Scrapbooks; "Actors' Meeting Ends in a Melee"; "Last Red Hot Mama, Stars Flee Actors' Union Harmony Riot," *Boston American*, June 20, 1939, MWEZ + n.c. 10,922, Sophie Tucker Scrapbooks.

6. "Actors' Finances Sifted by Dewey," *New York Times*, June 22, 1939, 25.

7. "Actors Union Trial on Funds Ordered," 30.

8. "Miss Tucker Leads Walkout at Trial," *New York Times*, July 11, 1939, 18.

9. "Stage Union Loses Its A.F.L. Charter," *New York Times*, July 15, 1939, 1.

10. "Outsted Stage Union Starts Court Fight," *New York Times*, July 20, 1939, 4.

11. Tucker, *Some of These Days*, 306.

12. "A.F.L. Stage Unions Face Serious Rift," *New York Times*, July 24, 1939, 11.

13. "Stage Unions Open Threatened War," *New York Times*, August 1, 1939, 21.

14. "Equity Suspends Sophie Tucker Pending Her Trial on Aug. 22," *New York Times*, August 5, 1939, 10.

15. "Stage Union Linked to 'Public Enemy,'" *New York Times*, August 2, 1939, 24.

16. "Union Threatens Hollywood Strike," *New York Times*, August 7, 1939, 16; "Stage Stars Hurl Charges in Labor Row," *Brooklyn Citizen*, August 7, 1939, MWEZ + n.c. 10,923, Sophie Tucker Scrapbooks; "A.A.A.A. Defended by Miss Hepburn," *New York Times*, August 6, 1939, 36.

17. "A.F.L. Upholds 4As in Actors' Dispute," *New York Times*, August 16, 1939, 1.

18. "Resignation Urged on Sophie Tucker," *New York Times*, August 21, 1939, 14.

19. "Actors to Close 11 Shows Tuesday If Feud Continues," *New York Times*, August 31, 1939, 1.

20. "Stagehands Defy Actors to Strike," *New York Times*, September 1, 1939, 17.

21. Ibid.

22. "Actors Ask Mayor for Peace Parley," *New York Times*, September 3, 1939, 2; "Stage War Ended; Strike Prevented," *New York Times*, September 4, 1939, 18.

23. Brooks Atkinson, "The Actors Win Their Point: The Theatre Settles Down After Its Near Strike," *New York Times*, September 10, 1939, X1.

24. "Miss Tucker Quits Whitehead Group," *New York Times*, September 15, 1939, 31; "Miss Tucker Joins New Stage Guild," *New York Times*, September 21, 1939, 29; Armond Fields, *Sophie Tucker: First Lady of Show Business* (Jefferson, NC: McFarland, 2003), 193.

25. Tucker, *Some of These Days*, 305–306.

26. Ibid., 306.

27. "The Night Hawk," *Shreveport Journal*, January 31, 1940, MWEZ 10,929,

Sophie Tucker Scrapbooks; "Musical Comedy Set," *Birmingham Age Herald*, January 29, 1940, MWEZ + n.c. 10,929, Sophie Tucker Scrapbooks.

28. "State, N.Y.," *Variety*, November 6, 1940, 46.

29. Noel Coward to Sophie Tucker, May 9, 1940, MWEZ + n.c. 12,930, Sophie Tucker Scrapbooks.

30. "Sophie Tucker Writing Her Life Story," n.d., MWEZ + n.c. 10,929, Sophie Tucker Scrapbooks; "Red Hot Mama's Book Will Sport Asbestos Cover," *Milwaukee Journal*, September 25, 1941, MWEZ + n.c. 12,940, Sophie Tucker Scrapbooks.

31. Linton Martin, "'High Kickers' Opens at the Forrest," *Philadelphia Inquirer*, October 14, 1941, MWEZ + n.c. 12,940, Sophie Tucker Scrapbooks.

32. Robert Sensenderfer, "The Living Theater," *Evening Bulletin*, October 14, 1941, 26, MWEZ + n.c. 12,940, Sophie Tucker Scrapbooks; "'Kickers' Fine, $26,300 in Final Philly Week," *Variety*, October 29, 1941, 51; "Studios Acquire 34 Story Properties in September," *Motion Picture Herald*, October 24, 1942, 59.

33. David Ware Stowe, *Swing Changes: Big-Band Jazz in New Deal America* (Cambridge, MA: Harvard University Press, 1998), 148.

34. "Comedies Lead Long-Run Shows," *Motion Picture Herald*, February 14, 1942, 44.

35. Ralph Warner, "Inspiring Salute to U.S.A. Negro Troops," *Daily Worker*, January 13, 1942, MWEZ + n.c. 10,943, Sophie Tucker Scrapbooks.

36. "Powell and Mrs. Roosevelt Call for Negro Equality in Services," *New York Herald Tribune*, January 12, 1941, MWEZ + n.c. 10,943, Sophie Tucker Scrapbooks; "Broadway Honors Soldiers Guarding New York City," *Chicago Defender*, January 17, 1942; Lauren Rebecca Sklaroff, *Black Culture and the New Deal: The Quest for Civil Rights in the Roosevelt Era* (Chapel Hill: University of North Carolina Press, 2014).

37. Sophie Tucker, *Sophie Tucker: The Very Best Of* (Master Classics Records, 2009).

38. "Boxing Wrestling Tournament U.S. Naval Receiving Station, Boston, MA," March 18, 1943, MWEZ + n.c. 10,947, Sophie Tucker Scrapbooks; "Sailor Guest of Sophie Tucker," *Jersey City Journal*, January 13, 1944, MWEZ + n.c. 10,951, Sophie Tucker Scrapbooks.

39. H. B. Watson Jr. to Sophie Tucker, January 14, 1945, MWEZ + n.c. 10,968, Sophie Tucker Scrapbooks; Fields, *Sophie Tucker*, 207.

40. Robert B. Westbrook, "'I Want A Girl, Just Like the Girl Who Married

Harry James': American Women and the Problem of Political Obligation in World War II," *American Quarterly* 42, no. 4 (December 1990): 587–614.

41. "Soph's Spice at Buff Navy Relief Benefit Shocks City-Fathers," *Variety*, July 29, 1942, 1, 52.

42. "Soph Rebukes Crix of 'Spicy' Buff Show," *Variety*, August 5, 1942, 3.

43. Sophie Tucker, *Red Hot Mama* (Gralin Music, 2012).

44. Tucker, *Some of These Days*; Tucker, *Sophie Tucker: The Very Best Of*; Bette Midler, *Bette Midler: Live At Last* (Rhino Atlantic, 1977).

45. Sophie Tucker, *The Complete Early Sophie Tucker (1910–1937)* (Superbatone Records, 2002); Samuel Lesner, "Chez Paree, Tucker Find 'It's Mutual,'" November 2, 1942, MWEZ + n.c. 12,946, Sophie Tucker Scrapbooks; Bob Locke, "Buxom Sophie Tucker Still a 'Red Hot Mama,'" *Chicago Sun*, November 1, 1942, MWEZ + n.c. 12,946, Sophie Tucker Scrapbooks.

46. Judy Tzu-Chun Wu, *Doctor Mom Chung of the Fair-Haired Bastards: The Life of a Wartime Celebrity* (Berkeley: University of California Press, 2005), 119–135.

47. Lillian Faderman, *Odd Girls and Twilight Lovers: A History of Lesbian Life in Twentieth-Century America* (New York: Penguin, 1992), 123.

48. Wu, *Doctor Mom Chung*, 174–183; "Margaret Chung Aids Bond Drive," January 24, 1944, MWEZ + n.c. 10,951, Sophie Tucker Scrapbooks.

49. Wu, *Doctor Mom Chung*, 174–177; Don Blessing to Sophie Tucker, December 1, 1952, MWEZ + n.c. 14,674, Sophie Tucker Scrapbooks.

50. "Sophie Tucker at Reception for Nephew," *Dayton Journal*, July 15, 1942, MWEZ + n.c. 10,945, Sophie Tucker Scrapbooks.

51. "Sophie Tucker's Son Back in Profession," *Variety*, April 15, 1942, 3; "Sophie Tucker's Son, Bert, Succeeds Drafted WM Agent," *Billboard*, August 28, 1943, 18.

52. "Liberty Goes to the Movies," *Motion Picture Herald*, May 20, 1944, 50.

53. "Stone Stars Work on Production Program," *Motion Picture Herald*, June 24, 1944, 97.

54. Fields, *Sophie Tucker*, 208.

55. "Sophie Tucker Interview" (Chicago: WIND Radio, October 29, 1946), L (Special) 88-67, Sophie Tucker private recordings collection, the Rodgers and Hammerstein Archives of Recorded Sound, the New York Public Library for the Performing Arts.

56. William Green to Sophie Tucker, March 14, 1945, MWEZ 10,956, Sophie Tucker Scrapbooks.

57. Abel Green, "Sophie Tucker's Biog a Lusty Cavalcade," *Variety*, March 24, 1945, 2, 44.

58. John Cavanagh to Sophie Tucker, January 15, 1947, MWEZ + n.c. 10,973, Sophie Tucker Scrapbooks.

59. "Vaudeville: Sophie Tucker's $14,000 from Book Sales to Charity," *Variety*, October 29, 1947, 52.

60. "BBC Review of Some of These Days" (BBC, July 17, 1948), L (Special) 88-67, Sophie Tucker private recordings collection, the Rodgers and Hammerstein Archives of Recorded Sound, the New York Public Library for the Performing Arts.

61. "Soph's Brother Dies," *Variety*, May 16, 1945, 47.

62. "La Tucker Suing Relatives in Conn. for 500G in Stock," *Billboard*, June 16, 1945; Lois Young-Tulin, *Sophie and Me: Some of These Days* (San Jose: iUniverse.com, 2001), 176–179.

63. Young-Tulin, *Sophie and Me*, 176.

64. "Soph Sees Same Postwar Cafe Trends Now as in '18," *Variety*, August 21, 1946, 55.

65. Clinton H. Johnson, "Sophie's $15,000 New Peak in Skyrocketing Night Club Salaries," *Baltimore American*, May 26, 1946, MWEZ 10,968, Sophie Tucker Scrapbooks.

66. "Soph Tucker's 80G in Two Weeks New Record for H'Wood Nitery," *Variety*, October 1, 1947, 43.

67. Jonathan D. Sarna, *American Judaism: A History* (New Haven, CT: Yale University Press, 2004), 258–282.

68. Albert Einstein to Sophie Tucker, September 25, 1945, MWEZ + n.c. 10,961, Sophie Tucker Scrapbooks.

69. Ernest Trattner to Sophie Tucker, January 6, 1946, MWEZ + n.c. 10,965, Sophie Tucker Scrapbooks.

70. Abel Green, "40th Anni Salute to Sophie Tucker Her 'Greatest One Night Stand,'" *Variety*, May 7, 1947, MWEZ + n.c. 10,976, Sophie Tucker Scrapbooks.

71. "Soph Follows Mrs. F.D.R. As 'Woman of The Year,'" *Variety*, October 3, 1951, 60.

72. Samuel Braunstein to Sophie Tucker, August 21, 1947, MWEZ + n.c. 10,977, Sophie Tucker Scrapbooks.

73. B. Mindel to Sophie Tucker, April 22, 1948, MWEZ + n.c. 10,982, Sophie Tucker Scrapbooks.

74. Adele Thompson to Sophie Tucker, May 24, 1948, Sophie Tucker Scrapbooks.

75. Ryvka Slodjinska to Sophie Tucker, May 24, 1948, MWEZ + n.c. 10,982, Sophie Tucker Scrapbooks.

76. "Sophie Tucker Interview with Louella Parsons," May 12, 1951, L (Special) 88–67, Sophie Tucker private recordings collection, Rodgers and Hammerstein Archives of Recorded Sound, New York Public Library for the Performing Arts.

77. "Sophie Tucker Souvenir Programme—Casino Theater JNF Benefit," June 7, 1948, MWEZ + n.c. 10,984, Sophie Tucker Scrapbooks; "Sophie Tucker among Orphans," *Musical Express*, June 18, 1948, MWEZ + n.c. 10,984, Sophie Tucker Scrapbooks; "Sophie Tucker Triumphs: Superb 'Yiddisher Momma,'" June 5, 1948, MWEZ + n.c. 10,984, Sophie Tucker Scrapbooks.

78. Earl Calloway, "George Kirby: Impressionist Extraordinaire!," *Pittsburgh Courier*, December 3, 1977; "Home-Grown George Kirby to Star in Giant Regal Stage Show Tomorrow," *Chicago Defender*, July 26, 1962.

79. "Sophie Tucker to Anglicise Songs for London Benefit," *Daily Mail*, May 21, 1948, MWEZ + n.c. 10,982, Sophie Tucker Scrapbooks; "Sophie Tucker Triumphs: Superb 'Yiddisher Momma,'" June 5, 1948, MWEZ + n.c. 10,984, Sophie Tucker Scrapbooks; "British King and Queen Thank Sophie Tucker," June 15, 1948, MWEZ + n.c. 10,984, Sophie Tucker Scrapbooks.

80. Lee Mortimer, "Soph Packs 'Em In on Coast," *New York Mirror*, December 23, 1947, MWEZ + n.c. 10,980, Sophie Tucker Scrapbooks.

81. Peter Bizzigotti to Sophie Tucker, November 25, 1948, MWEZ + n.c. 10,987, Sophie Tucker Scrapbooks.

82. Thomas F. Brady, "Metro to Do Film of Sophie Tucker," *New York Times*, January 21, 1948, MWEZ + n.c. 10,981, Sophie Tucker Scrapbooks; "MGM to Make Film of Life of Sophie Tucker," January 20, 1948, n.d., MWEZ + n.c. 10,981, Sophie Tucker Scrapbooks; "Movies Buy Book on Tucker's Life," *Hudson Register*, January 21, 1948, MWEZ + n.c. 10,981, Sophie Tucker Scrapbooks.

83. "Soph's 10G Charity," *Variety*, November 30, 1949, 43; "Sophie Tucker Booked Solid Until Next May," *Variety*, February 16, 1949, 51.

84. "Sophie Tucker Unloads Trunks of Nostalgia," *New York World Telegram*, January 3, 1949, MWEZ + n.c. 11,154, Sophie Tucker Scrapbooks;

"Sophie Tucker in N.Y. Debut with Clippings," *Christian Science Monitor*, January 4, 1949, MWEZ + n.c. 11,154, Sophie Tucker Scrapbooks; "Sophie Tucker Gives Library Scrapbook Pile," *New York Herald Tribune*, January 4, 1949, MWEZ + n.c. 11,154, Sophie Tucker Scrapbooks.

85. "Sophie and Family," *Hollywood Citizen News*, March 30, 1946, MWEZ + n.c. 10,968, Sophie Tucker Scrapbooks.

86. "Soph Gifts Son With Hotel," *Variety*, April 21, 1948, 51; "Sophie Tucker Now Owns Hotel," *Cincinnati Post*, April 26, 1948, MWEZ + n.c. 10,982, Sophie Tucker Scrapbooks.

87. Fanny Brice to Sophie Tucker, July 20, 1949, MWEZ + n.c. 11,622, Sophie Tucker Scrapbooks.

88. Eddie Cantor to Sophie Tucker, January 13, 1950, MWEZ + n.c. 11,766, Sophie Tucker Scrapbooks.

89. "Soph Shatters Friars Club 'No Women Rule,'" *Inglewood News*, November 25, 1949, MWEZ + n.c. 11,766, Sophie Tucker Scrapbook Collection.

90. "Negro Actors Planning Benefit," *New York Times*, November 20, 1950; "Sophie Tucker Steals Show at NAG Benefit," *New York Amsterdam News*, December 15, 1951, MWEZ + n.c. 14,180, Sophie Tucker Scrapbook Collection; "Negro Actors' Benefit Dec. 9," *New York Times*, November 23, 1951.

91. "Famous Stars Bill Robinson Clinic," *New York Amsterdam News*, December 6, 1952, MWEZ + n.c. 14,674, Sophie Tucker Scrapbook Collection.

92. Quoted in Jean-Claude Baker and Chris Chase, *Josephine: The Hungry Heart* (New York: Cooper Square, 1993); John A Diaz, "Paris' Josephine Playing Copa City," *Pittsburgh Courier*, December 30, 1950, 6; "Briefs," *Chicago Defender*, October 21, 1950, 21; "'Toast of Paris' Josephine Baker at Copa Tonight," December 1950, MWEZ + n.c. 12,513, Sophie Tucker Scrapbooks.

8. SOPHIE TUCKER FOR PRESIDENT

1. S. Regensberg, "A Conversation With Sophie Tucker," *Forward*, May 8, 1955, MWEZ + n.c. 16,331, Sophie Tucker Scrapbooks,*T-Mss 1966-004, Billy Rose Theater Division, New York Public Library (hereafter Sophie Tucker Scrapbooks).

2. "The Money-Makers," January 1952, MWEZ + n.c. 14,183, Sophie Tucker Scrapbooks.

3. "Sophie Tucker Bio in Nostalgic Disk," *The Billboard*, September 30, 1950, 3; Armond Fields, *Sophie Tucker: First Lady of Show Business* (Jefferson, NC: McFarland, 2003), 219.

4. Lynn Spigel, *Make Room for TV: Television and the Family Ideal in Postwar America* (Chicago: University of Chicago Press, 1992), 1, 6, 32–73.

5. John Lester, "Sophie Tucker Makes Terrific Debut on TV," *Newark Star-Ledger*, April 19, 1951, MWEZ + n.c. 14,919, Sophie Tucker Scrapbooks.

6. "Bob Lanigan's TV Review," *Brooklyn Eagle*, May 11, 1951, MWEZ + n.c. 14,919, Sophie Tucker Scrapbooks.

7. Ed Sullivan, "My 10 Greatest Acts," *TV Forecast*, January 17, 1953, MWEZ + n.c. 14,757, Sophie Tucker Scrapbooks; "Human Touch Is Vital Element in TV Success, Says Ed Sullivan," *New Haven Register*, April 6, 1952, MWEZ + n.c. 14,346, Sophie Tucker Scrapbooks.

8. "No TV for Me, Says Sophie," *Birmingham Gazette*, June 23, 1952, MWEZ + n.c. 14,349, Sophie Tucker Scrapbooks.

9. Sophie Tucker, "Looking Ahead," n.d., MWEZ + n.c. 14,350, Sophie Tucker Scrapbooks; "Sophie Tucker Story" (NBC, October 16, 1953), RWC 7573 B1–3, NBC Radio Collection, Division of Recorded Sound, Library of Congress.

10. "Let Men Wear the Pants, Advises Tucker, 68," *Lebanon News-Times*, April 29, 1952, MWEZ + n.c. 14,346, Sophie Tucker Scrapbooks.

11. Charles Mund to Sophie Tucker, November 25, 1952, MWEZ + n.c. 14,415, Sophie Tucker Scrapbooks.

12. A. L. Sachar to Sophie Tucker, January 19, 1953, MWEZ + n.c. 14,723, Sophie Tucker Scrapbooks.

13. "Sophie Tucker Speech at Brandeis University," September 20, 1955, MWEZ + n.c. 16,143, Sophie Tucker Scrapbooks.

14. "Royalties 'Music' to Songwriter, 73," *Los Angeles Examiner*, May 12, 1959, Box 3, Sophie Tucker scrapbooks and other material, 1957–1966, Robert D. Farber University Archives and Special Collections Department, Brandeis University (hereafter Sophie Tucker scrapbooks and other material, 1957–1966); Chappy Gardner, "Along the Rialto: Shelton Brooks—Bud Allen," *Pittsburgh Courier*, March 1, 1930, 16.

15. Noble Sissle to Sophie Tucker, January 21, 1953, MWEZ + n.c. 14,723, Sophie Tucker Scrapbooks.

16. Sophie Tucker, "How Negroes Influenced My Career," *Ebony*, December 1953, 80–93.

17. "Vaudeville: Soph Holds Own in Fun Barrage as Sole Femme Guest at Friars' Fete," *Variety*, September 23, 1953, 57.

18. "On the American Stage," *Day-Jewish Journal*, October 4, 1953, MWEZ + n.c. 15,006, Sophie Tucker Scrapbooks.

19. Jim Walsh, "Soph's 50th Anni Discography Goes Back to 1910 Cylinder Era," November 18, 1953, MWEZ + n.c. 15,105, Sophie Tucker Scrapbooks.

20. Fannie Mae candy advertisement, *Chicago Tribune*, April 30, 1954, MWEZ + n.c. 15,536, Sophie Tucker Scrapbooks; Bob Hull, "Sophie Tucker, Eartha Kitt, Battle 'Ziegfeld' Follies," *Los Angeles Herald Express*, April 3, 1954, MWEZ + n.c. 15,319, Sophie Tucker Scrapbooks; "Television Followups," *Variety*, December 2, 1953, MWEZ + n.c. 15,105, Sophie Tucker Scrapbooks.

21. "Vaudeville: Schuyler's Takeover of Beachcomber Cues Talent War; Bids 71/2G for Soph," *Variety*, July 15, 1950, 50.

22. Herb Rau, "Sophie Checks in at Miami Beach," *Boston Morning Globe*, December 6, 1953, MWEZ + n.c. 15,106, Sophie Tucker Scrapbooks; George Bourke, "Exodus to Florida Starts as First Cold Weather," *New York Herald Tribune*, November 8, 1953, MWEZ + n.c. 15,105, Sophie Tucker Scrapbooks; "Beachcomber Program," December 1953, MWEZ + n.c. 15,106, Sophie Tucker Scrapbooks.

23. "Nat King Cole Is Smash Hit at Miami's Beachcomber," 1954, MWEZ + n.c. 15,318, Sophie Tucker Scrapbooks.

24. Allan McMillian, "Miami Spots Plan Groovy Showbills; Jim Crow Out," *Chicago Defender*, June 11, 1955, 18.

25. Gene Knight, "Sophie a Sensation," *New York Journal American*, April 18, 1955, MWEZ + n.c. 15,850, Sophie Tucker Scrapbooks.

26. Dick Osgood, "Are Football and Fights Fading from TV," *Detroit Free Press*, January 27, 1955, MWEZ + n.c. 15,731, Sophie Tucker Scrapbooks.

27. "Sophie Tucker to Visit Berle Show," *Texarkana Gazette*, April 13, 1955, MWEZ + n.c. 15,928, Sophie Tucker Scrapbooks; Frank Morris, "Thunderous Applause Greets 'Queen' Sophie," *Winnipeg Free Press*, October 1, 1955, MWEZ + n.c. 16,145, Sophie Tucker Scrapbooks.

28. Tom Donnelly, "They Don't Build 'Em Like Sophie These Days," *Washington Daily News*, June 14, 1955, MWEZ + n.c. 15,989, Sophie Tucker Scrapbooks.

29. "R and R 'Killing' Cafe Biz, Soph Laments," *Variety*, August 11, 1965, 2.

30. Ken Tichenor, "Night Clubs? They're for Teens, Too, Says Mamma," *Los Angeles Mirror-News*, January 1957, MWEZ + n.c. 16,690, Sophie Tucker Scrapbooks.

31. "I Like People Who Stay the Pace Says Sophie Tucker," *Melody Maker*, March 30, 1957, MWEZ + n.c. 16,772, Sophie Tucker Scrapbooks; Kay Murphy, "Sophie's a Rock and Roll Mama, Now: 'Those Bopsters Love Me,' She Says," 1956, MWEZ + n.c. 16,331, Sophie Tucker Scrapbooks.

32. "But Here's Sophie Tucker's Special Favourite," *Picturegoer*, May 25, 1957, 19.

33. Abel Green, "New Acts," *Variety*, January 15, 1958, Box 1, Sophie Tucker scrapbooks and other material, 1957–1966; Doc Quigg, "Carol Channing Can't Understand Why Marlene Is Angry at Her," *Falls River Herald News*, January 7, 1958, Box 1, Sophie Tucker scrapbooks and other material, 1957–1966.

34. Carol Channing to Sophie Tucker, 1958, Box 1, Sophie Tucker scrapbooks and other material, 1957–1966.

35. "Barbra Thrills Sophie," *Miami Beach Daily Sun*, April 25, 1964, Box 22, Sophie Tucker scrapbooks and other material, 1957–1966.

36. Franklin D. Walker, "Last of the Red Hot Mamas," *New Yorker*, 1961, Box 14, Sophie Tucker scrapbooks and other material, 1957–1966.

37. "Sophie Tucker Declares TV Isn't Show Business," *Louisville Times*, January 12, 1957, MWEZ + n.c. 16,751, Sophie Tucker Scrapbooks.

38. Donnelly, "They Don't Build \'Em."

39. "Sophie Tucker Says Success Comes from Loving People," *Dayton Journal Herald*, January 1, 1957, MWEZ + n.c. 16,752, Sophie Tucker Scrapbooks.

40. Cecil Smith, "Legendary Ted Lewis, Sophie Tucker Return," *Los Angeles Times*, August 2, 1959, Box 3, Sophie Tucker scrapbooks and other material, 1957–1966; "Sophie Tucker, Spry 71, Will Travel," *New York Herald Tribune*, August 30, 1959, Box 3, Sophie Tucker scrapbooks and other material, 1957–1966.

41. Henry Ward, "'Sophie for President' Has Catchy Theme Song," *Pittsburgh Press*, August 9, 1960, Box 7, Sophie Tucker scrapbooks and other material, 1957–1966.

42. Sophie Tucker, *Sophie Tucker: The Very Best Of* (Master Classics Records, 2009); Earl Wilson, "Sophie in the White House," *Times Recorder*, September 29, 1964, Box 23, Sophie Tucker scrapbooks and other material, 1957–1966; Herbert Mueller to Sophie Tucker, October 11, 1964, Box 23, Sophie Tucker scrapbooks and other material, 1957–1966.

43. Louella O. Parsons, "'Sophie Tucker' Roles Won by Betty Hutton," 1952, MWEZ + n.c. 14,350, Sophie Tucker Scrapbooks.

44. Jimmie Garland Thompson to Sophie Tucker, 1956, MWEZ + n.c. 16,331, Sophie Tucker Scrapbooks.

45. Wayne Allen, "Sophie's Saga to Reach Screen?—Possibly Some of These Days," June 5, 1956, MWEZ + n.c. 16,482, Sophie Tucker Scrapbooks; Fields, *Sophie Tucker*, 228–229.

46. Milt Freudenheim, "Redhead from Southern Illinois," *St. Louis Post-Dispatch*, June 3, 1962, Box 15, Sophie Tucker scrapbooks and other material, 1957–1966; Joe Hyams, "How Producers Persuaded 'Sophie,'" *Miami News*, May 27, 1962, Box 15, Sophie Tucker scrapbooks and other material, 1957–1966; Louis Calta, "Sophie Approves of 'Sophie' Lead," *New York Times*, May 18, 1962, Box 14, Sophie Tucker scrapbooks and other material, 1957–1966; Paul Speegle, "What Bugs Sophie Will Fill a Musical," *News-Call Bulletin*, 1962, Box 15, Sophie Tucker scrapbooks and other material, 1957–1966.

47. Ernest Schier, "Book Troubles Mar Two New Musicals," *Philadelphia Bulletin*, March 31, 1963, Box 19, Sophie Tucker scrapbooks and other material, 1957–1966; Ron Pataky, "New Musical Has Mood of Early Sophie Tucker," *Youngstown Vindicator*, March 2, 1963, Box 19, Sophie Tucker scrapbooks and other material, 1957–1966; Sam Zolotow, "'Sophie' Road Tryout Shortened; Advanced Opening Here Likely," *New York Times*, April 5, 1963, Box 19, Sophie Tucker scrapbooks and other material, 1957–1966; Irven Scheibeck, "'Sophie' Contains 'Hit' Ingredients," *Columbus Dispatch*, March 1, 1963, Box 19, Sophie Tucker scrapbooks and other material, 1957–1966; Nora Ephron, "Sophie Tucker Looks Ahead," *New York Post*, September 6, 1964, Box 23, Sophie Tucker scrapbooks and other material, 1957–1966.

48. Rosalind Rush, "Mama Loves Her Family," *Miami News*, February 17, 1960, Box 6, Sophie Tucker scrapbooks and other material, 1957–1966; Lois Young-Tulin, *Sophie and Me: Some of These Days* (San Jose: iUniverse.com, 2001), 96; Lois Young-Tulin, author interview, July 30, 2012.

49. Ted Shapiro, "My 31 Years with Sophie Tucker," December 1952, MWEZ + n.c. 14,676, Sophie Tucker Scrapbooks.

50. Margaret Chung to Sophie Tucker, January 11, 1958, Box 1, Sophie Tucker scrapbooks and other material, 1957–1966.

51. "Dwight Eisenhower to Margaret Chung," November 28, 1958, Box 3, Sophie Tucker scrapbooks and other material, 1957–1966.

52. "A Queen of Entertainment," June 1952, MWEZ + n.c. 14,349, Sophie Tucker Scrapbooks.

53. Wayne Allen, "Sophie Tucker Plans 'Farewell Tour'—Not Retirement," June 1956, MWEZ + n.c. 16,482, Sophie Tucker Scrapbooks; "Sophie Is Here to Rock n Roll," *Daily Echo*, March 26, 1957, MWEZ + n.c. 16,772, Sophie Tucker Scrapbooks.

54. "Variety News and Gossip: Sophie Tucker Captivates the Cafe," *The Stage*, April 4, 1957; "Sophie Tucker in Eamonn Andrews Show," *New Musical Express*, April 5, 1957.

55. Robert Weltsch, "The Yiddishe Momme Today," *Jewish Chronicle*, April 3, 1957, MWEZ + n.c. 16,772, Sophie Tucker Scrapbooks.

56. Doris Davis to Sophie Tucker, June 25, 1952, MWEZ + n.c. 14,349, Sophie Tucker Scrapbooks; "Sophie Tucker Meets Bobbies and Zeides," *Jewish Telegraph*, July 25, 1952, MWEZ + n.c. 14,349, Sophie Tucker Scrapbooks.

57. "The 'Yiddishe Momme' in London," *Jewish Chronicle*, April 5, 1957, MWEZ + n.c. 16,772, Sophie Tucker Scrapbooks.

58. "Tucker First Again as Trustee in Field," January 1955, MWEZ + n.c. 15,731, Sophie Tucker Scrapbooks.

59. "Sophie Tucker to Irving Berlin," November 14, 1955, Box 362, Irving Berlin Collection, ML31.B48, Music Division, Library of Congress, Washington, DC.

60. Tikvah Weinstock, "The Jewish Grandmother, Sophie Tucker," *Maariv*, April 24, 1959; "Itinerary for Israel Trip, April 1959," n.d., Box 3, Sophie Tucker scrapbooks and other material, 1957–1966; Paul Kohn, "The Last Red-Hot Mama," *Jerusalem Post*, April 1959, Box 3, Sophie Tucker scrapbooks and other material, 1957–1966.

61. Shalom Cohen, "Sophie Tucker Dedicates Centre for Beit Shemesh Children," *Jerusalem Post*, April 20, 1959, Box 3, Sophie Tucker scrapbooks and other material, 1957–1966.

62. "The Israeli Children Call Me Momma," May 15, 1959, Box 3, Sophie Tucker scrapbooks and other material, 1957–1966.

63. "Memorial Speech for Headstone of Annie Abuza Aronson," August 27, 1961, Box 11, Sophie Tucker scrapbooks and other material, 1957–1966.

64. "Sophie Tucker to Irving Berlin," December 15, 1960, Box 362, Irving Berlin Collection, ML31.B48, Music Division, Library of Congress, Washington, DC; "Irving Berlin to Sophie Tucker," February 14, 1961, Box 362, Irving Berlin Collection, ML 31.B48, Music Division, Library of Congress,

Washington, DC; Betty Burroughs, "Jessel Lights Cigar, Fires Away at TV, Racial Bias," *Wilmington News*, June 12, 1963, Box 19, Sophie Tucker scrapbooks and other material, 1957–1966; Joseph Schwartz to Sophie Tucker, February 28, 1962, Box 15, Sophie Tucker scrapbooks and other material, 1957–1966.

65. "Sophie's Here," *The Sun*, June 19, 1962, Box 15, Sophie Tucker scrapbooks and other material, 1957–1966; "Sophie Tucker 'Incomparable,'" June 1962, Box 15, Sophie Tucker scrapbooks and other material, 1957–1966; Tivoli Theatre advertisement, June 1962, Box 15, Sophie Tucker scrapbooks and other material, 1957–1966; Vera Howe to Sophie Tucker, June 29, 1962, Box 15, Sophie Tucker scrapbooks and other material, 1957–1966; Sol Schwartz to Sophie Tucker, June 15, 1962, Box 15, Sophie Tucker scrapbooks and other material, 1957–1966; "Soph Sets New High Pay Mark for Femme Talent in Aussie—$2,240 Wkly," *Variety*, July 4, 1962.

66. "Her Long Distance Welcome for Sophie," *Cape Times*, August 31, 1962, Box 17, Sophie Tucker scrapbooks and other material, 1957–1966; "Sophie Tucker to Appear Here in August," *Cape Times*, June 23, 1962, Box 17, Sophie Tucker scrapbooks and other material, 1957–1966; "'No Sex,' Says Sophie, 'Only Philosophy,'" *Cape Times*, August 16, 1962, Box 17, Sophie Tucker scrapbooks and other material, 1957–1966; "Sophie Has Recovered Today," *Daily News*, September 14, 1962, Box 16, Sophie Tucker scrapbooks and other material, 1957–1966; Debra, "Sophie Tucker—a Real Yiddishe Mamma," *South African Jewish Times*, August 31, 1962, Box 17, Sophie Tucker scrapbooks and other material, 1957–1966; "Sophie Tucker Scores in Initial South Africa Tour; Heads for Israel Vacash," *Variety*, September 26, 1962.

67. "Sophie Tucker Dedicates Her Forest in Israel," September 1962, Box 16, Sophie Tucker scrapbooks and other material, 1957–1966.

68. "Bob Hope Tells Queen U.S. Has No Titles," *Colorado Springs-Gazette Telegraph*, October 31, 1962, Box 16, Sophie Tucker scrapbooks and other material, 1957–1966; "Sophie Steals the Show," *Daily Mail*, October 30, 1962, Box 16, Sophie Tucker scrapbooks and other material, 1957–1966; "Royal Performance Program," October 29, 1962, Box 16, Sophie Tucker scrapbooks and other material, 1957–1966; Harold Myers, "Sophie Tucker 'Saga' Wows Aud at Britain's Royal Command Variety Gala," *Variety*, November 7, 1962.

69. Harold Stern, "A Junior at 76," *Time*, August 28, 1964, Box 23, Sophie Tucker scrapbooks and other material, 1957–1966; William Stoneman,

"Sophie Wows British, Nearly Collapses," *Akron Beacon Journal*, August 8, 1964, Box 23, Sophie Tucker scrapbooks and other material, 1957–1966; William Stoneman, "A Triumph for Sophie in London," *Des Moines Register*, August 23, 1964, Box 23, Sophie Tucker scrapbooks and other material, 1957–1966.

70. Jack Zucker to Sophie Tucker, January 16, 1961, Box 10, Sophie Tucker scrapbooks and other material, 1957–1966; Harry Emerson Fosdick to Sophie Tucker, November 13, 1961, Box 14, Sophie Tucker scrapbooks and other material, 1957–1966.

71. "Sophie Tucker Gives $10,000 to Hebrew Home," *Hartford Courant*, 1959, Box 4, Sophie Tucker scrapbooks and other material, 1957–1966; Shep Sterling to Sophie Tucker, August 24, 1959, Box 3, Sophie Tucker scrapbooks and other material, 1957–1966.

72. Sophie Tucker Free Maternity Clinic pamphlet, March 1960, Box 6, Sophie Tucker scrapbooks and other material, 1957–1966; "Speech at Latin Quarter," May 3, 1964, Box 22, Sophie Tucker scrapbooks and other material, 1957–1966.

73. Sophie Tucker Free Maternity Clinic pamphlet.

74. "Speech at Latin Quarter."

75. Ibid.; Burroughs, "Jessel Lights Cigar."

76. Sidney Zion, "Sophie's the Star as an M.C.," *New York Post*, June 12, 1964, Box 22, Sophie Tucker scrapbooks and other material, 1957–1966; "WD Volunteers to Spend Afternoon with Sophie Tucker at Carnegie Hall," June 1964, Box 22, Sophie Tucker scrapbooks and other material, 1957–1966; "Sophie Tucker at Carnegie Hall Speech," June 11, 1964, Box 22, Sophie Tucker scrapbooks and other material, 1957–1966.

77. Myer Feldman to Sophie Tucker, September 22, 1964, Box 23, Sophie Tucker scrapbooks and other material, 1957–1966.

78. "La Sophie to Mark 75th on Television," *Oneonta Star*, January 12, 1963, Box 18, Sophie Tucker scrapbooks and other material, 1957–1966; Harvey Pack, "Red Hot Mama to Appear in Rare TV Guest Shot," *Portland Oregonian*, January 13, 1963, Box 18, Sophie Tucker scrapbooks and other material, 1957–1966; Edward Boyd to Sophie Tucker, January 14, 1963, Box 18, Sophie Tucker scrapbooks and other material, 1957–1966; Mrs. Henry Heyer to Ed Sullivan Show, January 16, 1963, Box 18, Sophie Tucker scrapbooks and other material, 1957–1966.

79. "Funeral Today for Eddie Cantor," *Bergen Evening Record*, October 12, 1964, Box 23, Sophie Tucker scrapbooks and other material, 1957–1966.

80. Louis Sobol, "Vaudeville—Gone but Not Forgotten," *Journal American*, September 6, 1964, Box 23, Sophie Tucker scrapbooks and other material, 1957–1966; Maureen Englin, "Good Old Days of Seattle Vaudeville," *Seattle Post-Intelligencer*, May 31, 1964, Box 23, Sophie Tucker scrapbooks and other material, 1957–1966.

81. Ephron, "Sophie Tucker Looks Ahead."

82. Marie Moreau, "Femininity Has No Age Limit—Sophie," *Toronto Daily Star*, January 26, 1965, Box 25, Sophie Tucker scrapbooks and other material, 1957–1966.

83. Hy Gardner, *New York Herald Tribune*, January 18, 1965, Box 25, Sophie Tucker scrapbooks and other material, 1957–1966; Phyllis Battelle, "Assignment: America," February 20, 1965, Box 26, Sophie Tucker scrapbooks and other material, 1957–1966.

84. Earl Wilson, "It Happened Last Night," *New York Post*, n.d., MWEZ + n.c. 26,583, Sophie Tucker Scrapbooks.

85. Lillian Tucker and Bert Tucker to Sophie Tucker, January 16, 1966, Box 28, Sophie Tucker scrapbooks and other material, 1957–1966.

86. Shalom Cohen, "Sophie Tucker Dedicates Centre for Beit Shemesh Children," *Jerusalem Post*, April 20, 1959, Box 3, Sophie Tucker scrapbooks and other material, 1957–1966.

87. Yale School of Drama Fortieth Anniversary Commemoration, November 6, 1965, Box 28, Sophie Tucker scrapbooks and other material, 1957–1966.

EPILOGUE

1. Albert Tucker, "Scrapbook Cover—Sophie Tucker Death," n.d., MWEZ + n.c. 26,583, Sophie Tucker Scrapbooks,*T-Mss 1966-004, Billy Rose Theater Division, New York Public Library (hereafter Sophie Tucker Scrapbooks).

2. Earl Wilson, "It Happened Last Night," *New York Post*, n.d., MWEZ + n.c. 26,583, Sophie Tucker Scrapbooks.

3. "How They Remember Billy and Sophie," *The New York Post*, February 11, 1966, MWEZ + n.c. 26,583, Sophie Tucker Scrapbooks.

4. David Nathan, "Twin Fires Go Out on Old Broadway," *London Sun*, February 11, 1966, MWEZ + n.c. 26,583, Sophie Tucker Scrapbooks.

5. "Miss Sophie Tucker 'Last of the Red Hot Mamas,'" *London Times*, February 11, 1966, MWEZ + n.c. 26,583, Sophie Tucker Scrapbooks.

6. "Sophie on Why They Don't Last," *The Cape Times*, February 11, 1966, MWEZ + n.c. 26,583, Sophie Tucker Scrapbooks.

7. Nathan, "Twin Fires Go Out."

8. "1,000 Hear George Jessel Eulogize Sophie Tucker," *The New York Times*, February 12, 1966, MWEZ + n.c. 26,583, Sophie Tucker Scrapbooks.

9. Lois Young-Tulin, *Sophie and Me: Some of These Days* (San Jose: iUniverse .com, 2001), 145.

10. Armond Fields, *Sophie Tucker: First Lady of Show Business* (Jefferson, NC: McFarland, 2003), 247.

11. "Sophie Tucker Estate Tops $500,000," *New York Post*, February 20, 1966, MWEZ + n.c. 26,583, Sophie Tucker Scrapbooks; Fields, *Sophie Tucker*, 248–249.

12. Moses Abuza; US Find a Grave Index, 1600–Current, February 14, 2017; http://www.findagrave.com/cgi-bin/fg.cgi (Ancestry.com). Bert Tucker; US Social Security Death Index, 1935–2014, n.d.; Social Security Administration; Social Security Death Index, Master File (Ancestry.com, February 14, 2017). Fields, *Sophie Tucker*, 248.

13. Obituary for Yitzhak Bar-Shasheet, February 9, 1970, *Izkor: The Commemorative Website for the Fallen of Israel's Military Campaigns*, http://www .izkor.gov.il/HalalKorot.aspx?id=92406.

14. Mrs. Alfred Herz to Sophie Tucker, November 6, 1964, Box 23, Sophie Tucker scrapbooks and other material, 1957–1966, Robert D. Farber University Archives and Special Collections Department, Brandeis University.

15. David Denby, "Spielberg at 70," *New Yorker*, January 16, 2017.

PHOTO CREDITS

Tucker with Judy Garland: Clarence Sinclair-Bull (1896–1979)/Museum of the City of New York. F2017.27.224

Tucker greets crowds in Los Angeles: Stagg Photo Service/Museum of the City of New York. F2017.27.248

Tucker on the beach with Bert and Lillian: Fred Hess & Son/Museum of the City of New York. F2017.27.251

Tucker and Margaret Chung: Billy Rose Theatre Division, The New York Public Library for the Performing Arts, Astor, Lenox and Tilden Foundations

Sophie Tucker for President: Billy Rose Theatre Division, The New York Public Library for the Performing Arts, Astor, Lenox and Tilden Foundations

Ballot for Tucker for President: Maurice Jeymaw/Robert D. Farber University Archives & Special Collections Department, Brandeis University

Tucker singing: Photographer unknown/Museum of the City of New York. F2017.27.452

Tucker's funeral: Billy Rose Theatre Division, The New York Public Library for the Performing Arts, Astor, Lenox and Tilden Foundations

Scrapbook: Lauren Rebecca Sklaroff

INDEX